IMAGES
of America

LAVA BEDS
NATIONAL MONUMENT

On the Cover: Two Lava Beds National Monument visitors are pictured crawling through one of the monument's more than 700 lava tubes—the largest concentration of these types of caves in the continental United States. Only one cave at Lava Beds National Monument is lighted with illuminated interpretive signs. Several in the Cave Loop Road area and elsewhere have trails and entrances with signs.

IMAGES
of America

LAVA BEDS
NATIONAL MONUMENT

Lee Juillerat

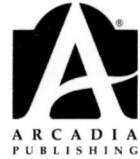

Copyright © 2015 by Lee Juillerat
ISBN 978-1-4671-3407-1

Published by Arcadia Publishing
Charleston, South Carolina

Printed in the United States of America

Library of Congress Control Number: 2015935764

For all general information, please contact Arcadia Publishing:
Telephone 843-853-2070
Fax 843-853-0044
E-mail sales@arcadiapublishing.com
For customer service and orders:
Toll-Free 1-888-313-2665

Visit us on the Internet at www.arcadiapublishing.com

This book is dedicated to J.D. "Judd" Howard, the person most responsible for Lava Beds being designated as a national monument.

Because of Howard's efforts to preserve the unique features of Lava Beds, he is called "The Father of Lava Beds." I have a special appreciation and link to Howard. Years ago, after a day of exploration with then–park ranger Mac Hebner, I was in the park library rummaging through boxes searching for historical tidbits. It was after midnight, I was tired, and I wanted to be done. I grabbed the final box, which was stuffed with original and mimeographed letters and papers written by Howard, who had settled in nearby Klamath Falls, Oregon, in the early 1900s. That night, I scanned through Howard's typewritten papers. As I turned one letter aside, something hit home—literally. I flipped back the page and reread the letterhead that began, "From the desk of J.D. Howard," with his address. My address. That was when I learned I live in Howard's old house, where he died in 1961 at age 81. I am sure it was my imagination, but as I stared at the letterhead, I thought I heard an old man's laugh.

CONTENTS

Acknowledgments		6
Introduction		7
1.	Geology	9
2.	Early Inhabitants	25
3.	The Modoc War	35
4.	After the Modoc War	59
5.	Cave Discoverers	65
6.	The CCC Influence	75
7.	Development of a National Monument	85
8.	Still Learning	107
Bibliography		127

Acknowledgments

Mike Reynolds, the former superintendent at Lava Beds National Monument, was the motivational force in creating this book to help visitors better understand the monument. Reynolds is the most recent in a series of superintendents—including David Kruse, Craig Dorman, Doris Omundsen Bowen, James Sleznick, Paul Haertel, and William Kennedy—who have encouraged me to learn more about Lava Beds and its rich history. I thank them also for their friendship and eagerness to help me and others appreciate the monument. My thanks also to Jessica Middleton, the monument's chief of natural resources, who was instrumental in providing access to historical photographs.

I have also enjoyed the friendship of dozens of Lava Beds personnel over the past 40-plus years, including James Blaisdell, Gary Hathaway, Mac Hebner, Steve Underwood, Kale Bowling, John Krambrink, Angela Sutton, Terry Harris, Nancy Nordensten, Jesse Barden, and many, many others. The wealth of publications about the area provides great insight into the monument's multidimensional history. Delightfully, I have had the pleasure of working with and knowing some of the authors of those publications, including Carrol B. Howe, Keith Murray, Charlie Larson, Frederick Brown, Boyd Cothran, Cheewa James, and Daniel Woodhead. Their histories help keep the stories of Lava Beds alive.

All images in this volume appear courtesy of Lava Beds National Monument.

INTRODUCTION

Lava Beds National Monument is often called the "Land of Burnt Out Fires," and for good reason. Lava Beds is a region shaped—some might say tormented—by volcanic events and a fiery human history highlighted by California's only Indian war, the Modoc War, fought in 1872 and 1873. The Modoc War drew international attention, resulted in the death of an Army general, and led to the hanging deaths of three key Modoc leaders and the forced relocation of most of the tribe.

In far northern California, the landscape hints at what exists below the surface. It is a landscape that begs exploration above and below ground, whether for its unusual geology or its unique human history. The area below ground is truly fascinating, hosting an intricate network of more than 700 lava tube caves that reach out like underground tentacles. No two are exactly alike, and many are fascinatingly different. Some have ferns, while others have complex ice formations. Several contain seasonal populations of rare bats. Many caves show signs of human visitation ranging from pictographs created by ancestral Native Americans to markings made by J.D. "Judd" Howard, the early Lava Beds explorer who used white paint to record the caves' names and dates of discovery.

Lava Beds has a rich history and great potential for an even more impressive future. Ongoing studies of bats, wildlife, and lichen have created a greater understanding of the monument's natural resources. The use of GPS has allowed researchers to set the number of lava tube caves at Lava Beds at more than 700, when, years ago, the number of caves was estimated at more than 200.

Not all of the increased knowledge stems from technological advances. The number of fortifications and other features discovered in Captain Jack's Stronghold, which Modoc Indians occupied during the Modoc War, greatly increased following a fire that burned through the area and exposed structures made by the Modocs and, after they left the Stronghold, Army troops.

Howard and others who lived at or explored the Lava Beds would be surprised, and probably delighted, by the new insights and information.

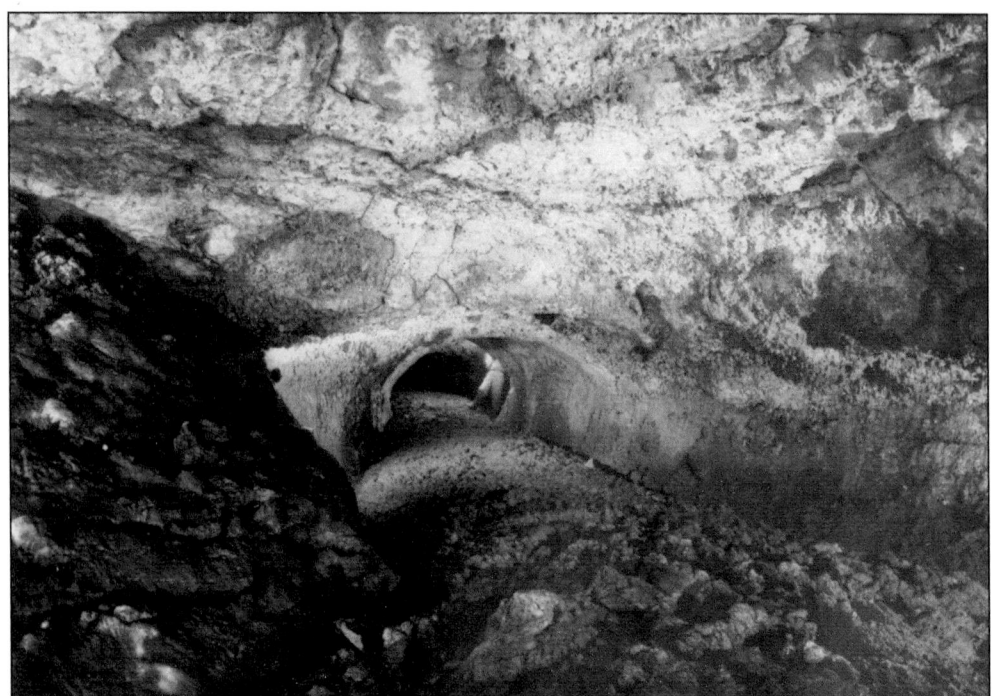

Valentine Cave, which Ross Musselman discovered on Valentine's Day in 1933, is among the easiest caves to access at Lava Beds. The cave is known for its relatively high ceilings and unusual floor. Cave discoverer Ross Musselman saw the cave "breathing" steam during a cool morning (the temperature was -12° F), grabbed a lantern, ran from Indian Wells, and located the cave entrance, which was small and obscured by a juniper tree. Wide passages make it easy for visitors to walk in Valentine Cave. Geologists say the final flow was a brief, highly fluid surge—about three feet deep—that, as it drained out the lower end, smoothly blanketed previous irregularities with a thin lining.

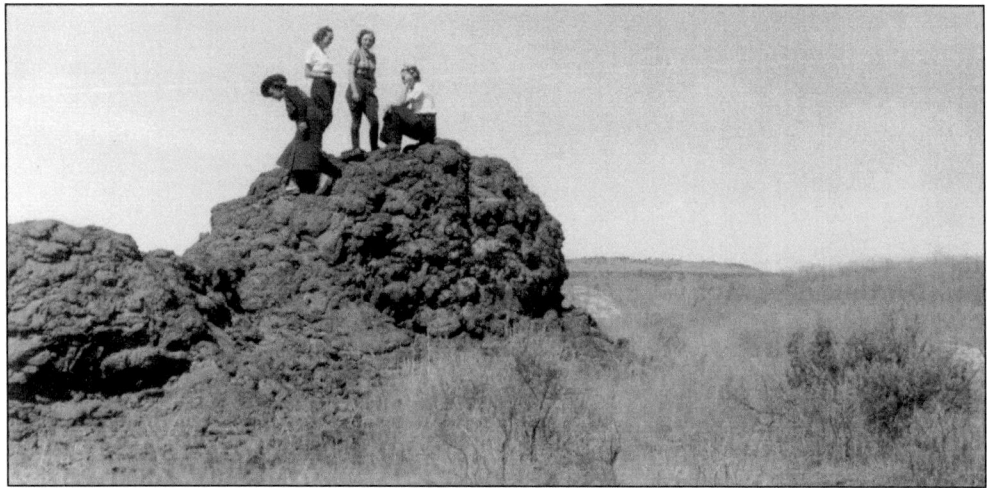

Among the curious volcanic features found throughout Lava Beds National Monument are spatter cones: low, steep-sided hills or mounds of welded lava fragments that form along a linear fissure or around a central vent. As lava fragments erupt into the air, they often do not have time to cool completely before hitting the ground.

One

GEOLOGY

Call it a case of cataclysmic chaos. Hundreds of thousands of years of volcanic activity have shaped and reshaped the tortured, often inhospitable landscape that encompasses the Lava Beds National Monument. It is a landscape created by repeated flows of magma that emerged from vents on the northern flank of the massive Medicine Lake shield volcano, which spreads across 900 square miles. Over millennia, and as recently as 1,100 years ago, recurring seismic events have created lava flows, including smooth and ropy pahoehoe and rough, ragged aa. These events also formed the monument's chimney-like spatter cones, 300-foot tall cinder cones, and more than 700 lava tube caves.

Most of the basaltic lava that created the network of caves came from Mammoth Crater, which experienced a major eruption about 30,000 years ago. Some of those caves feature ice deposits, while others feature lava stalactites. Some are filled with squeeze-through narrow passages; others have openings as grand as cathedrals.

The erratic landscape has also been significant in human history. Most notably, in the 1870s, a small force of Modoc warriors held off hundreds of US Army troops by using their knowledge of the lava-created fortress that has become known as Captain Jack's Stronghold to outmaneuver frustrated soldiers. In later years, settlers used ice caves to provide water for themselves, horses, and—during Prohibition—whiskey stills.

Visitors go to Lava Beds to explore those caves; to walk the Stronghold; and to experience the brooding, often harsh aboveground cataclysmically-created landscape. The lands within the monument's boundaries also include grasslands, sagebrush, juniper, and stands of ponderosa pine at higher elevations. But, Lava Beds National Monument remains an area dominated by lava, creating a landscape that is fractured and unforgiving but also unforgettable.

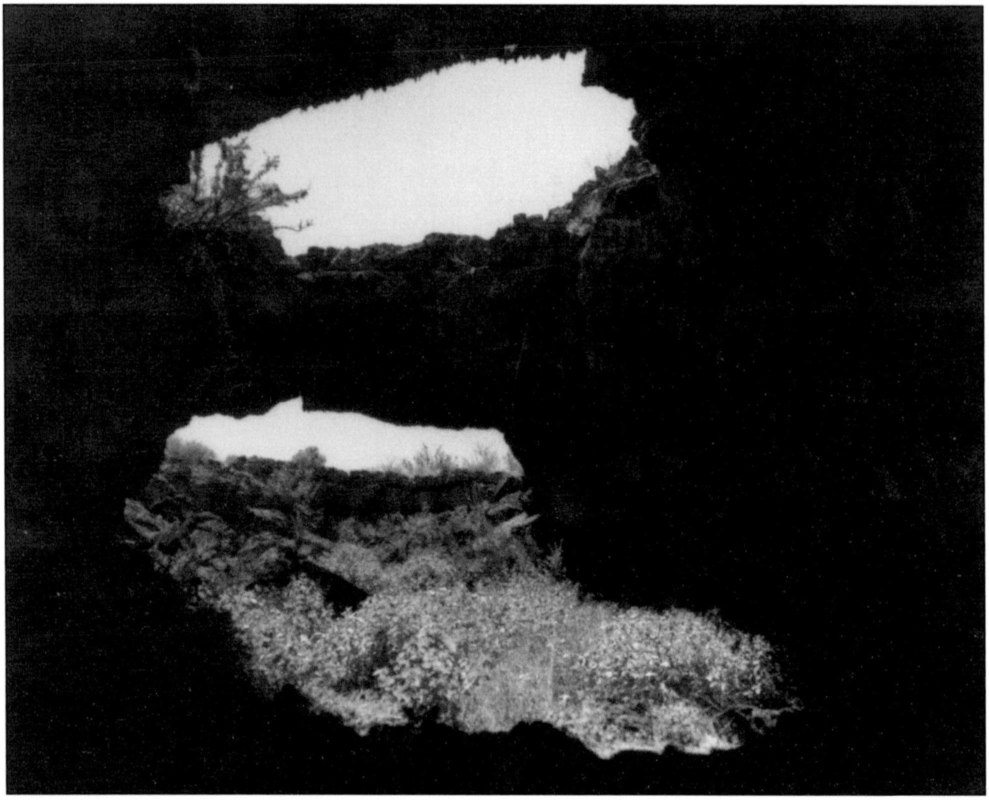

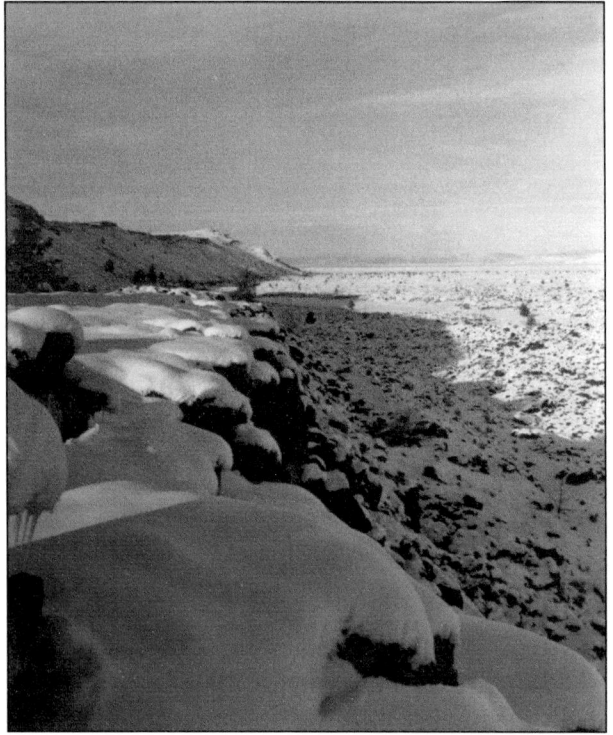

Garden Bridge is an area where a small remnant of a lava tube roof was left standing between collapses. Garden Bridge is one of the park's most outstanding bridges. J.D. Howard named the area the Six Garden Bridges "because of the garden under one of them." The "Six Garden" name is no longer in use.

Lava Beds' rugged landscape at Devil's Homestead, a ragged area of pahoehoe and aa lava, appears less harsh under a blanket of snow. Aa (pronounced "ah ah") is a Hawaiian term for a lava flow with an extremely rough, jagged, and irregular surface. In Hawaiian, aa is also an expression of pain as experienced walking barefoot on lava or other hard surfaces. Pahoehoe refers to lava with a smooth or ropy appearance.

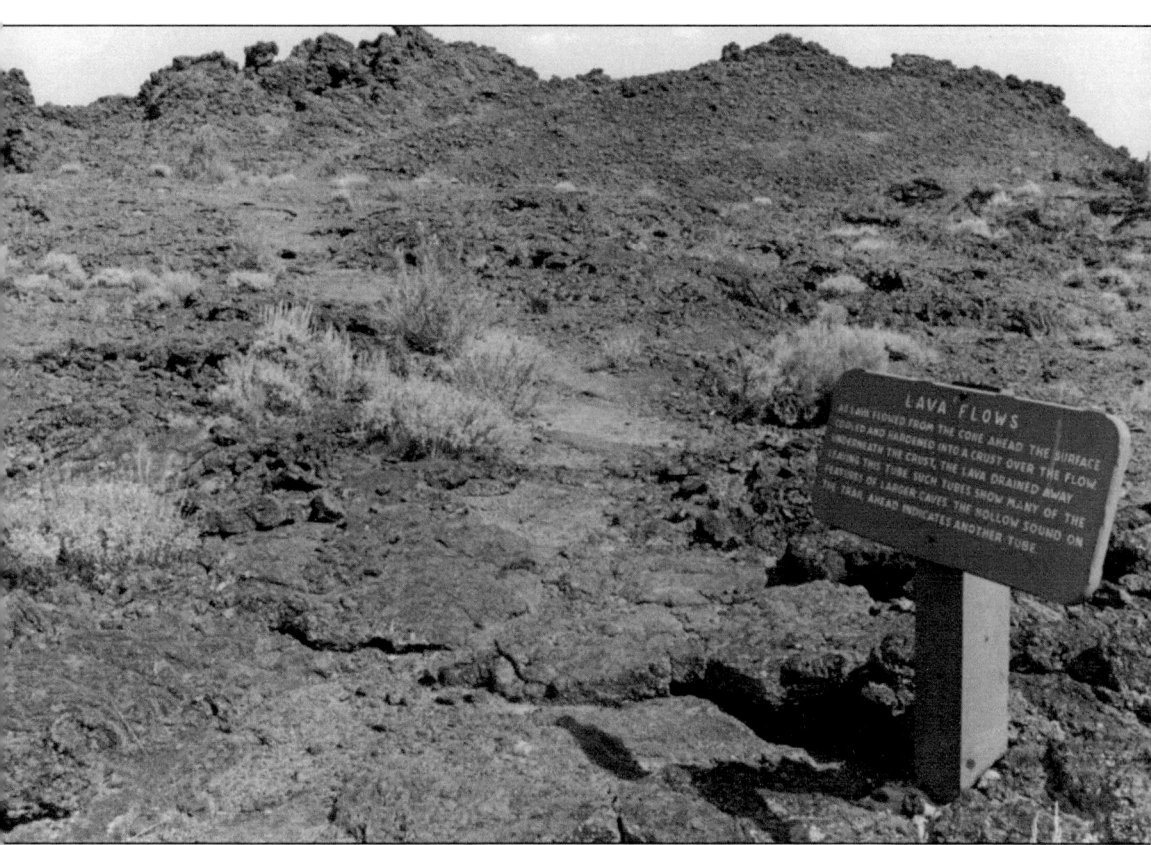

The Black Crater Trail is one of many that visitors can walk to learn more about the forces that created the monument's dramatic landscape. Signs help explain how flowing lava created specific features, including Black Crater. The monument's parking lot was improved and paved as part of the National Park Service's Mission 66 improvement program. Mission 66 was a large-scale capital improvement project launched by NPS director Conrad Wirth in 1955 with a goal of upgrading sites across the country before the National Park Service's 50th anniversary in 1966. In 1956, Congress approved a $700 million budget for 10 years of improvements. The figure eventually increased to about $1 billion and led to increased staffing and construction projects such as visitor centers and new park units.

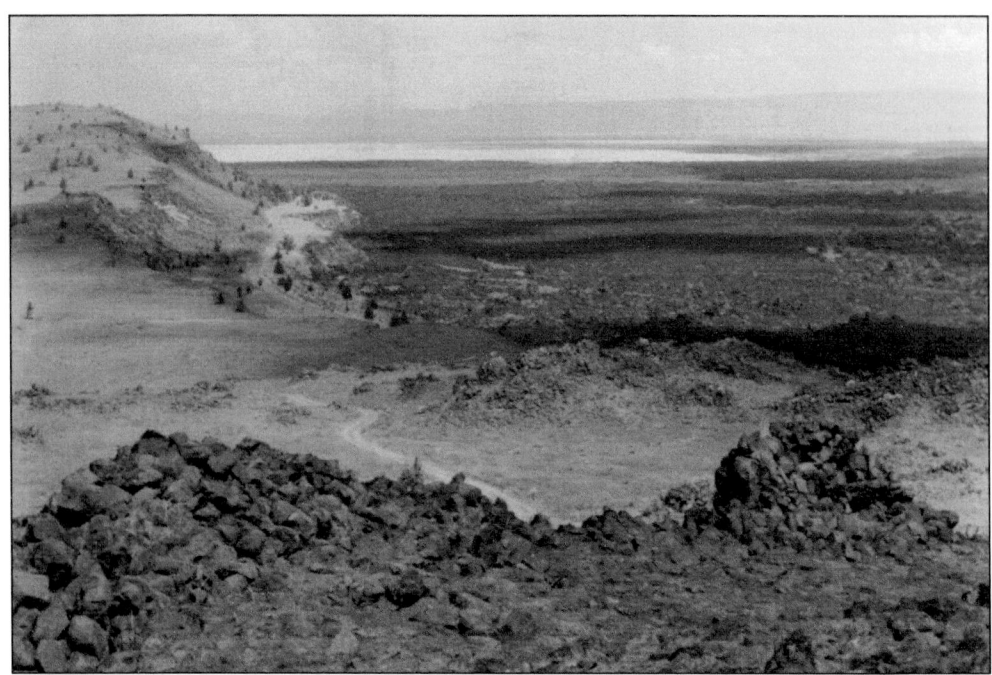

Expansive views of lands bordering what is now Lava Beds National Monument include the distant waters of Tule Lake, a body of water that flanked areas of the park until it was partially drained in the early 1900s. The remaining lake, which is a fraction of its original size, is part of the Tule Lake National Wildlife Refuge and serves as an important stop for migrating waterfowl.

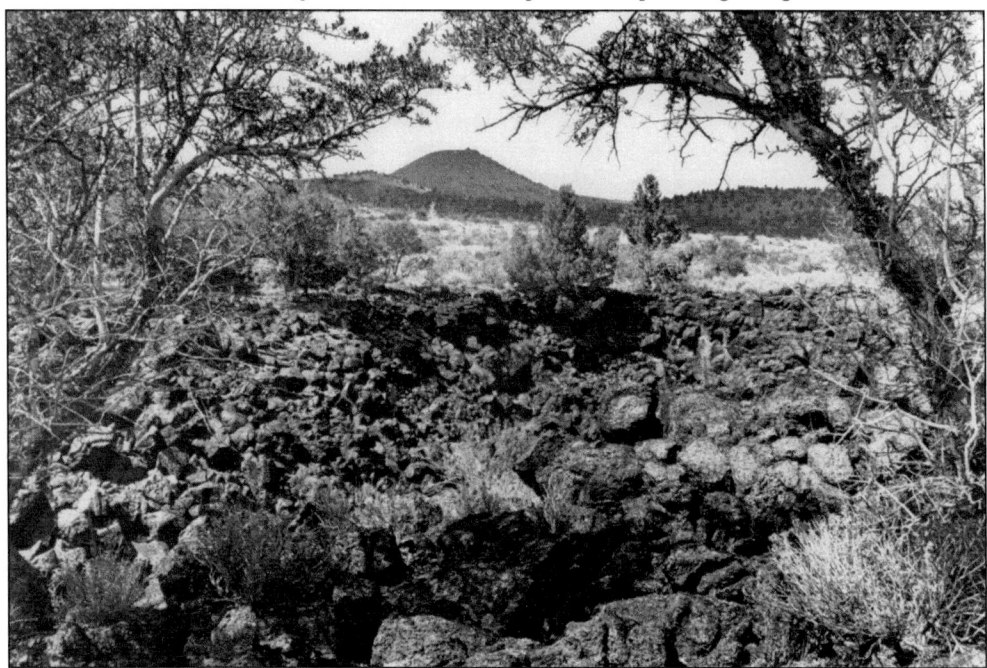

Schonchin Butte, one of the most recognizable buttes in Lava Beds, can be reached by a gentle trail. The view from the top, where a lookout is seasonally staffed, shows a large portion of the neighboring and distant terrain. The lookout was built by Civilian Conservation Corps crews.

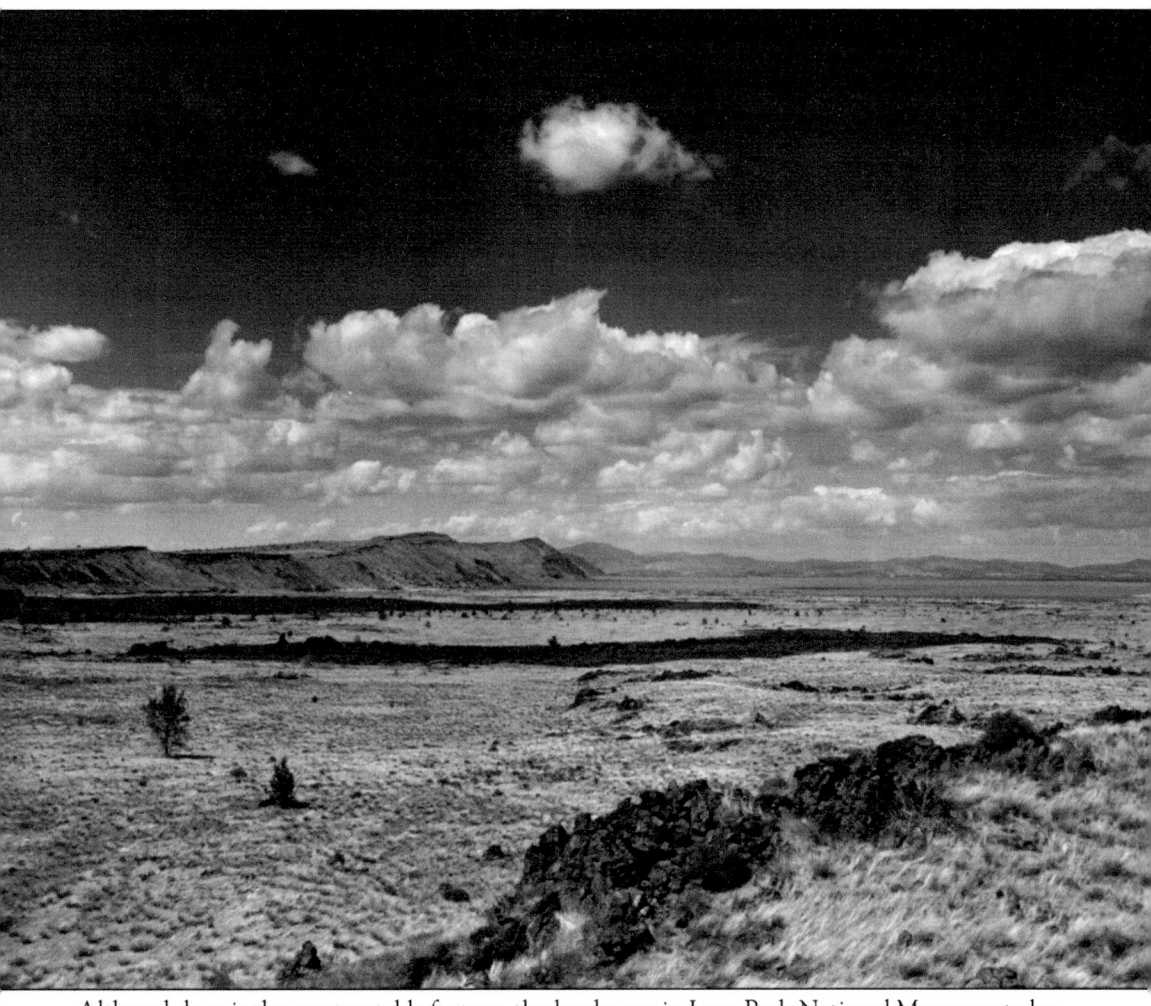

Although lava is the most notable feature, the landscape in Lava Beds National Monument also includes expansive grasslands, sagebrush and juniper (at lower elevations), and stands of ponderosa pine trees at higher elevations. Mule deer are frequently seen in the open terrain and along protected hillsides. Pronghorn antelope, which were once relatively common, are seldom seen. Although settlers passed through the area, most of them established farms on the more productive, fertile lands along Tule Lake. The Lava Beds area and neighboring forests were instead used for grazing sheep and horses. Early Modoc Indians traveled to Lava Beds, where they established seasonal villages and hunted deer.

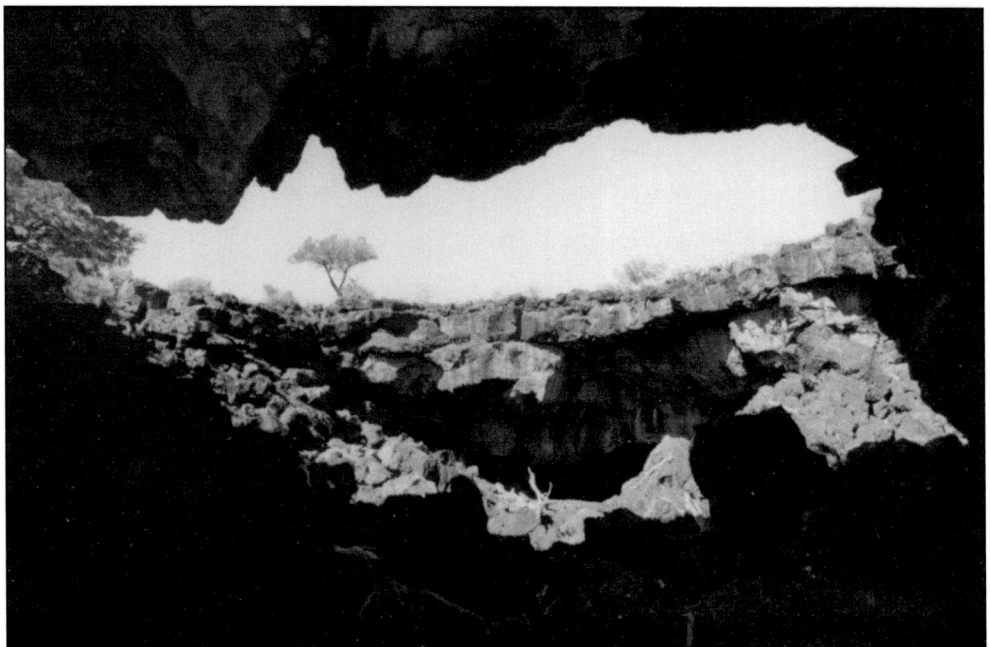

Hercules Leg is among the lava tube caves along Cave Loop Road. It is now one cave (with Juniper), but the two caves were discovered independently and treated separately until 1933, when Depression-era crews joined the two via excavation. The cave's features include several skylights and a large pillar.

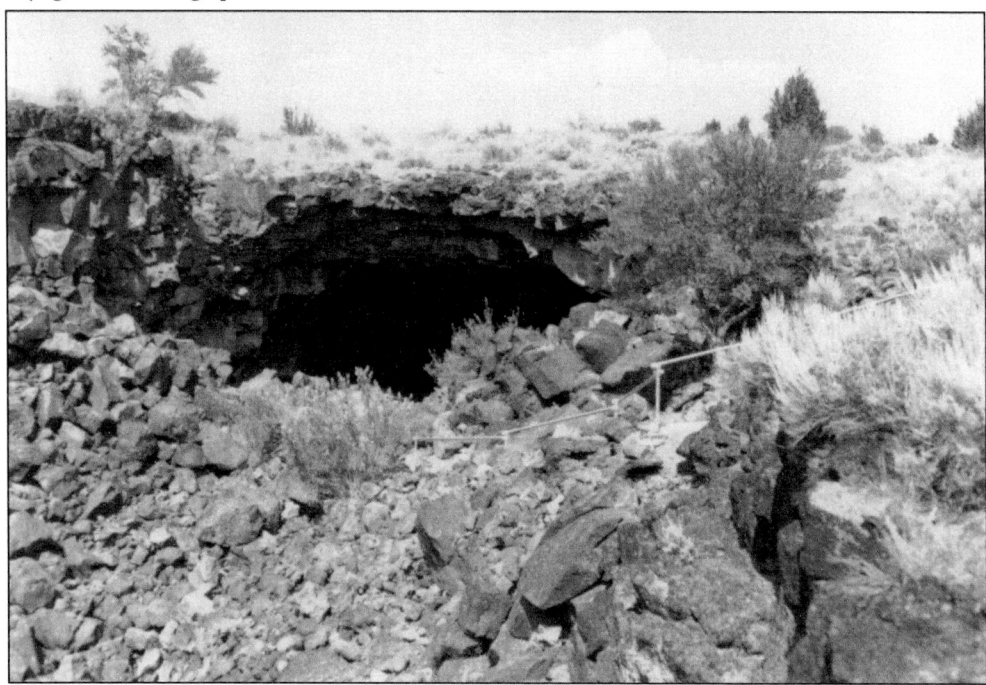

Skull Cave, a segment of the 10-mile long Modoc Crater lava tube system, has two main levels. The cave was named by E.L. Hopkins after the discovery of a large accumulation of bones at the bottom of the cave; most of the skulls were those of bighorn sheep, antelope, and mountain goats.

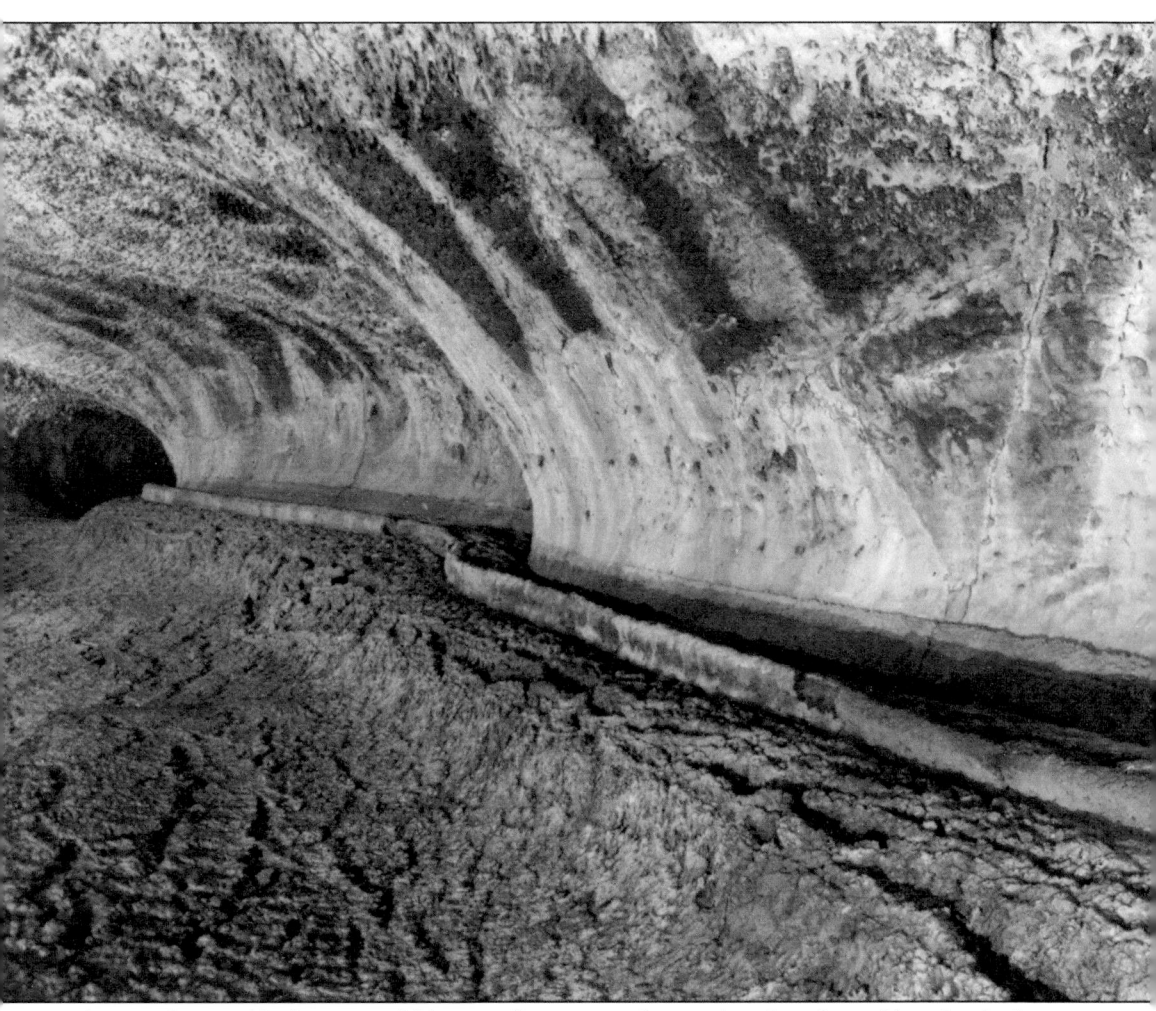

Among the notable features in Valentine Cave are its distinct benches, formed by a bank along the cave's lava tube. Benches join the cave's floor and wall. Along with its well-defined benches, Valentine is renowned for its well-preserved lava flow features, including symmetrical pillars and a ceiling with dark patches of lava stalactites separated by white bands of water-deposited minerals. Valentine is one of the few significant caves not discovered by J.D. Howard; it was discovered by Ross R. Musselman on Valentine's Day in 1933. The original entrance was quite small and obscured by a juniper tree. After his visit, Musselman described the cave as "the most beautiful thing I ever saw."

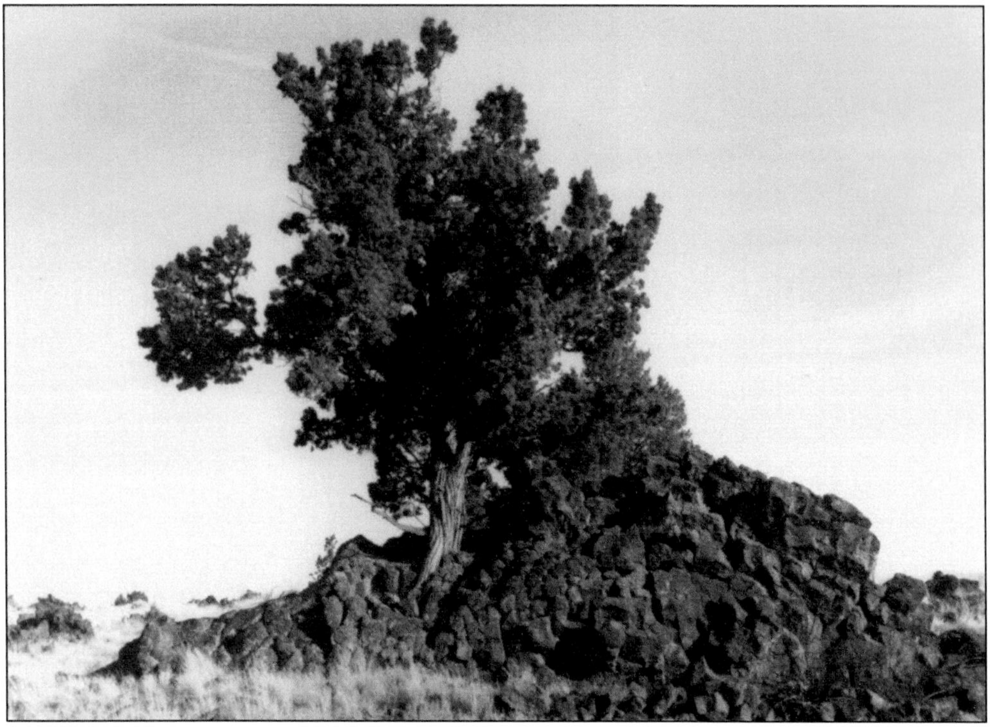

Not even lava from the Devils Homestead flow could prevent a hardy juniper tree from taking root. The flow, located near Gillems Camp, was created by volcanic events on the nearby Medicine Lake Highlands, which are located outside the monument's boundaries.

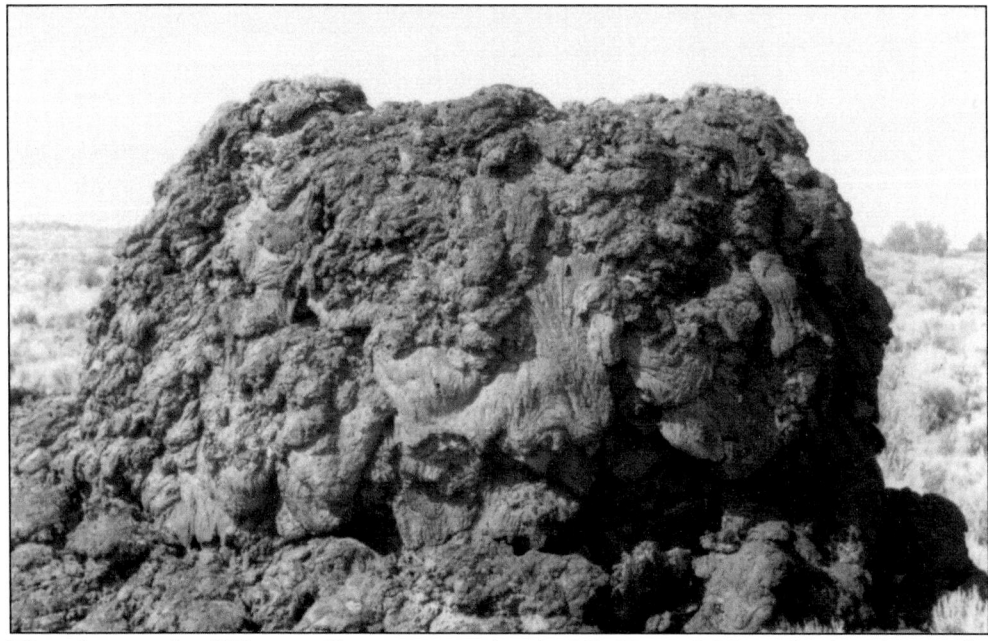

This photograph of Thomas Chimney was taken by J.D. Howard. Howard is best known for discovering many of the caves in what is now Lava Beds National Monument over a period that stretched from the mid-1910s into the 1930s.

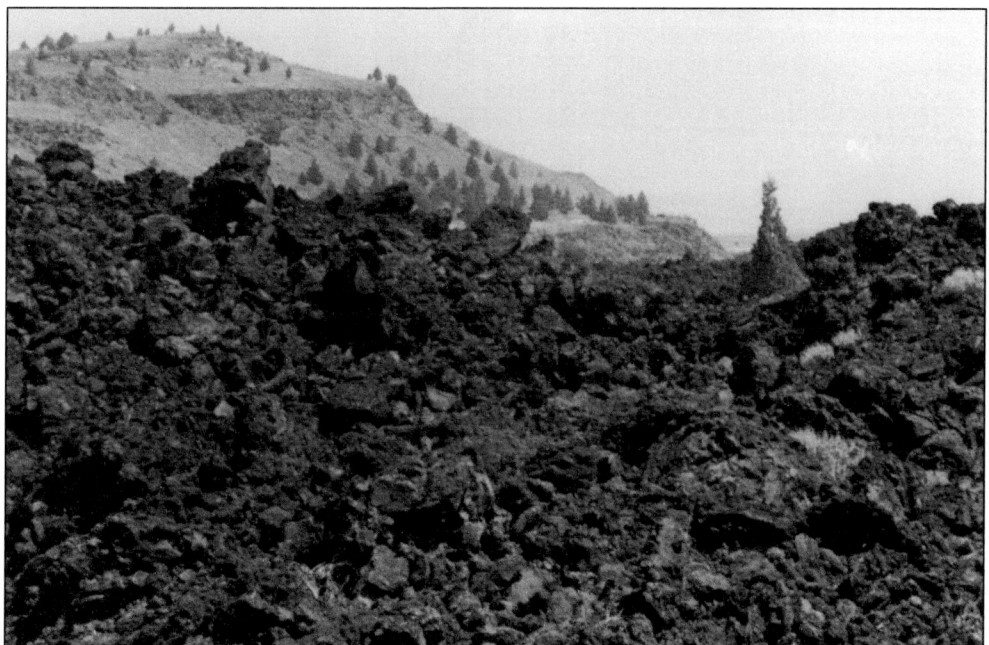

The aptly named Devils Homestead is a lava flow that extends for 3.5 miles. The pahoehoe lava flowed from its vent in a wide channel and, as it moved north, lost dissolved gasses and changed to aa lava. The main park road has an overlook that provides an expansive view of the flow.

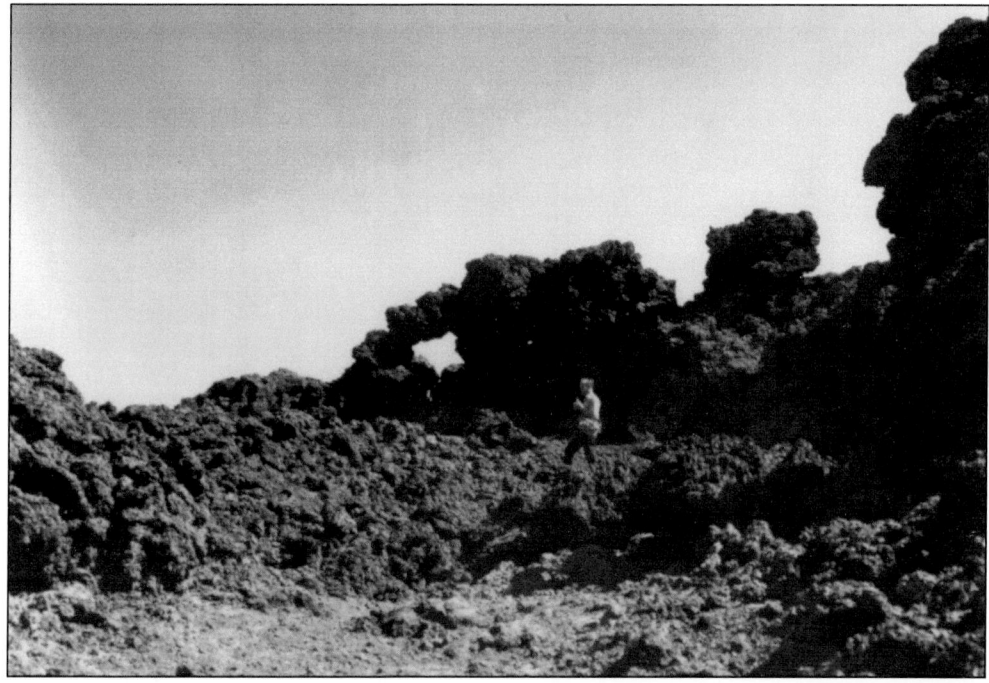

Access to the Black Crater, now just a short drive from the monument's main road, became possible in the late 1950s, when a new road was built; it was improved in 1962 as part of the National Park Service's Mission 66 effort to upgrade parks. The crater is a wondrous jumble of ragged lava. Some people believe the section of lava looks like a petrified cat or dragon.

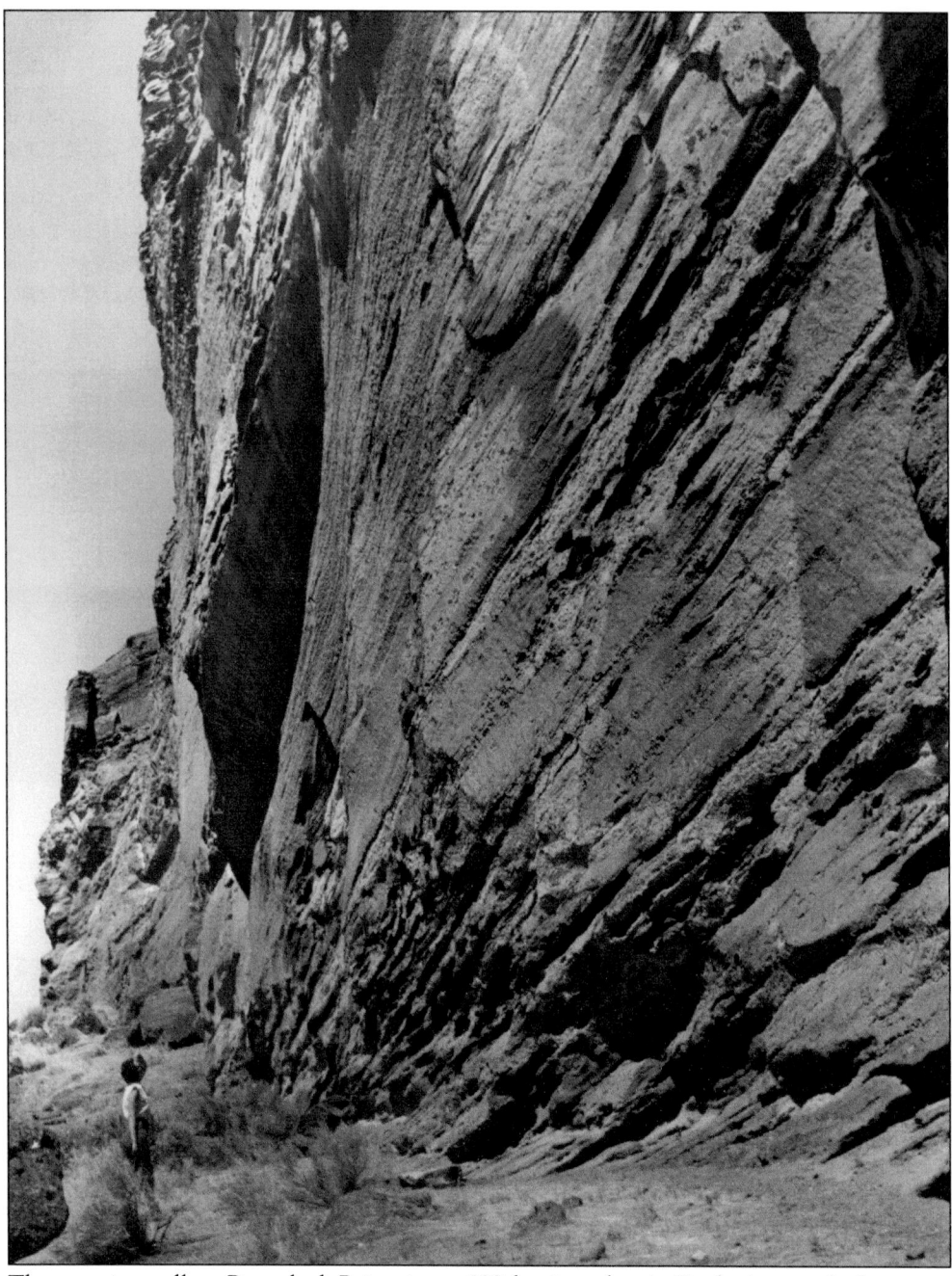

The towering walls at Petroglyph Point rise up 180 feet into the air. Geologists say the butte was created by underwater volcanic activity about 275,000 years ago. The sharp cliffs were formed 10,000 to 15,000 years ago by wave action from the formerly much larger Tule Lake. In Modoc legend, this was the place Gmukamps—the "creator"—built to view the world he made.

Petroglyph Point, a noncontiguous section of the monument, is remarkable for its geology and its use by native people, who incised petroglyphs into its calcified crust. The area around the large butte was once part of Tule Lake.

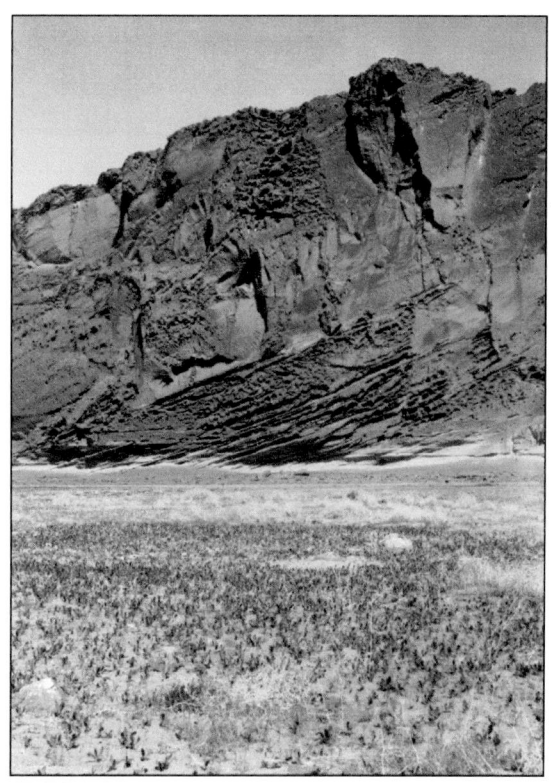

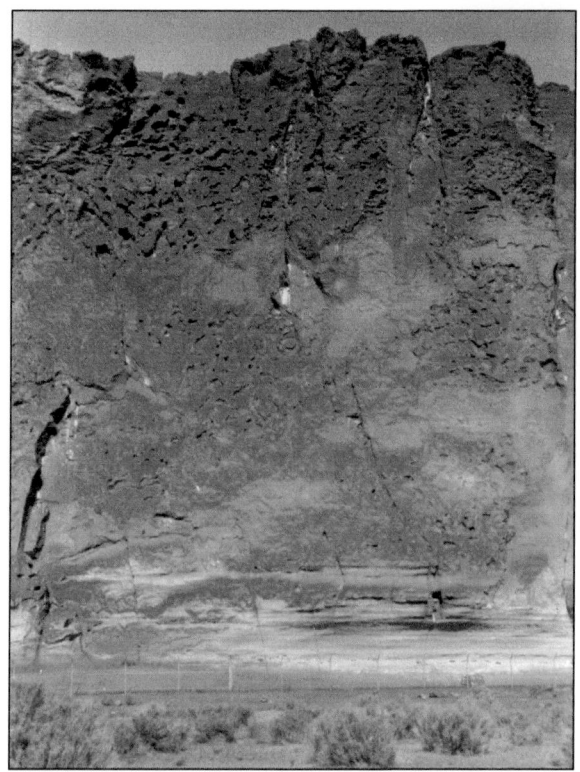

A fence near the base of Petroglyph Point was built by Civilian Conservation Corps work crews to help preserve the images carved by native people on the west and east faces of the butte. Over the years, some visitors have done irreversible damage to some of the images.

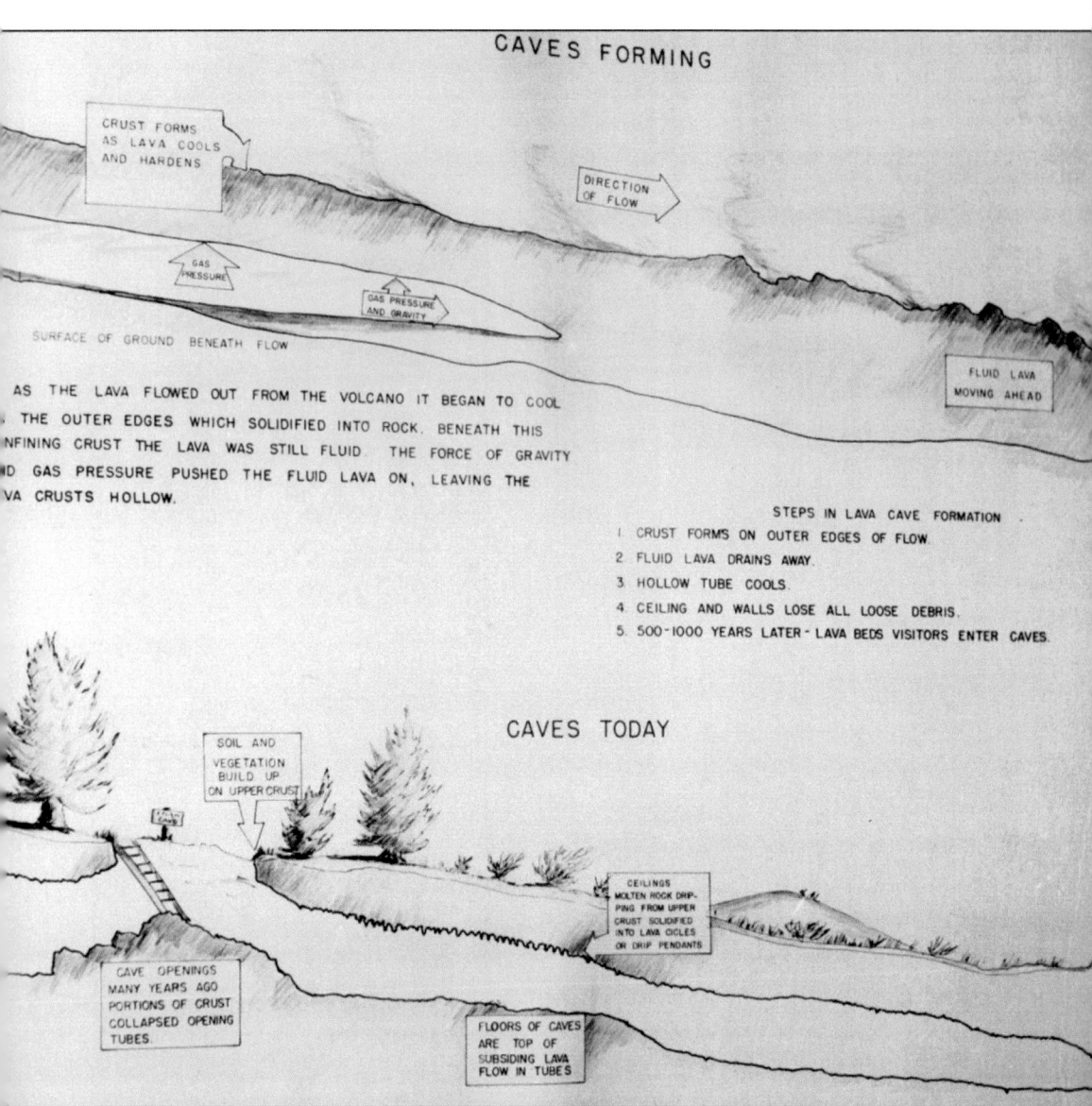

This simplified, illustrated explanation shows how lava tubes, like those at Lava Beds National Monument, are created. Much of the lava that created the monument's system of caves flowed from Mammoth Crater. As the lava flowed from the volcano, it began to cool on the outer edges, eventually solidifying into rock. However, the still-fluid lava underneath continued to flow, leaving hollow openings beneath the crust.

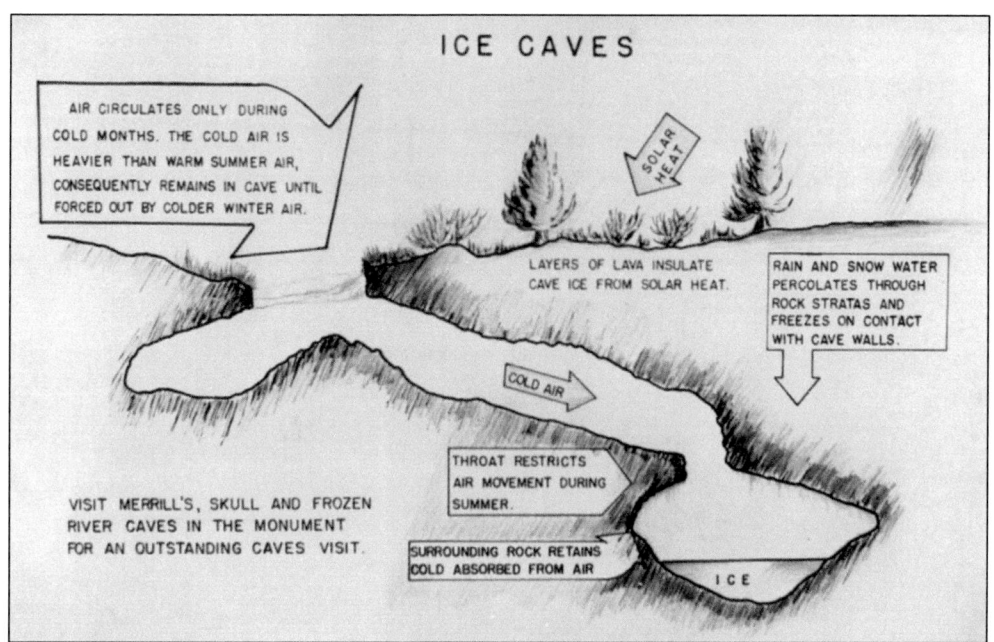

This diagram provides insight about how ice caves are created. Cold air is heavier than warm summer air, which remains in caves until it is forced out by colder winter air. The surrounding rock retains the cold. Rain and snow water percolates through the rock and freezes on contact with cave walls.

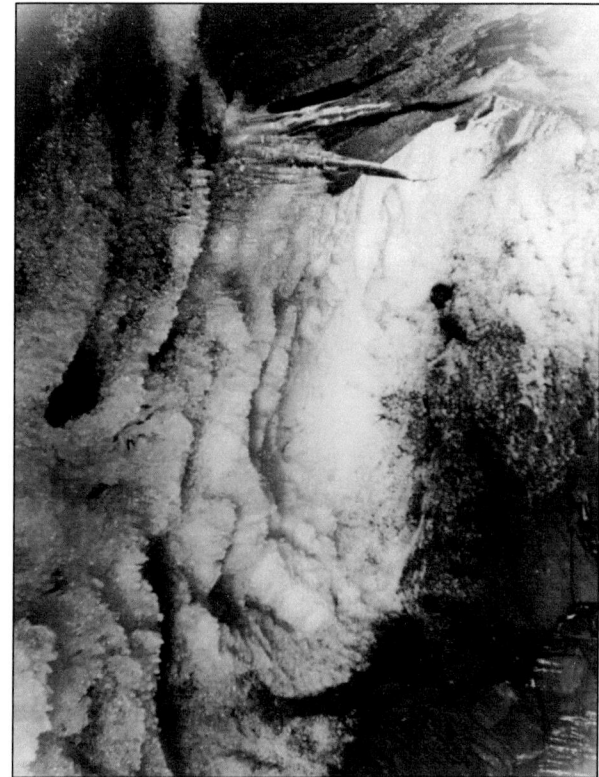

Ice crystals sparkle like diamonds in Crystal Ice Cave. Because of concerns about maintaining the cave's temperature, the entrance to the cave is locked. Limited numbers of visitors are allowed to tour the cave with a ranger during selected Saturdays in winter. Visiting the cave is physically demanding, because people must use ropes, clamber on ice, and slither through passages.

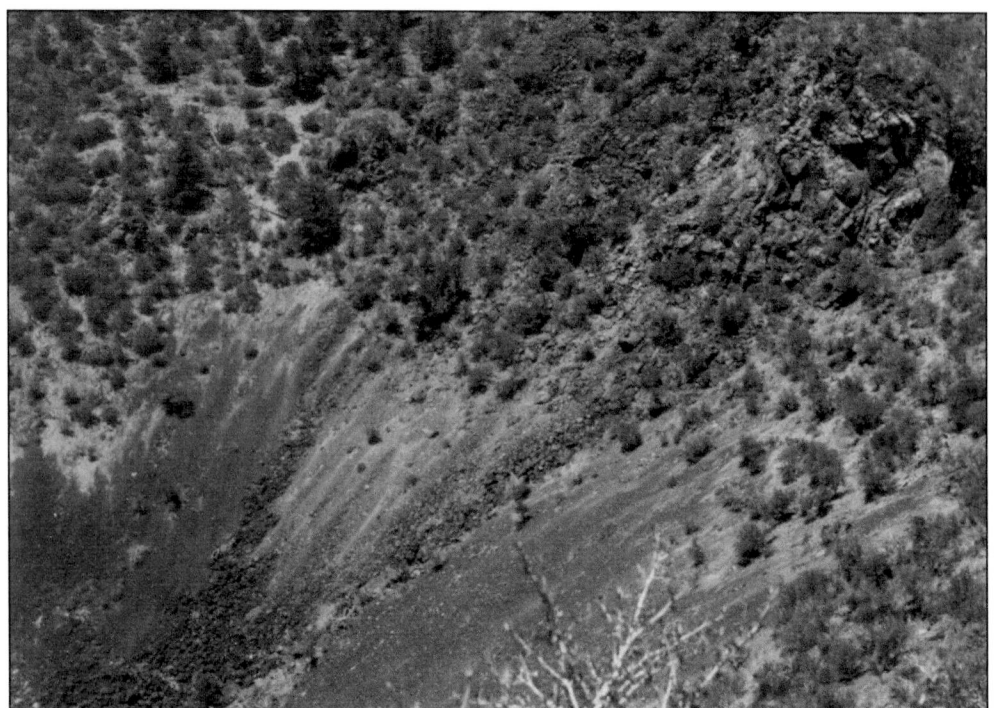

Geologists believe Mammoth Crater was created more than 30,000 years ago. Massive lava flows spilled as far as 15 miles downhill, creating an intricate network of lava tube caves and covering about 70 percent of the monument's surface area. The vast majority of the 700-plus caves, including all caves in the Cave Loop area, were created by flows from Mammoth Crater.

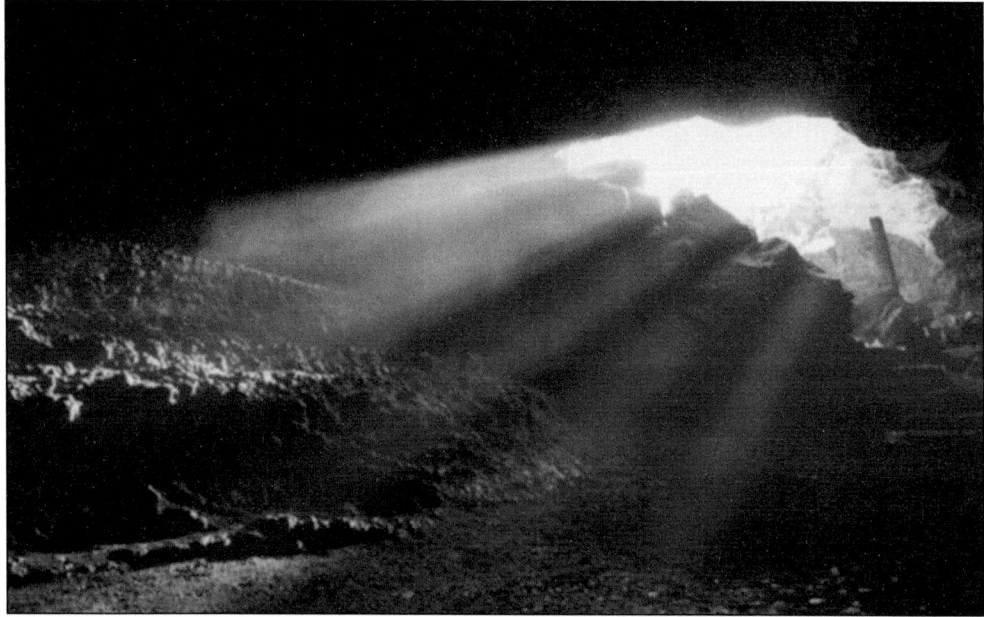

Valentine Cave's entrance seems to "breathe" steam on cold days. The cave is about 11,000 years old—relatively young compared to others at the monument. Because of its tall ceiling and somewhat smooth floor, it is one of the easiest caves for people to access.

Many areas of Lava Beds are seldom seen, including the Devils Homestead lava flow. Visitors sometimes view the area along its edges, but few people venture into the ragged lava flow because of the difficulty in trying to walk along its irregular, often jagged terrain. Pockets of bunchgrass, shrubs, and juniper trees have found ways to survive in the intervals of topsoil. Devils Homestead is part of Lava Beds National Monument's vast acreages of harsh, unforgiving landscape.

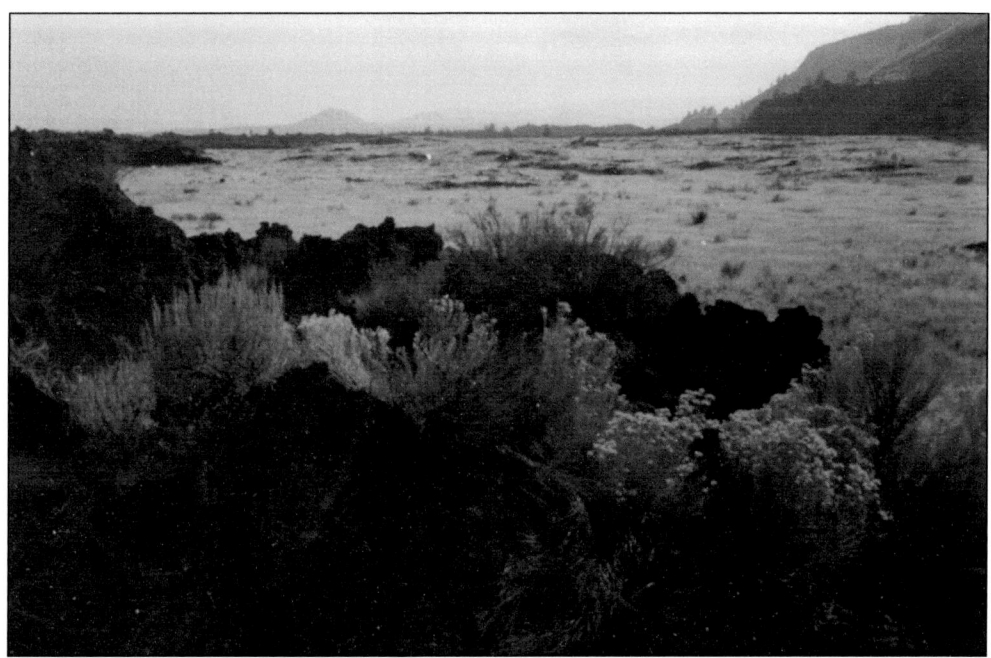

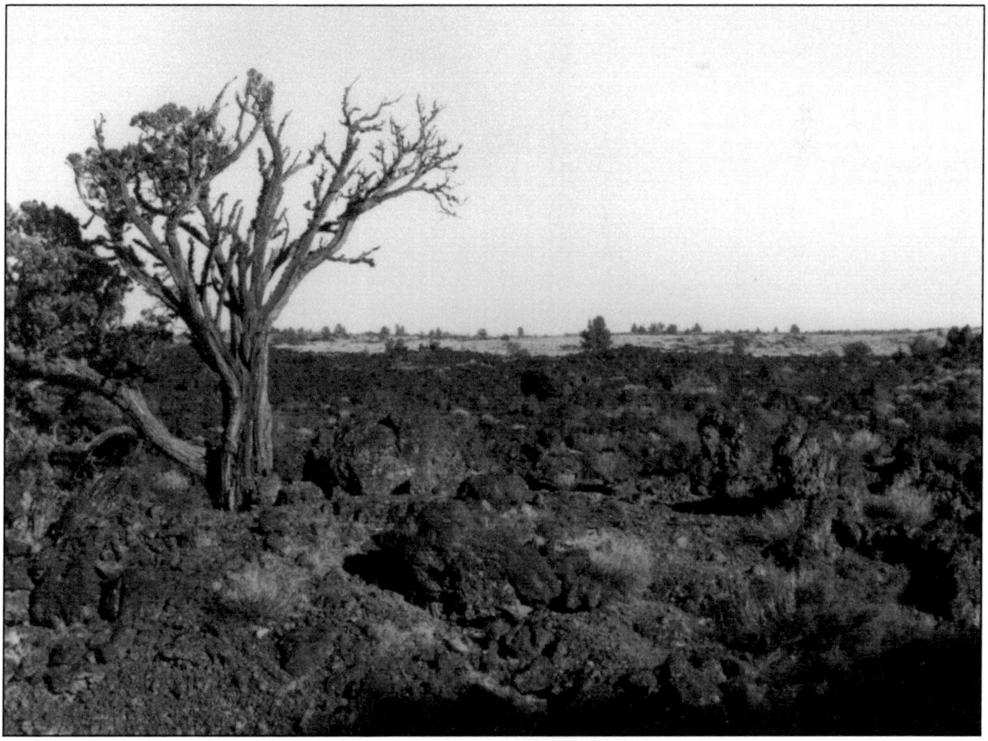

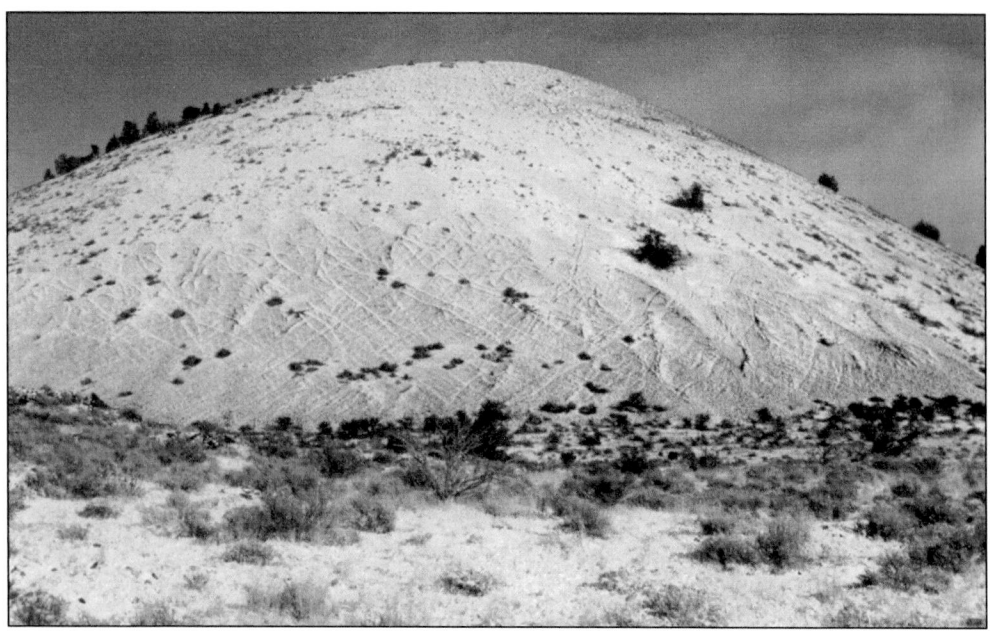

Coatings of winter snow add a softer dimension to Lava Beds' often bleak, barren landscape. Schonchin Butte (above), one of the monument's most prominent features, may appear less imposing under a blanket of white snow. In the monument's higher elevations, closer to Mammoth Crater and the Medicine Lake Highlands, the pine forest reveals a different personality. The monument does not typically receive extremely heavy snow, but during some winters, cross-country skiers can travel the Lyons Road and other areas.

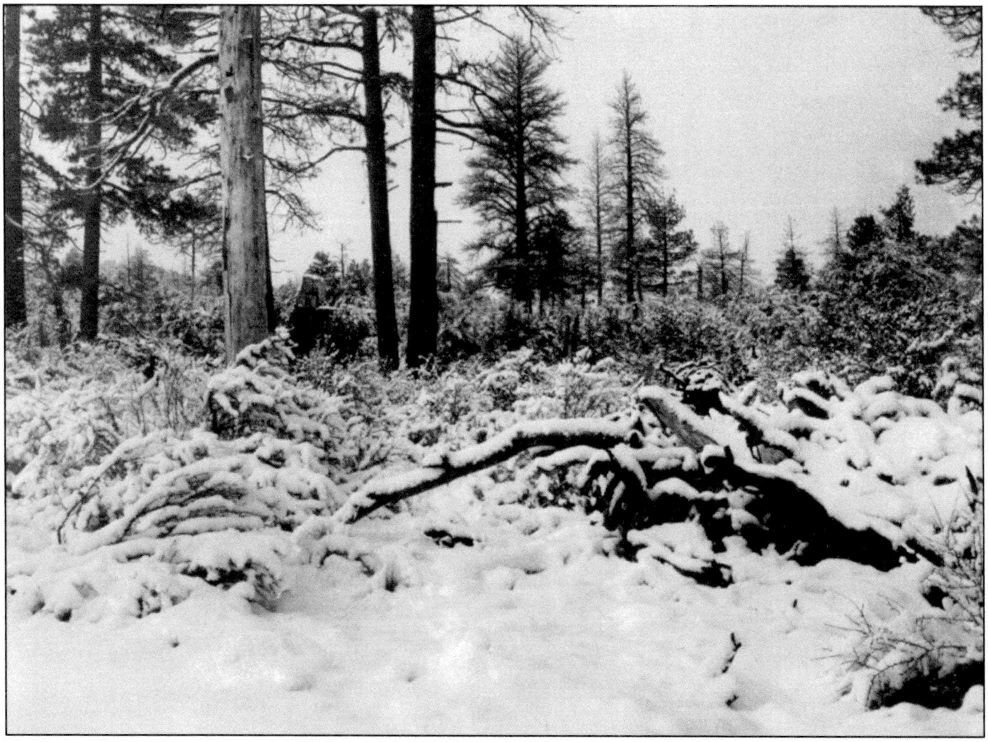

Two

EARLY INHABITANTS

Although geologists and scientists have explanations of how the region known as Lava Beds was created, so do Modoc Indians, whose ancestors inhabited the region at least 7,000 years ago. To the Modocs, the world was a disc with the eastern shore of Tule Lake at its center. Archeological studies show that groups of ancestral Modocs wintered in subterranean lodges in villages on the southern shore of Tule Lake and near Petroglyph Point. They dug earth-covered lodges that were entered through hatchways on top of the structures. During the winter, tribal elders passed along tales of Gmukamps, "the creator." According to Modoc legend, the people of the world were created from bones he threw from his basket. Gmukamps saved the bones for the Modocs for the last toss, telling them, "You will eat what I eat, you will keep my place when I am gone, you will be the bravest of all. Though you may be few, even if many and many people come against you, you will kill them."

A relatively small, loosely organized tribe, the Modocs lived in autonomous bands. Each band had a leader, but decisions affecting the entire group were voted on by adult men and women at community assemblies. The tribe's lifestyle was largely dictated by seasons, with members relocating village sites to hunt deer, elk, and waterfowl; to fish; and to gather edible plants, seeds, and bulbs. Tule reeds were used to weave baskets, make footwear, and help construct boats and homes. The Modocs have been estimated to have had at least 20 semi-permanent villages along the shores of lakes and rivers in the area until Euro-Americans eventually settled in the region.

The frequency of contact between the settlers and the Modocs grew with the discovery of gold at Sutter's Mill near Sacramento, California, in 1849, and, only a few years later, at Yreka. The Applegate Trail, a branch of the Oregon Trail, passed alongside Modoc lands. Most travelers continued west, but some stayed to grow crops and raise sheep. Hostilities increased between the two groups, with Modocs raiding and killing settlers and, in 1852, the slaughter of more than 30 Modoc men, women, and children by noted "Indian killer" Ben Wright. In the 1870s, the lands at the center of the Modoc world became the center of California's only Indian war.

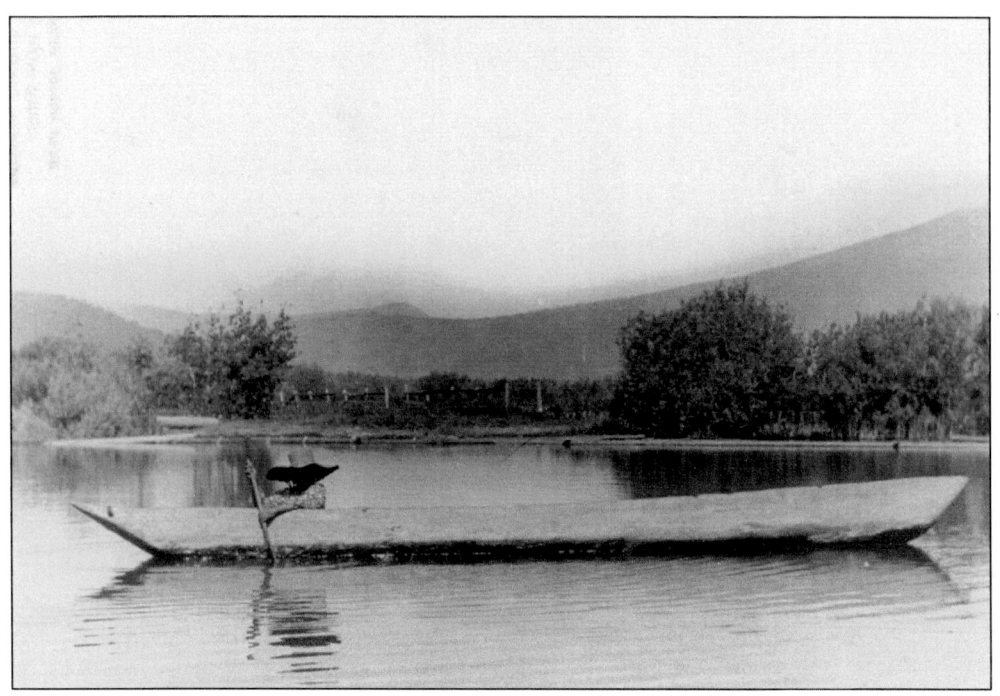

The natives used dugout canoes—carved from trees—for transportation, fishing, boating to areas to pick wocas (seed pods of the yellow water lily), and to escape to the rocky fortress known as Captain Jack's Stronghold at the start of the Modoc War.

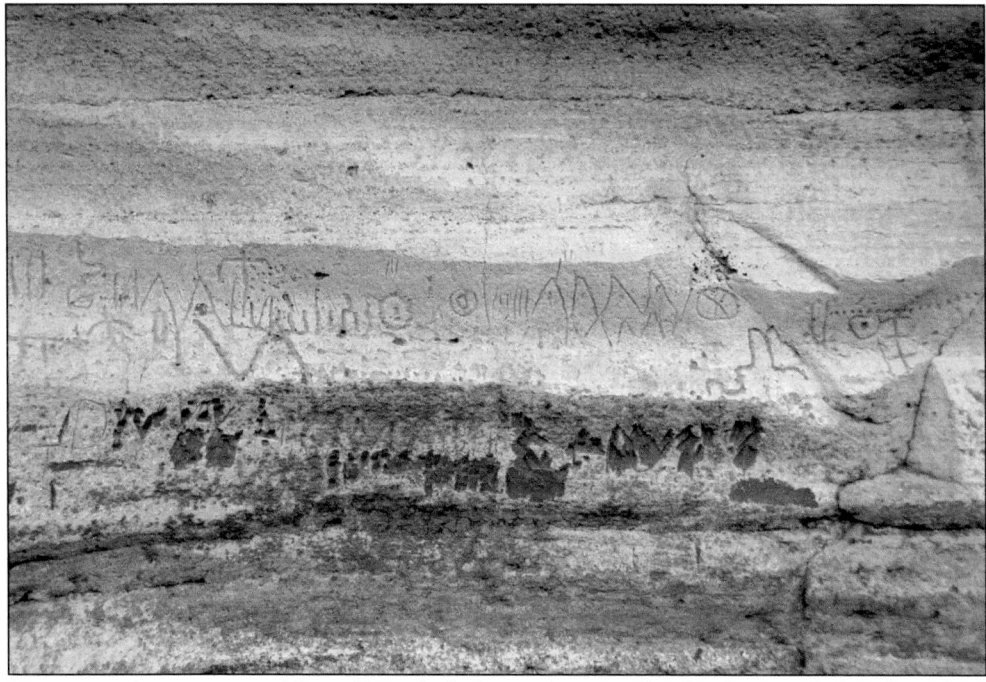

Natives used canoes to paddle to Petroglyph Point, then an island in historic Tule Lake, where they carved hundreds of images in the walls. Despite fences that installed by the CCC to protect the historic images, over the years, some visitors have defaced sections of the rock.

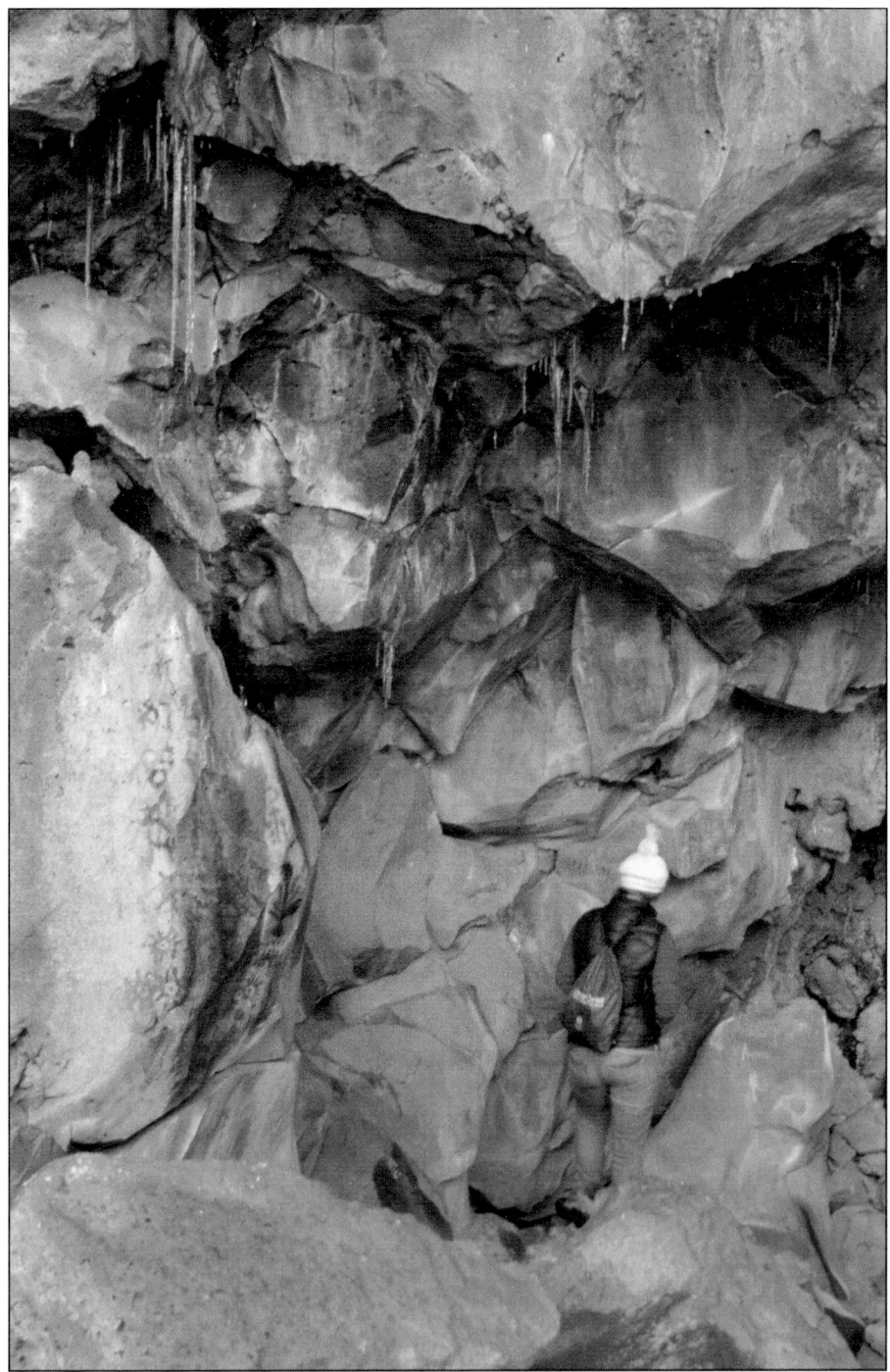
Visitors to Symbol Bridge can view pictographs—images painted on cave walls that may date to more than 1,000 years ago. The paintings are believed to be related to the spiritual activities of ancestral Modocs. Over the years, many of the pictographs have faded, and some have been obscured by water-deposited materials. Worse, some pictographs have been defaced by inconsiderate visitors. This area can be reached via a short trail.

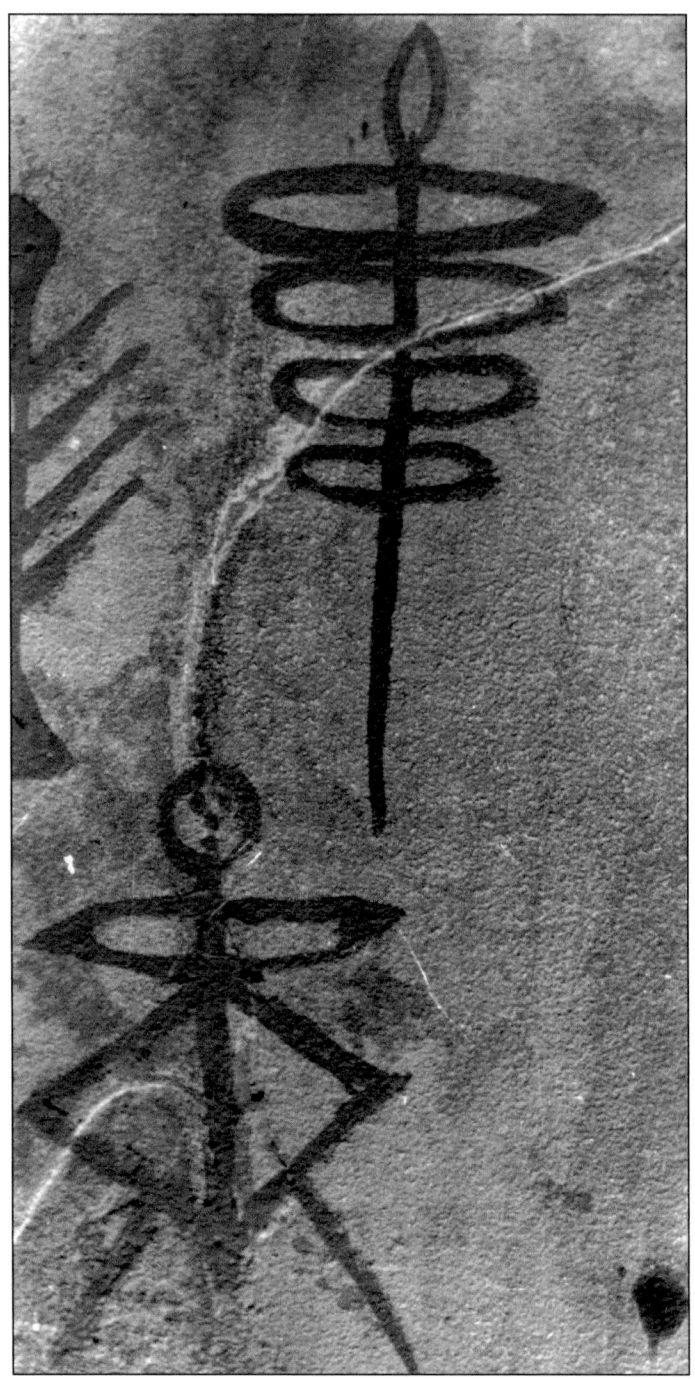

Some of the images created by ancestral native people at Petroglyph Point represented humans and lizards, while other images featured more abstract lines, circles, and curves. The pictographs cannot be dated with precision, and their meanings are unknown, although people are encouraged by rangers to develop their own theories. This undated photograph, taken by Lava Beds explorer J.D. Howard, shows a series of side-by-side images, one almost human-like and others featuring characteristic lines and circles.

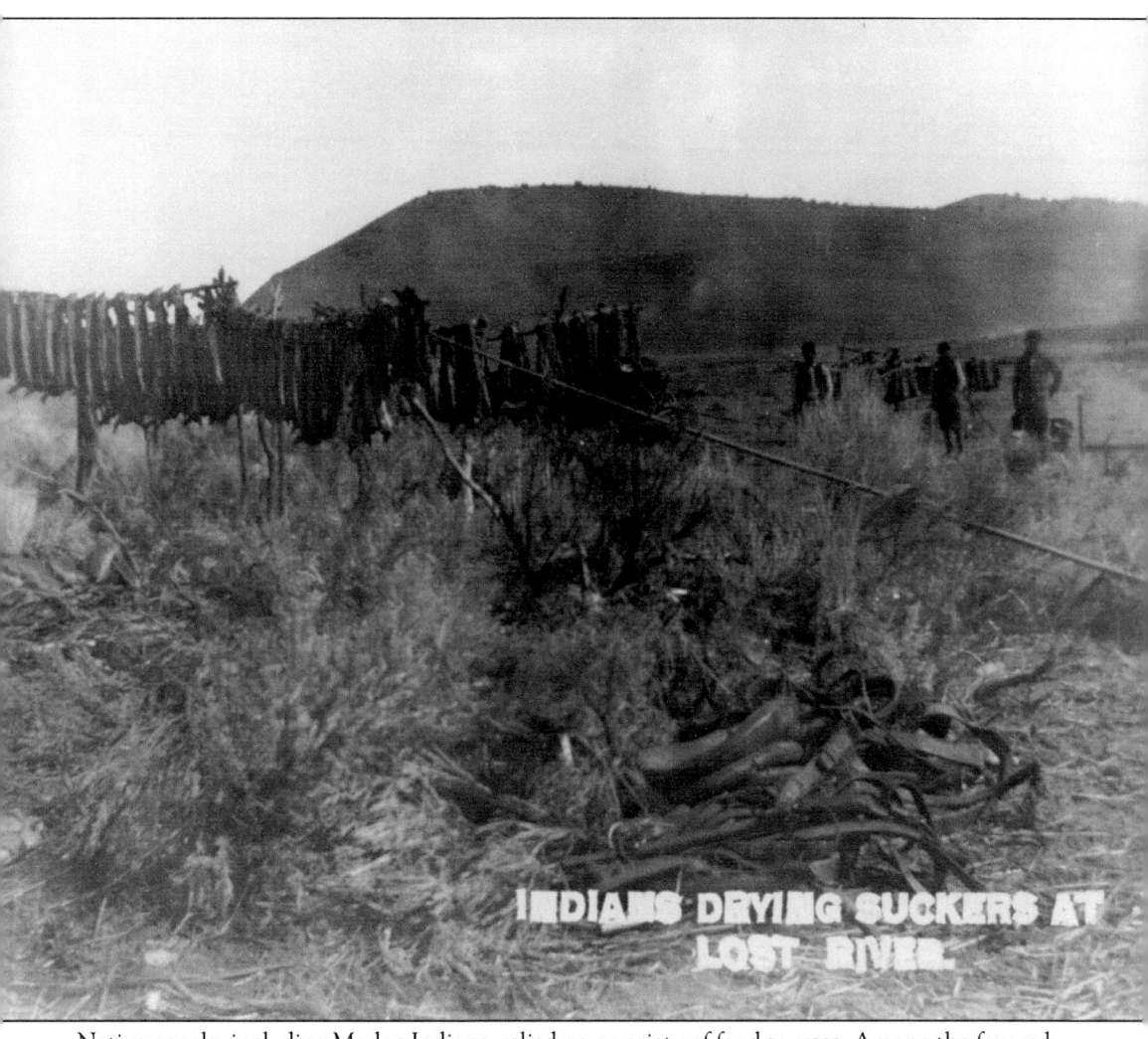

Native people, including Modoc Indians, relied on a variety of food sources. Among the favored items were suckers, found in area rivers, which were often dried and eaten. The photograph shows a sucker-drying station at the Lost River. Tule Lake also provided the natives with tules, wocas, cattails, reeds, trout, geese, ducks, coots, cranes, elk, and grizzly bears.

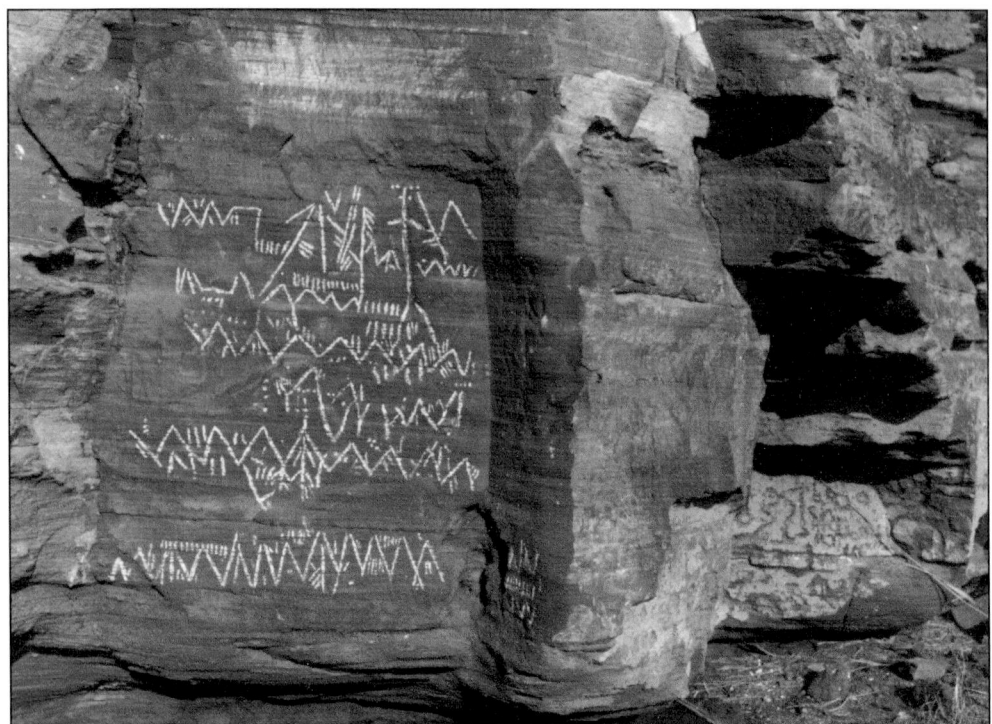

Petroglyphs, some enhanced and others simply carved into the walls, are easily viewed at Petroglyph Point. About 5,000 have been counted on the west and east walls at the former island. No one knows what the lines, circles, and other images mean

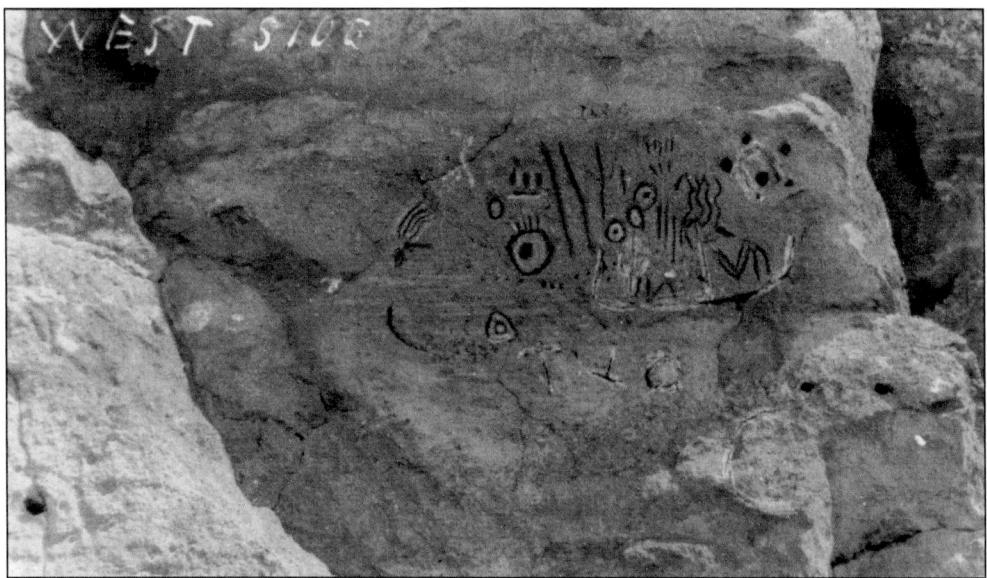

Circles, ovals, straight lines, and wavy lines are typical of the images pierced and scraped into the walls at Petroglyph Point. It is believed that the various petroglyphs were made before the 1840s. Some archeologists posit that because fluctuating lake levels would quickly erode images, the drawings at Petroglyph Point may be no more than a few hundred years old, although others believe they were created thousands of years ago.

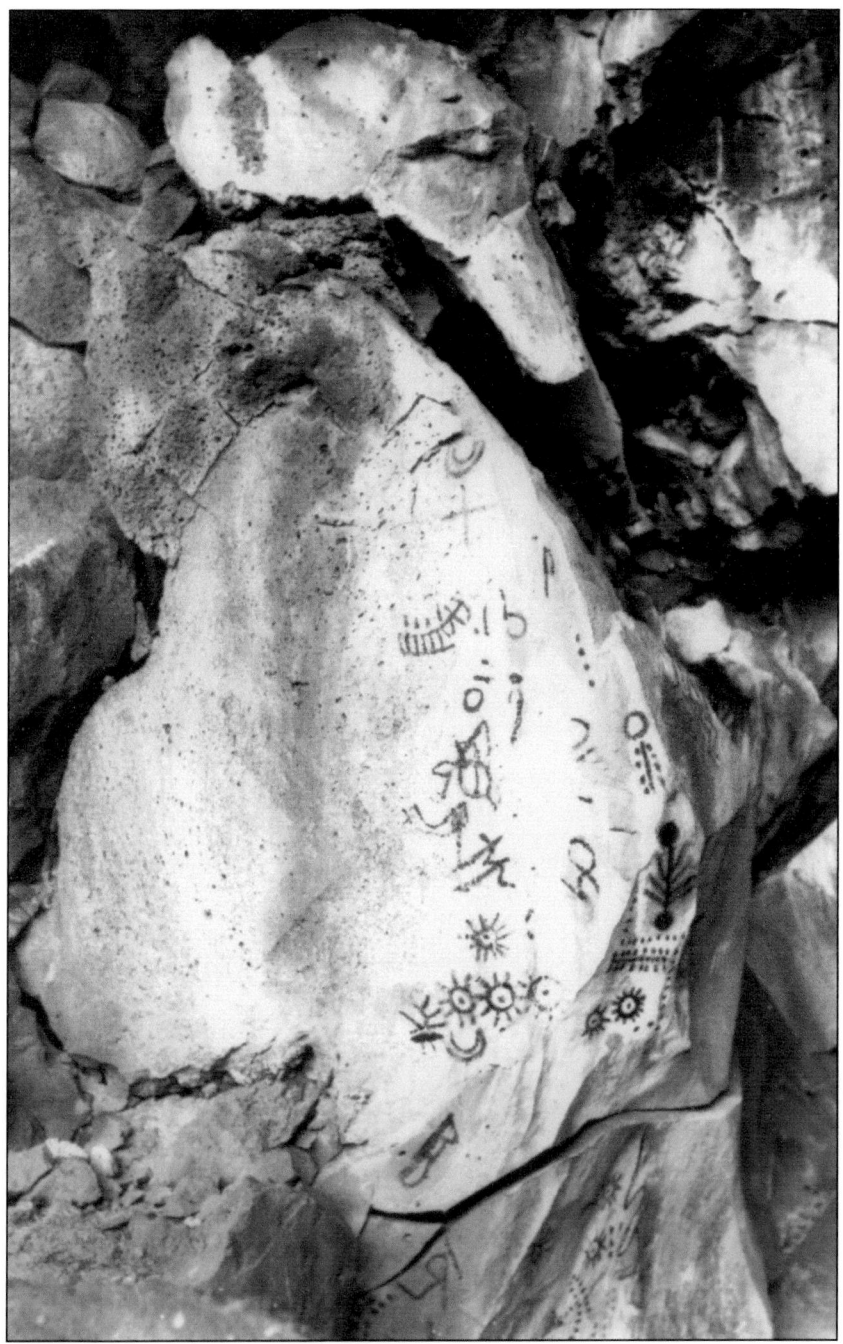

Stick-like human images, rows of dots, decorated circles some believe represent the sun or flowers, and a variety of other images are among the pictographs found at places like Symbol Bridge. A study indicated that most of the petroglyphs are abstract images, with relatively few showing humans, lizards, and/or insects. Most involved abstract images of circles, lines, and curves. Those who created the images most likely used a "pierce and scrape" technique, which involved piercing holes through the rock face or, less often, incising lines with a thin, sharp instrument. This photograph was taken by J.D. Howard, who expressed a fascination with pictographs and petroglyphs.

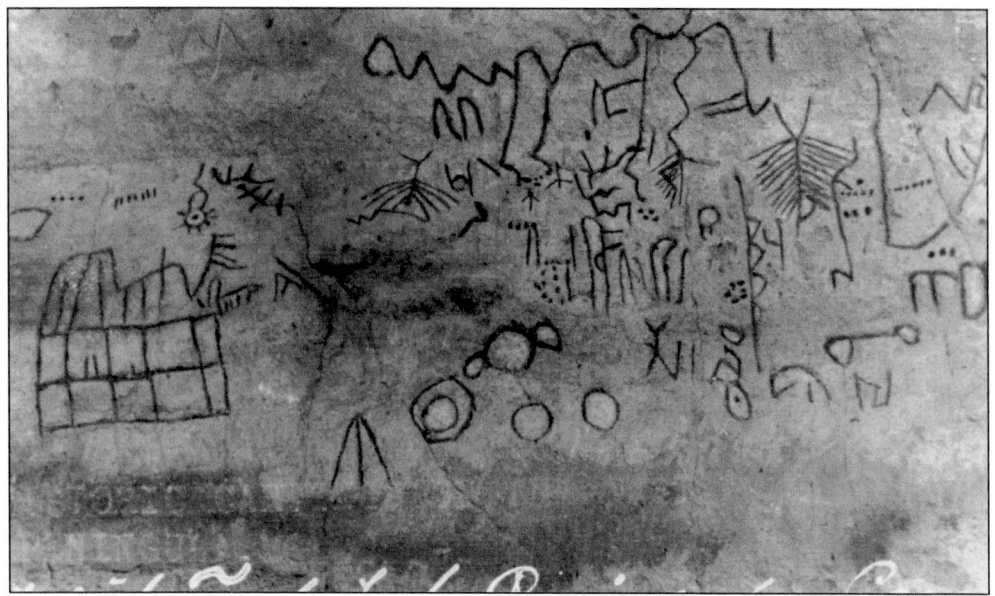

J.D. Howard, one of Lava Beds' earliest explorers, photographed many of the petroglyphs at Petroglyph Point. Howard produced an extensive collection of photographs that documented Lava Beds in the early 20th century and has proved valuable for historians.

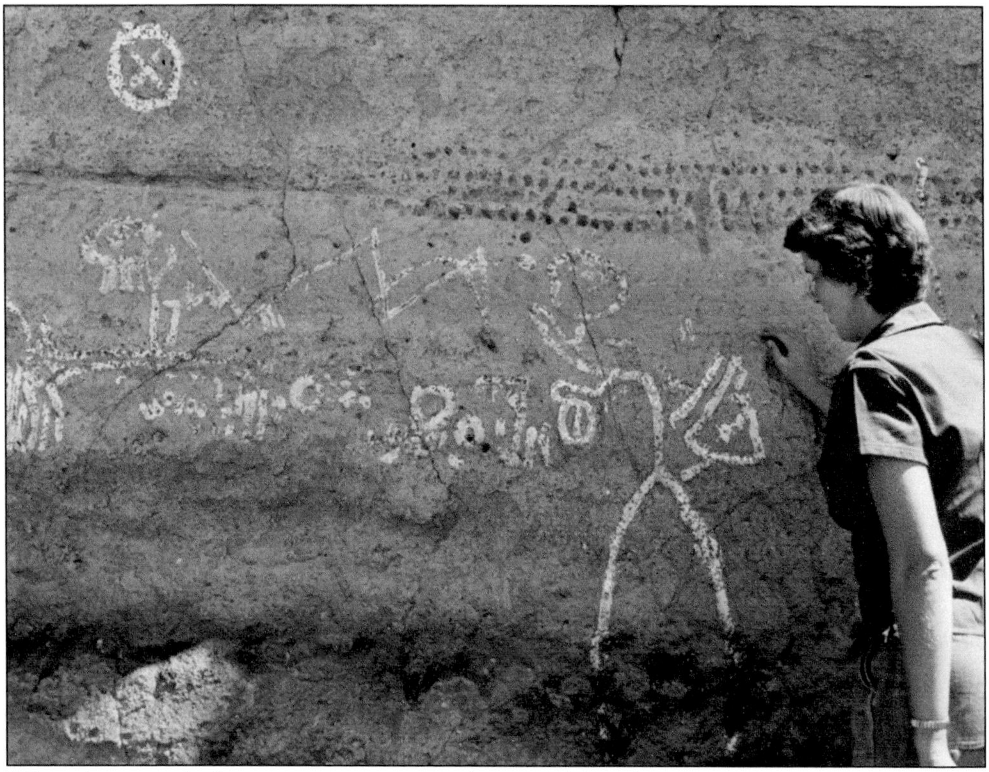

What the petroglyphs represent remains unknown, although some scholars believe they may be associated with the search for spiritual power through vision quests. Park rangers encourage visitors to formulate their own ideas of what they might mean or represent.

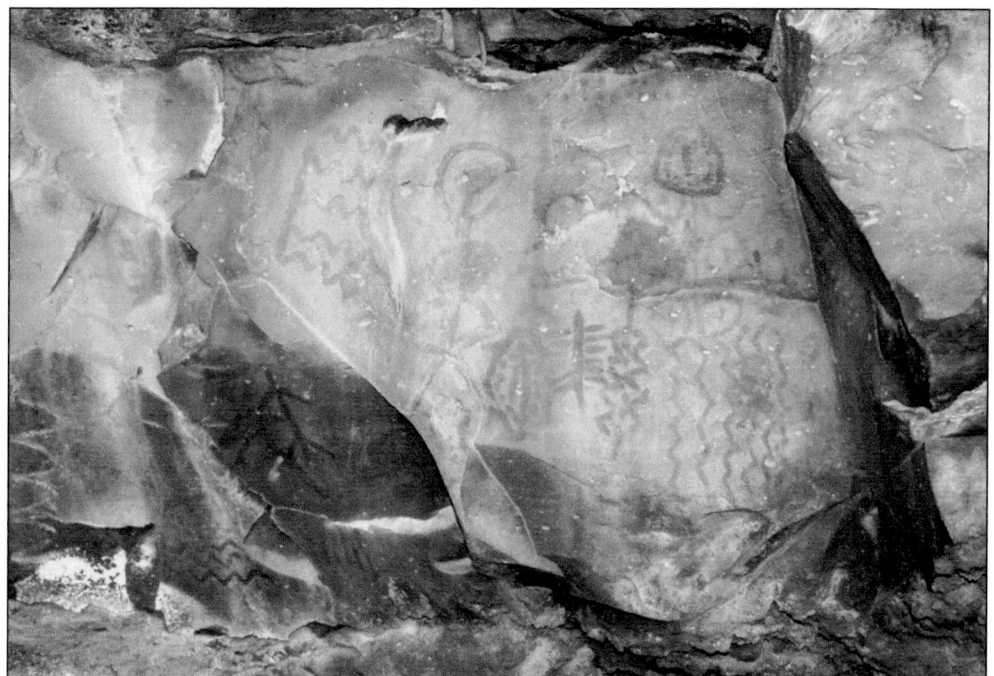

Multicolored art on the walls of Symbol Bridge indicates that the area was an important prehistoric culture site. J.D. Howard located the site, which he named, after being introduced to the area and neighboring Big Painted Cave by former Klamath Falls postmaster William Delzell in 1917. Symbol Bridge and Big Painted Cave are segments of the Modoc Crater lava tube system.

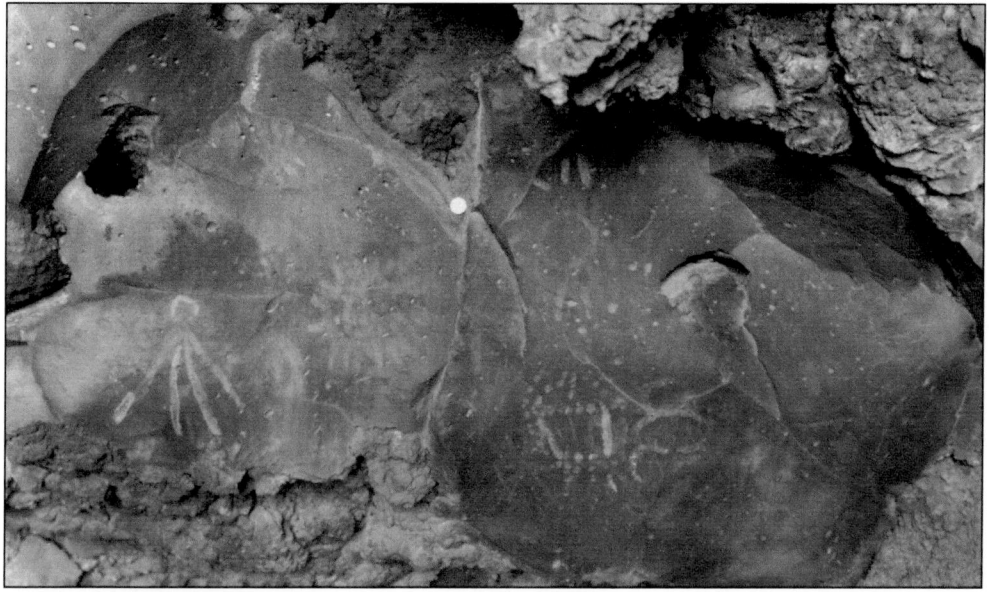

Visitors to Symbol Bridge are greeted by distinct pictographs near the right side of the entrance. These images are believed to have been created by prehistoric Modoc Indians, and the art may be related to the spiritual activities of ancestral Modocs. Charlie and Jo Larson suggest in their booklet, "Lava Beds Caves": "As you walk there, do so with honor. Spirits still sing there, and if you show respect to them and to their site, they, in turn, will honor you."

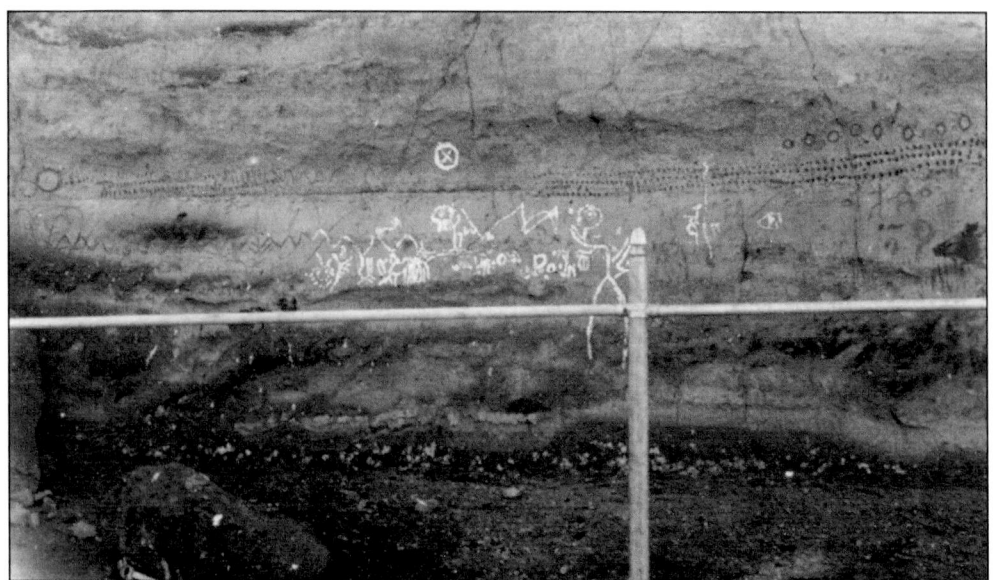

Modern humans have considered petroglyphs to represent a wide range of things, from graffiti to spiritual symbolism. People who view the petroglyphs carved into the walls of Petroglyph Point by ancestral natives have long debated their significance. In this undated photograph, construction had just begun on a wall intended to prevent vandalism.

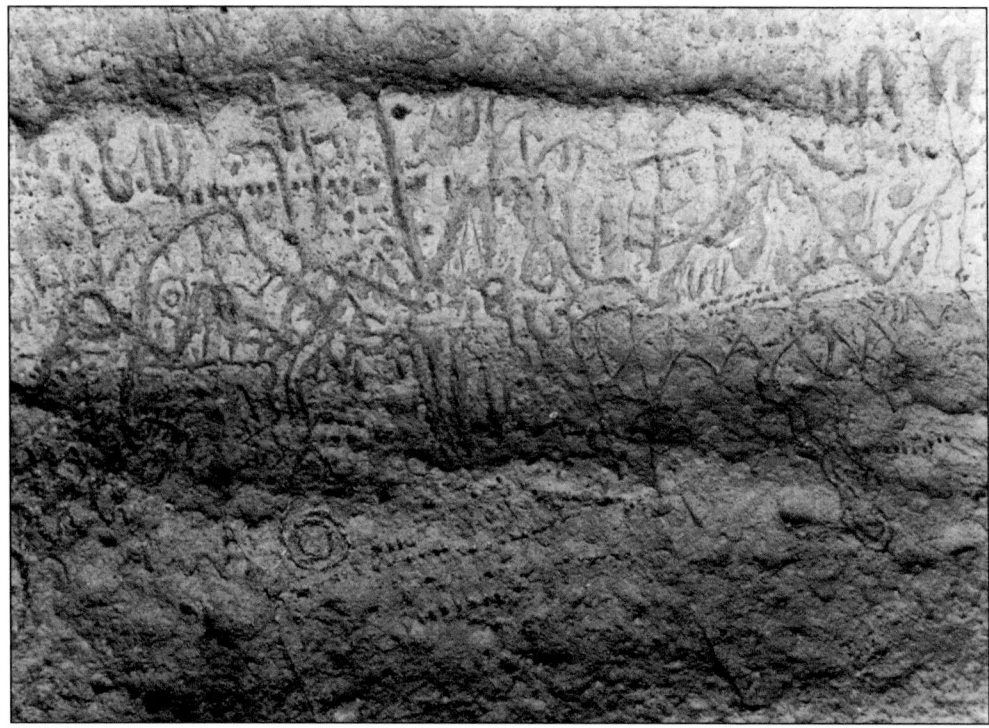

The size and scale of some of the petroglyphs at Petroglyph Point is impressive. The height of the images, which varies, reflects the water level of Tule Lake, which once enclosed the butte. Because fluctuating water levels would have eroded images, some archeologists believe they could be thousands of years old.

Three

THE MODOC WAR

Lava Beds became the venue for the major battles of the Modoc War—a war that reflected the struggles between Indians and whites throughout the American West.

The war began on November 29, 1872, with the Battle of Lost River, initiated by US Army troops attempting to force Modocs who had left the Klamath Reservation back to the reservation. The largest band of Modocs, led by Captain Jack (or Keint-poos), retreated to Lava Beds and what is now Captain Jack's Stronghold, a maze of natural lava fortifications. Another faction of Modocs killed 14 white male settlers before retreating to the stronghold. A third group of Modocs wanted to return to the reservation, but went to the stronghold to avoid a lynch mob.

On January 17, 1873, a cold, foggy morning, 320 Army soldiers, volunteers, and Indian scouts from other tribes (including Warm Springs) attacked the stronghold. The Modocs' knowledge of the rugged terrain, combined with the weather, proved disastrous for the invaders, who suffered a humiliating defeat. The 55 Modoc warriors were emboldened by their victory.

Months of peace negotiations followed, with the Modocs requesting a reservation in their Lost River homeland. The Army increased its troops, eventually to more than 1,000. The night before a peace commission meeting, Modocs voted on whether they should kill the commissioners. The faction led by Captain Jack, which pleaded for peace, was outvoted. Toby Riddle, a Modoc translator later known as Winema, warned peace commissioners; they ignored her pleas.

On April 12, the commissioners—Gen. E.R.S. Canby, Rev. Eleazar Thomas, Alfred Meacham, and Leroy Dyar—attended the peace commission meeting. After his reservation request was rejected, Captain Jack shot General Canby, who died. Other Modocs also opened fire, killing Thomas and wounding Meacham.

Four days later, Army troops invaded the stronghold but found it deserted. On April 26, a 69-man patrol, led by Capt. Evan Thomas and Lt. Thomas Wright, was attempting to locate the Modocs when it was fired on while stopped for lunch. Thomas and Wright and several other soldiers were killed.

The Modocs suffered their first defeat on May 10 while attacking troops at Dry Lake. Following the battle, bands of quarreling Modocs separated. The Hot Creek band surrendered on May 22. In exchange for amnesty, they helped track Captain Jack, who surrendered on June 1.

On October 3, 1873, Captain Jack, Schonchin John, Black Jim, and Boston Charley were found guilty of murder and hanged at Fort Klamath. Two others, Barncho and Slolux, had their death sentences commuted and were sent to Alcatraz. Within two weeks, 163 Modocs were sent to the Quapaw Agency in Oklahoma as prisoners.

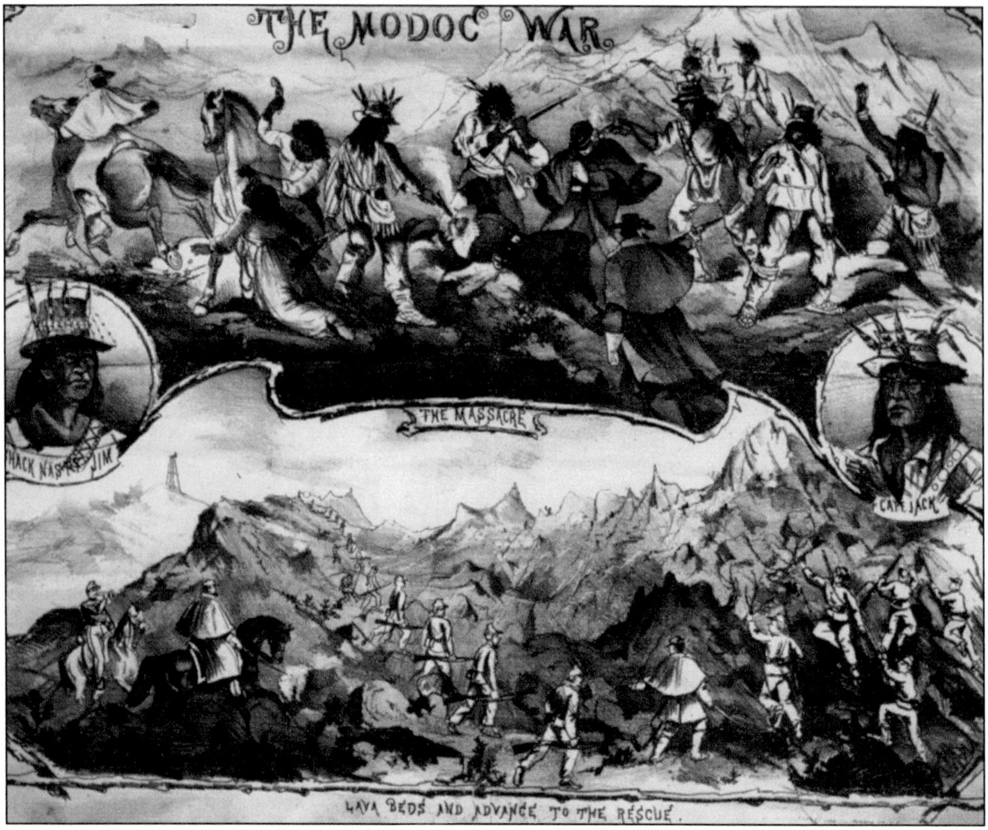

This drawing, exhibited at the Modoc County Courthouse in Alturas, dramatized scenes from the Modoc War, which began in 1872 and lasted until 1873. This image, from the collection of the Native Daughters of the Golden West, features a montage of scenes from the war.

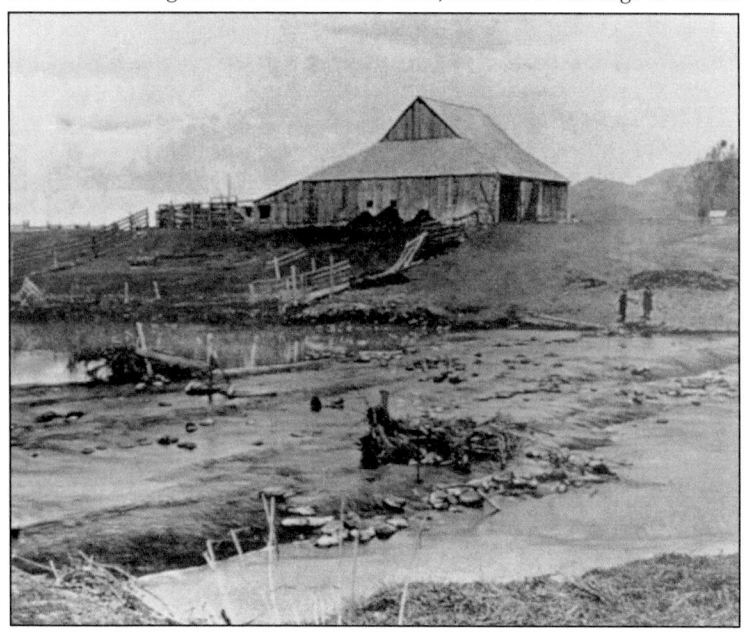

The Modoc War began on November 29, 1872, with the Battle of Lost River. US Army soldiers and Oregon volunteers went to the Modocs' camp after being told to return the Modocs to the Klamath Reservation. The question of who fired the first shot is still under debate, but it resulted in fierce fighting.

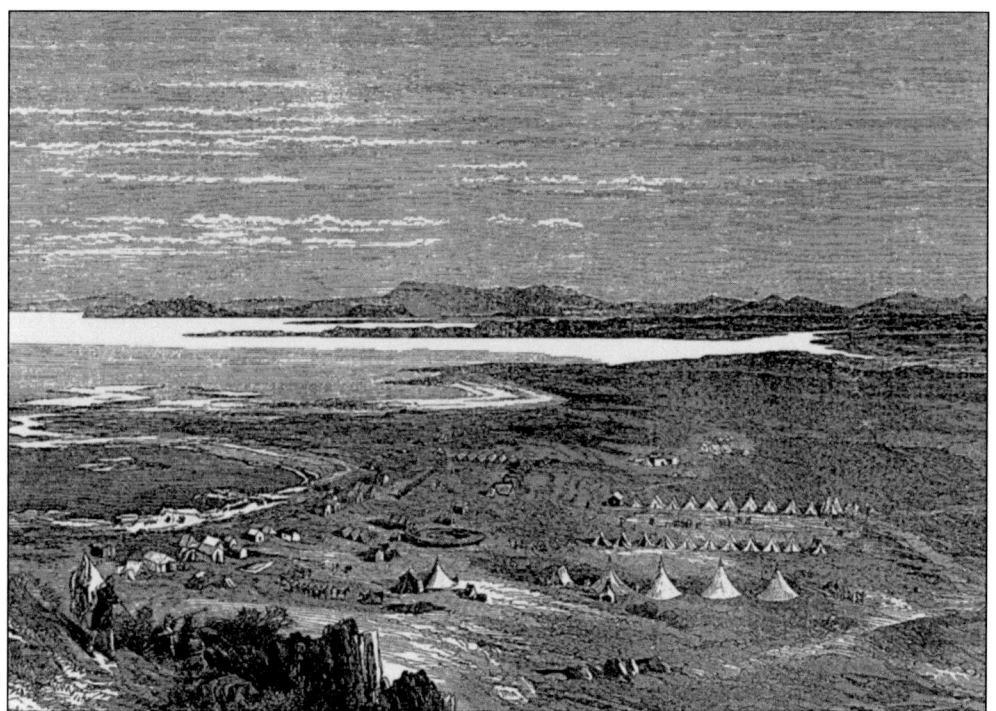
The Modoc War was extensively covered by reporters from the United States and England. Illustrators captured the scene in drawings, including this illustration of the US Army's headquarters at Gillems Camp; this appeared in the May 24, 1873, issue of the *Illustrated London News*.

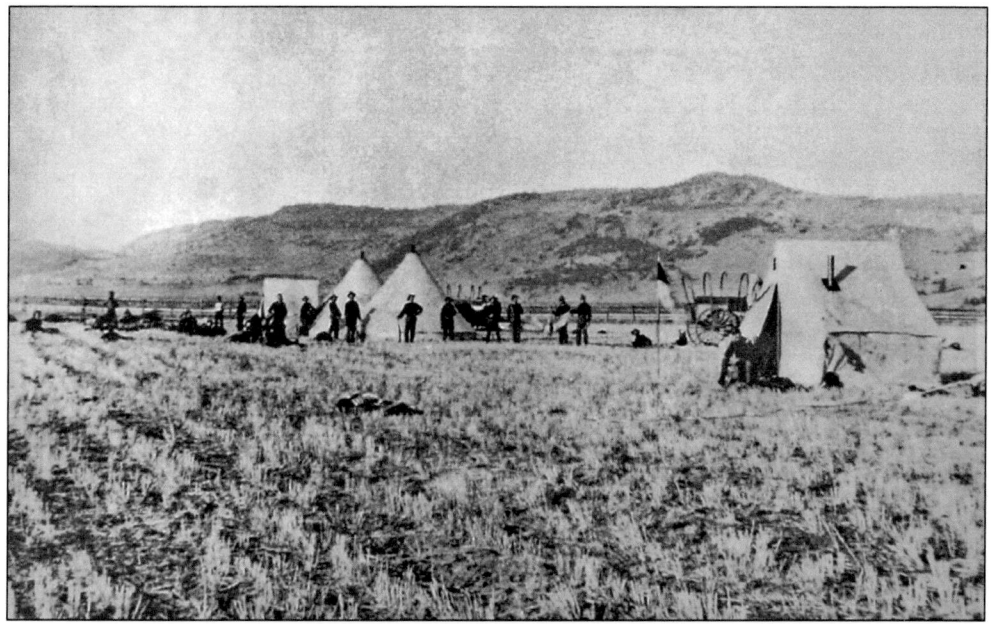
About 700 US Army troops were stationed at the Applegate Ranch (in the Tulelake area), the Dorris and Van Bremer ranches, and at Lost River when Army troop numbers were increased after the humiliating defeat at Captain Jack's Stronghold. Another 140 troops assembled at Fort Warner and Fort Harney.

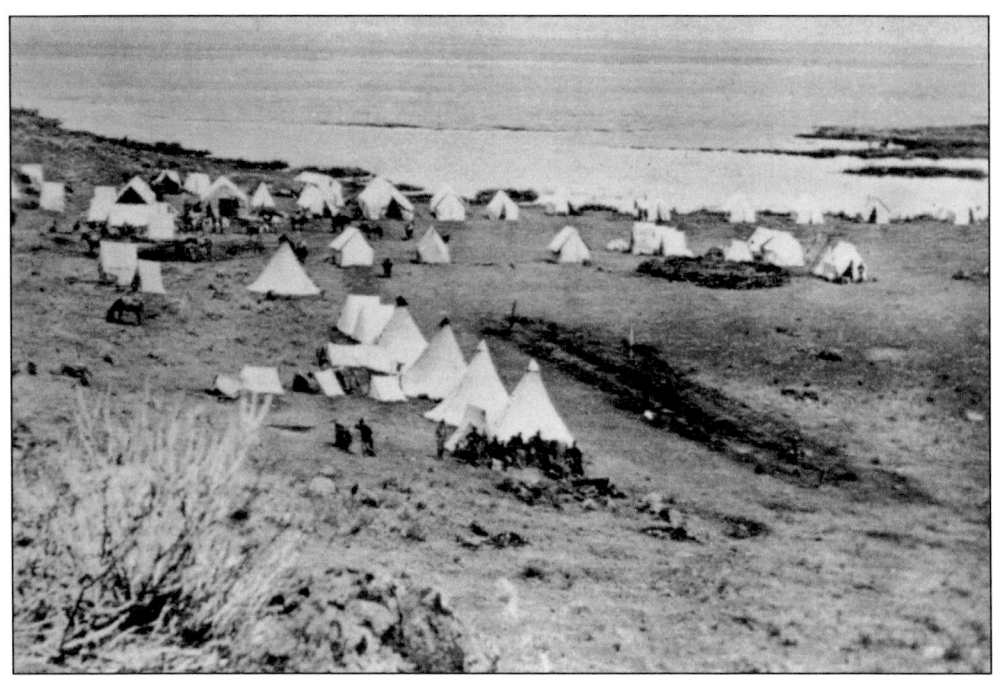

Gillems Camp, near Tule Lake, is shown here in the spring of 1873. At least 100 white canvas tents were erected. A rock circle, visible in the center-right portion of this photograph (and pictured below in close-up), may have been used as a corral. A rock corral was necessary because of the lack of junipers—trees that have since come prolific in the Lava Beds region.

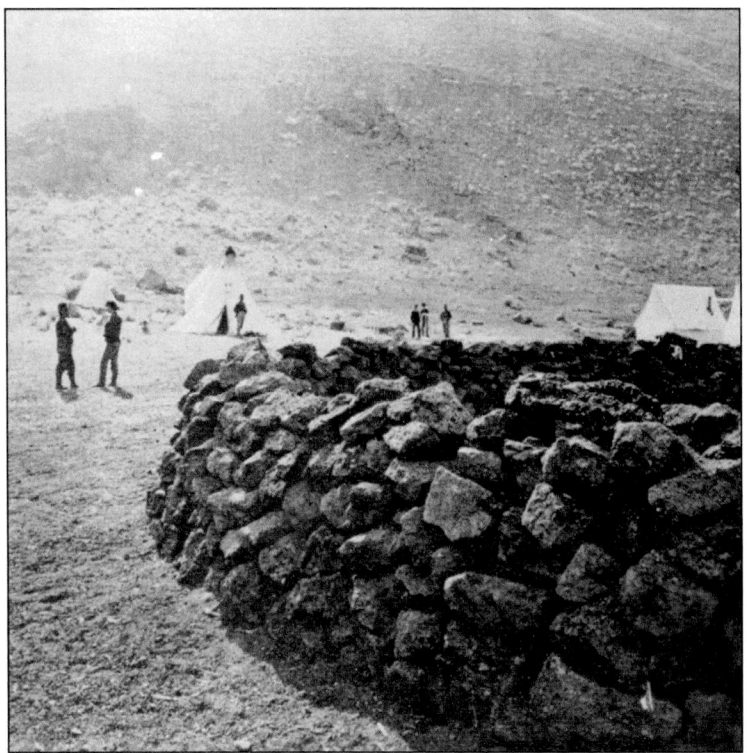

It is believed that this stone structure at Gillems Camp, the US Army's headquarters during the Modoc War, was used as a corral. This camp was located about three miles from Captain Jack's Stronghold, where the Modoc Indians used their knowledge of the terrain to withstand the invading troops for several months.

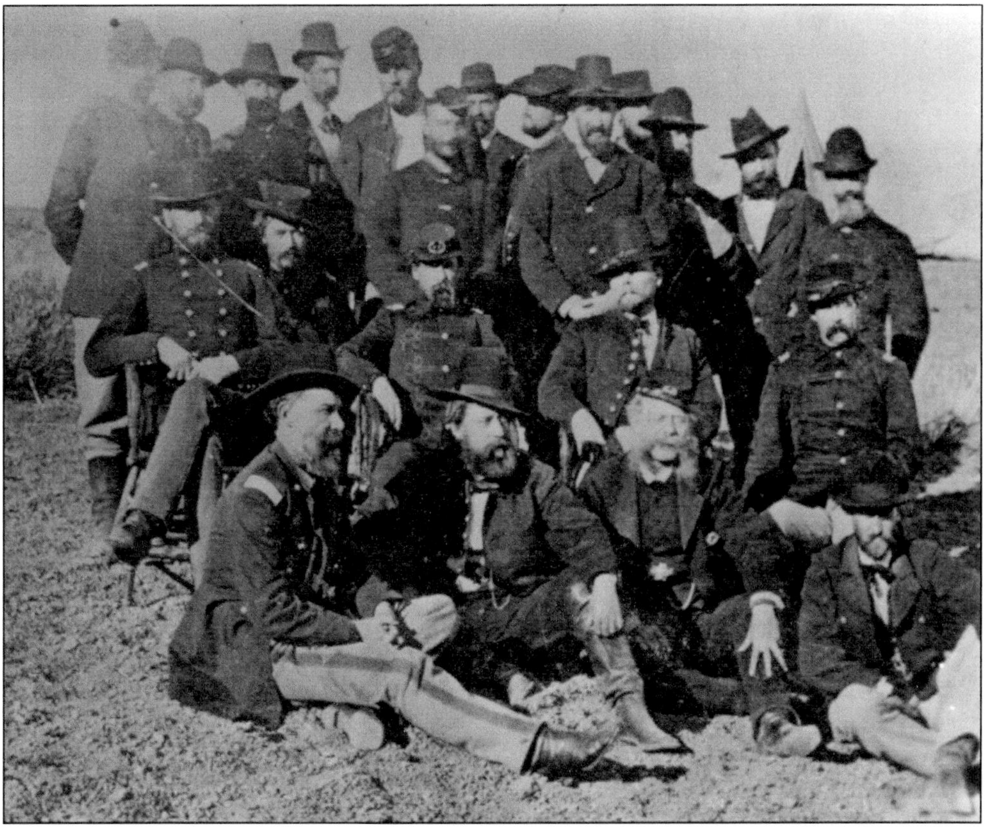

US Army officers were photographed at Gillems Camp in May 1873. They include, from left to right, (first row) Col. A.C. Gillem, Col. Jefferson C. Davis, Col. J.A. Hardie, and Major E.C. Mason. Maj. John Green is at farthest right in the second row. This photograph was taken by Eadweard Muybridge.

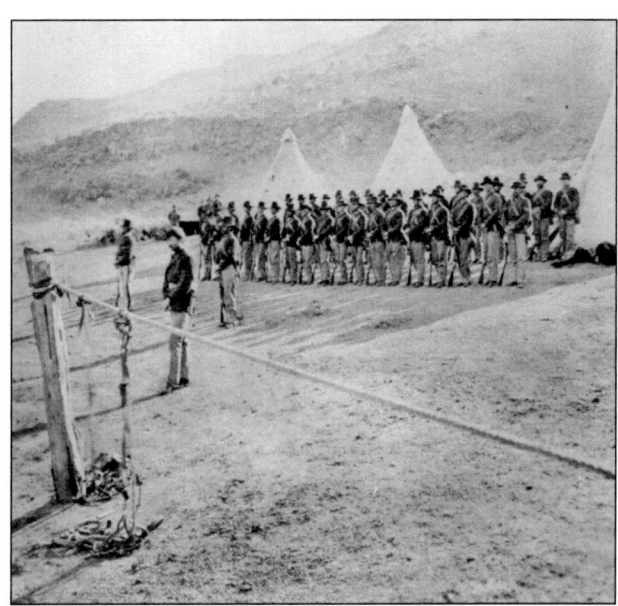

These Army soldiers are lined up for inspection at Gillems Camp. In all, more than 1,000 US Army soldiers participated in the Modoc War. In addition, it is believed that up to 200 civilian followers lived near the camps.

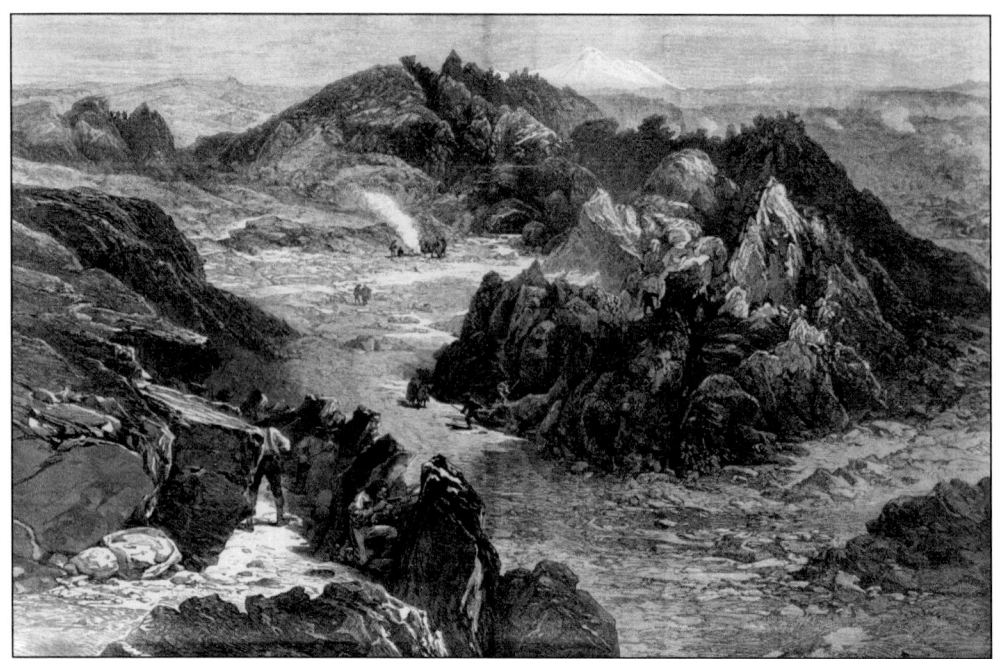

William Simpson, an illustrator for the *Illustrated London News*, was among the newspaper people stationed at Lava Beds during the Modoc War. His image of the Modocs defending the stronghold is regarded as one of the most accurate depictions of the battlefield. Simpson was known to visit the sites he illustrated and was in San Francisco when he learned about the peace commission killings; he spent a week sketching scenes for the *Illustrated London News*.

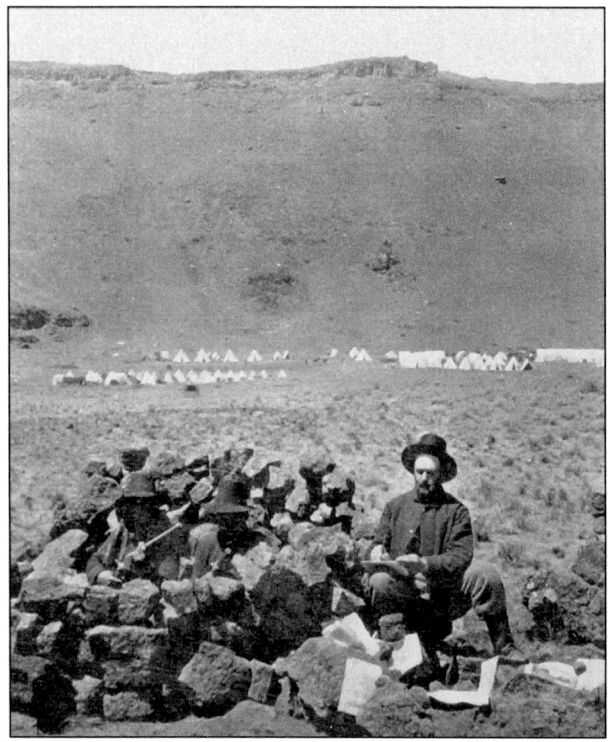

Reporter Alex McKay, who represented the *San Francisco Bulletin* and the *Yreka Union*, was photographed at a sentry post near Gillems Camp in the spring of 1873. Reporters began covering the war in February 1873 and produced stories on all the major events.

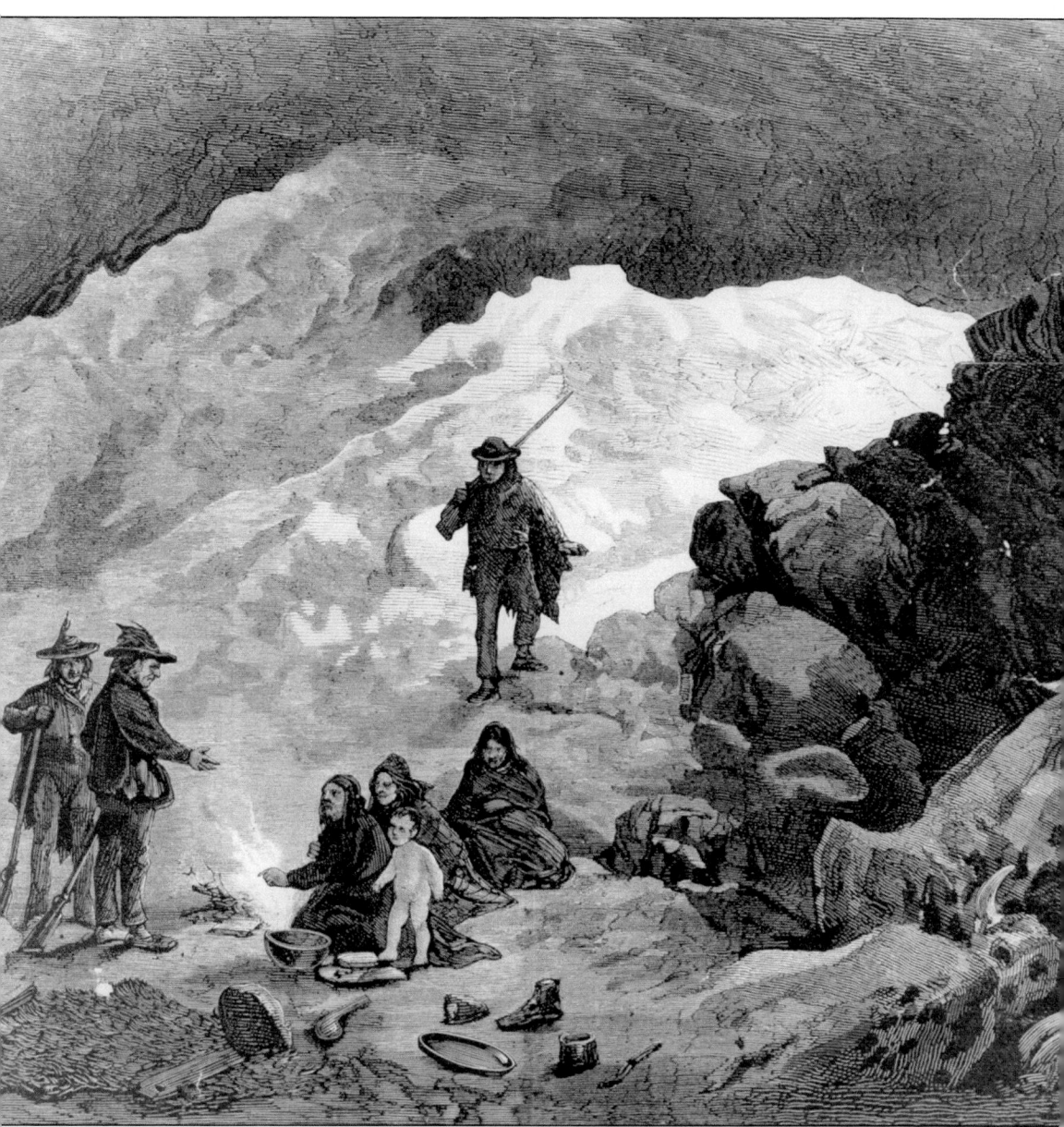

This illustration, created by William Simpson for the *Illustrated London News*, provides a sense of Captain Jack's Cave, where the Modoc leader and his family lived for several months. *New York Herald* correspondent Edward Cox, who arrived in February 1873, scored a major coup by being the first reporter to enter the stronghold and Captain Jack's cave. Simpson's illustrations were generally regarded as having accurate details because he visited the scenes or, if he was not able to see them for himself, relied on descriptions from others who had witnessed them.

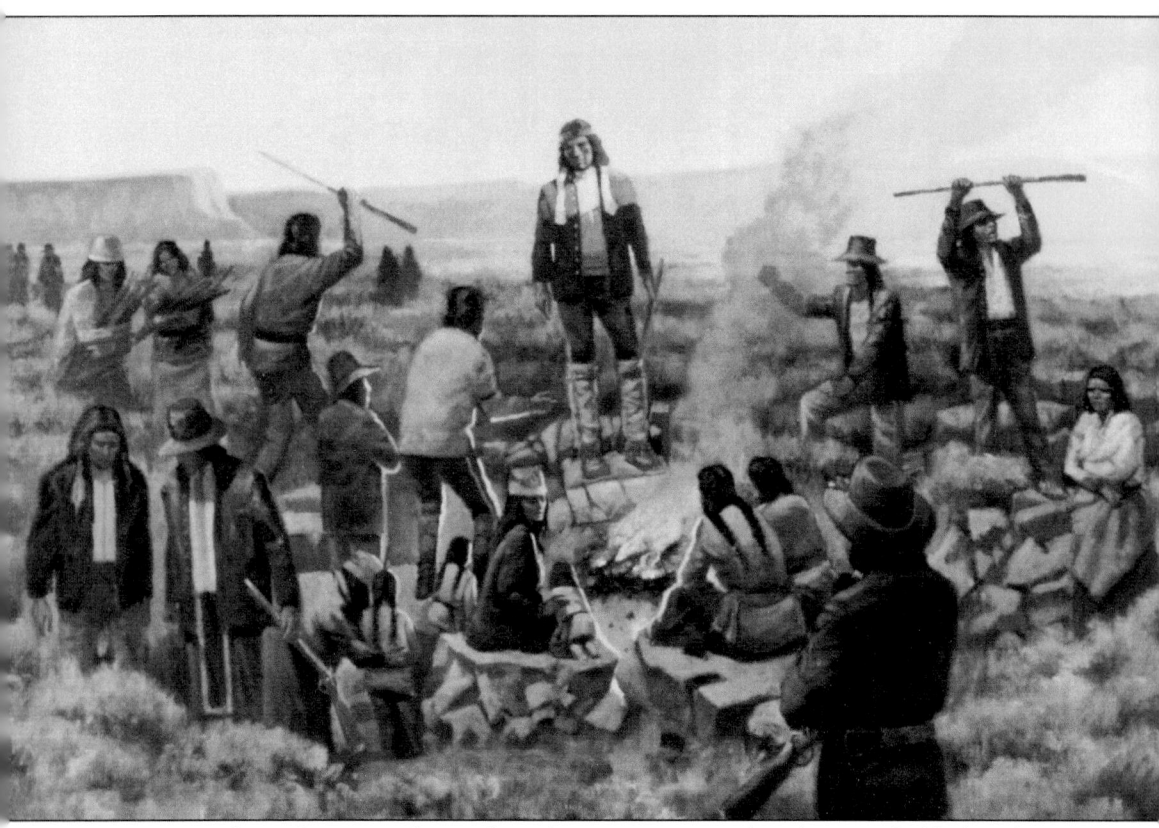

A painting shows Captain Jack, standing, during a war council in the stronghold where he was criticized for wanting to negotiate a surrender with the hope of having a reservation in Lava Beds. Those advocating war, including the Hot Creek Modocs, who had killed 17 male settlers after the Battle of Lost River, threw a woman's hat and shawl on Jack and mocked him, calling him a squaw. Because the majority of Modocs wanted to continue the war and murder members of the peace commission, Jack agreed, reportedly telling the Modocs, "I will kill Canby, although it will cost me my life and all the lives of my people."

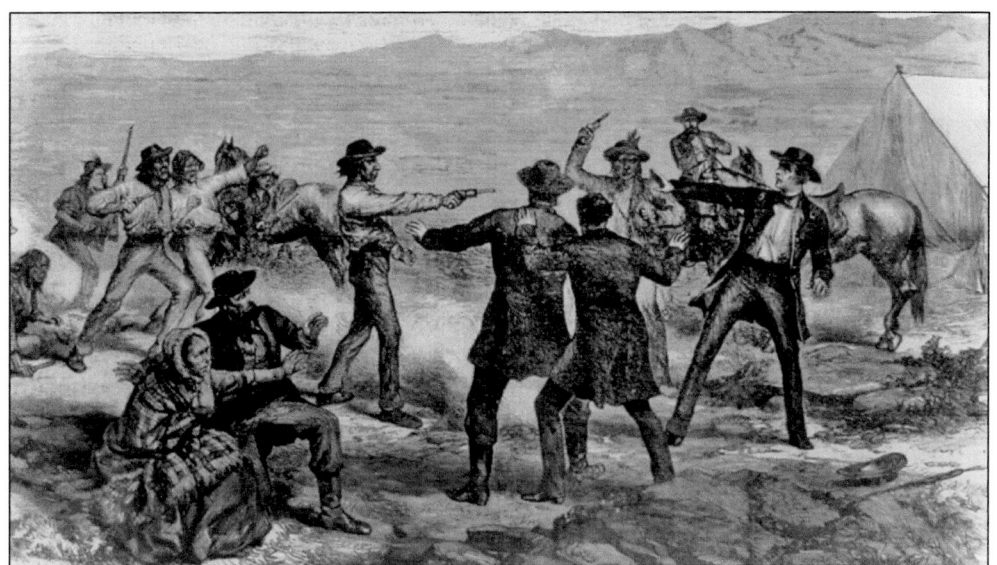

The murder of Army general E.R.S. Canby, as depicted by William Simpson for the *Illustrated London News*, turned much of the American public against the Modocs. Captain Jack is shown pointing a gun at Canby, who has his arm outstretched. Toby and Frank Riddle, who had warned Canby and the peace commission, are huddled at left.

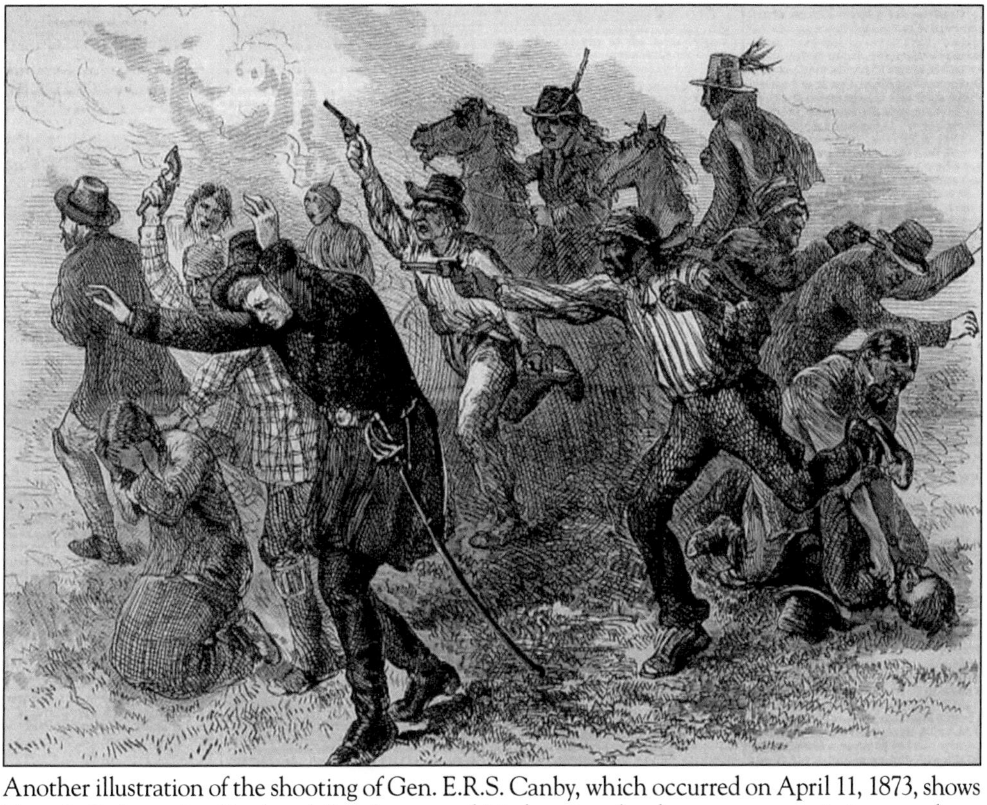

Another illustration of the shooting of Gen. E.R.S. Canby, which occurred on April 11, 1873, shows Captain Jack pursing Canby while other armed Modocs attack other peace commission members. Rev. Eleazar Thomas, a Methodist minister from Petaluma, California, was also killed.

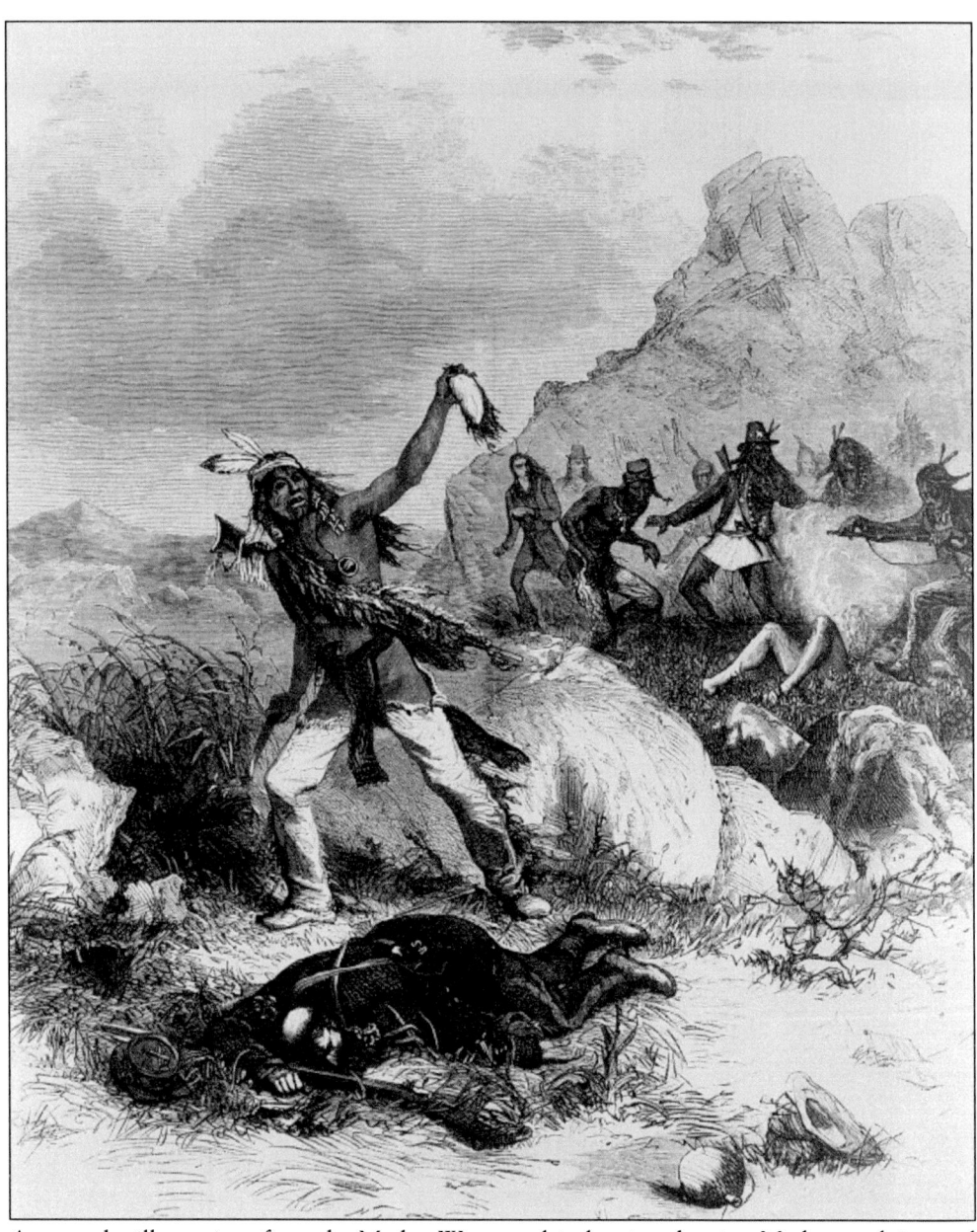

Among the illustrations from the Modoc War was this drawing showing Modocs scalping and torturing prisoners. Within two days of the killing of two peace commissioners on April 11, 1873, newspapers across the United States printed detailed stories about the incident. A story in the *San Francisco Chronicle* included a series of headlines stacked atop one another (see page 54) that declared: "The Red Judas," "Base Treachery of the Modoc Indians," "General Canby Murdered," "Shot Through the Head by Capt. Jack," "Commissioner Dyar's Flight from the Savages," "Repulse of the Redskins," and "The Soldiers Maddened by the Loss of Their Commander."

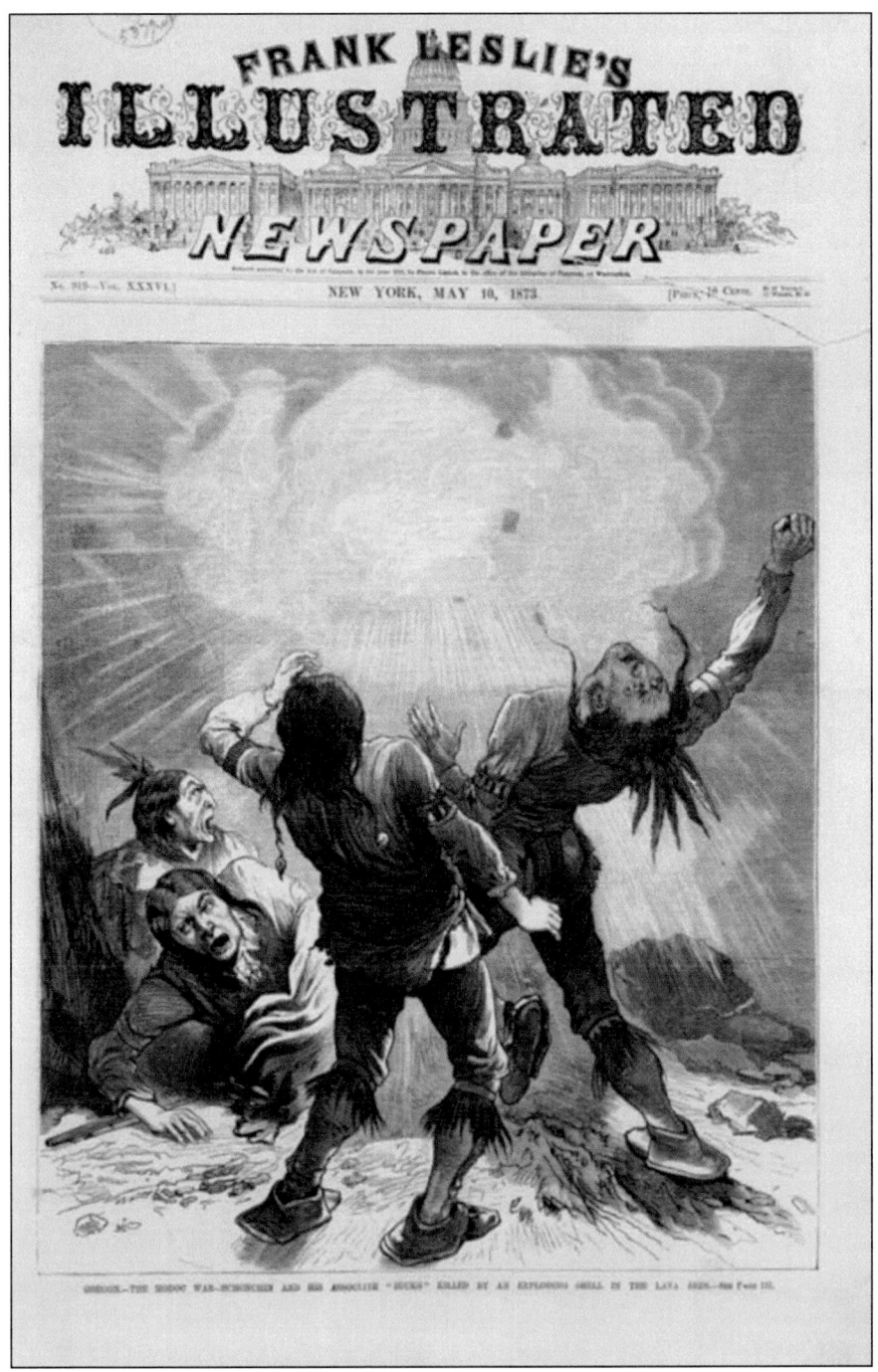

A drawing in the May 10, 1873, edition of *Frank Leslie's Illustrated Newspaper* purported to show Schonchin John and his associated "bucks" killed by an exploding shell during the Modoc War; this incident never happened. The artist also incorrectly showed the Modocs, who wore blue jeans and calico shirts, dressed as Plains Indians. The war was heavily covered and drew international interest, especially after the two peace commissioners were killed. At the time, four reporters—the largest press contingent ever to cover an Indian war—were writing about the war.

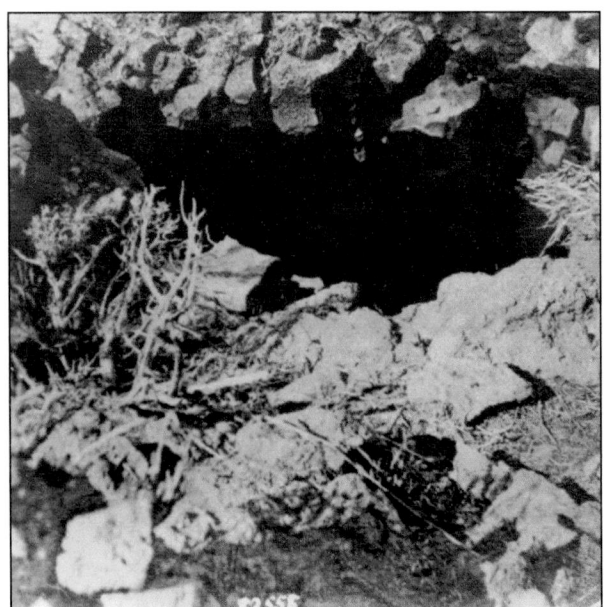

This photograph of Captain Jack's cave in the stronghold was taken by Eadweard Muybridge, a nationally prominent photographer who was hired by the US government to "prepare photographic views of the different approaches to the lava bed and of Captain Jack's famous cave and fortifications."

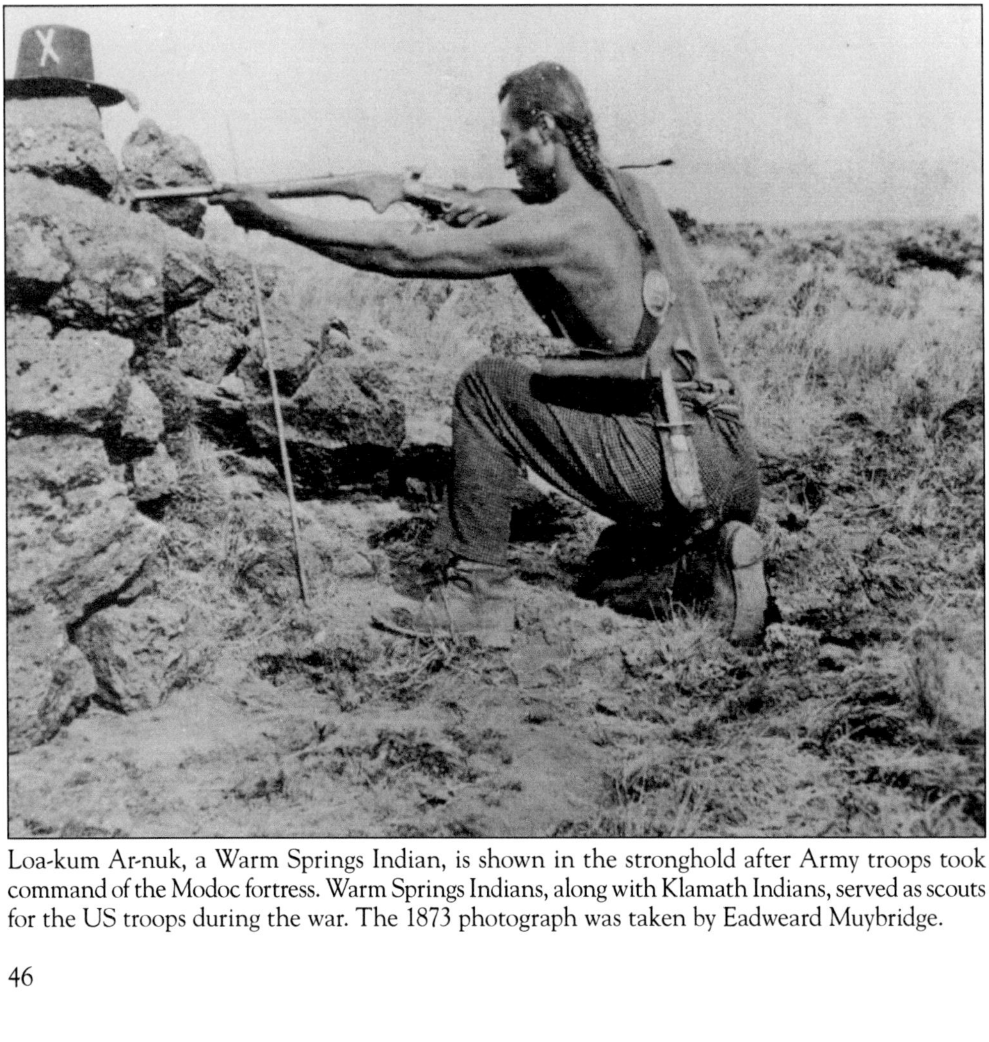

Loa-kum Ar-nuk, a Warm Springs Indian, is shown in the stronghold after Army troops took command of the Modoc fortress. Warm Springs Indians, along with Klamath Indians, served as scouts for the US troops during the war. The 1873 photograph was taken by Eadweard Muybridge.

A group of military personnel and others gather at a viewpoint in the stronghold, probably after the Modocs left their fortress in May 1873. After taking over the stronghold, the Army built up the existing fortifications in case the Modocs attempted to return.

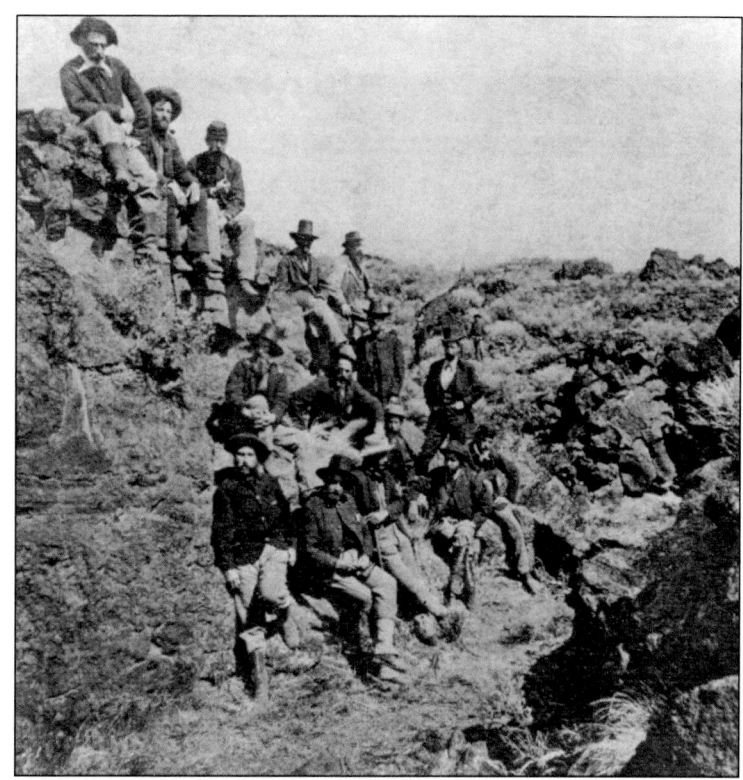

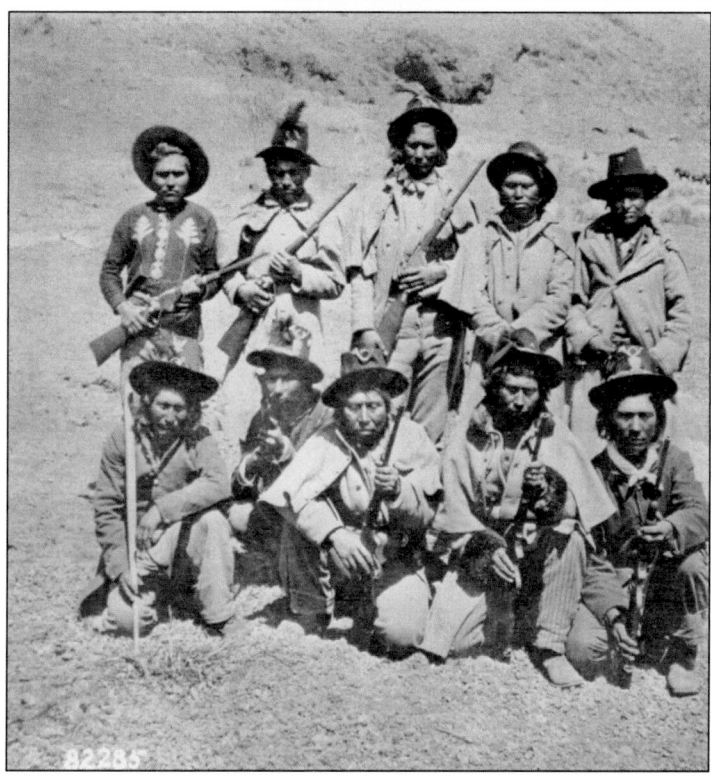

Warm Springs Indians pose with their rifles in the stronghold in an image taken by famed photographer Eadweard Muybridge in May 1873. Warm Springs tribal members worked for the US Army. On May 1, 1873, some of the Warm Springs scouts were killed during the Battle of Dry Lake.

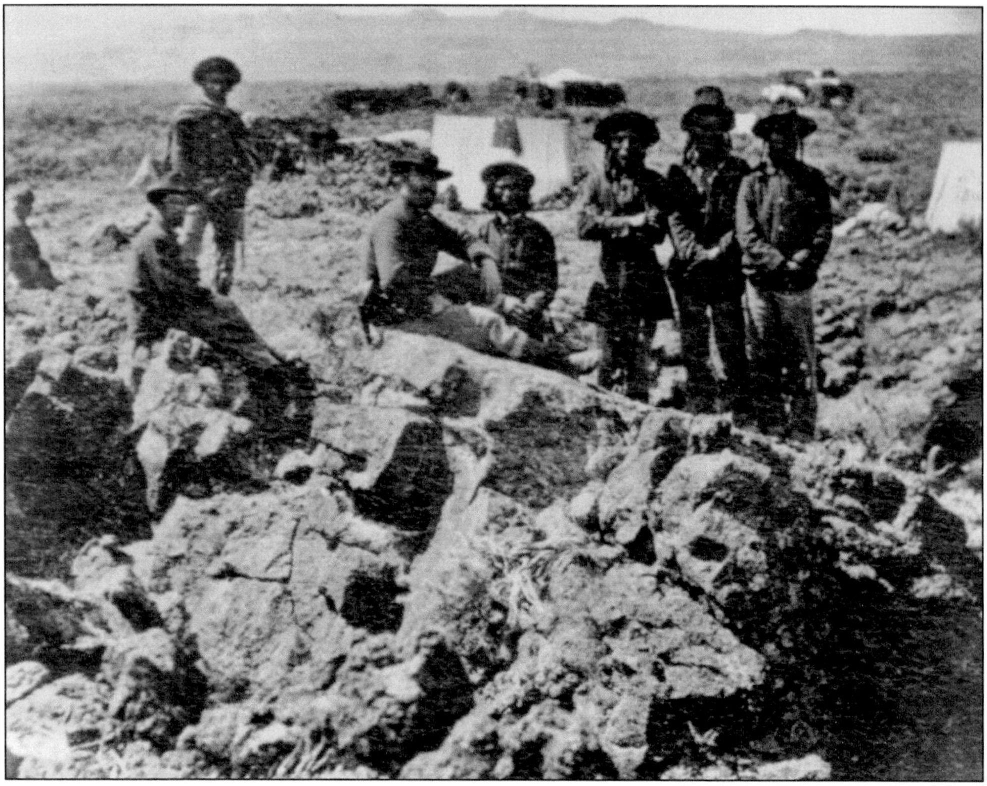

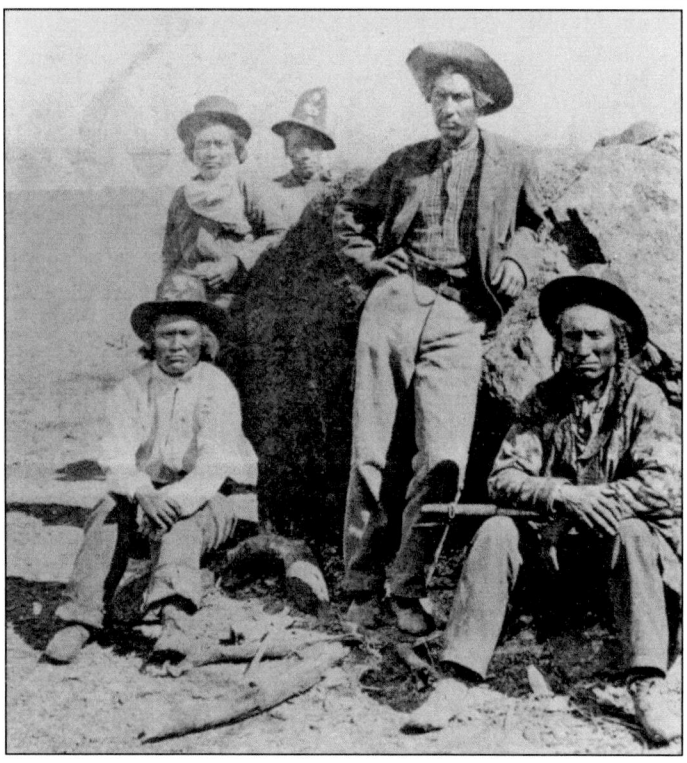

In the 1873 photograph above, Army troops and Warm Spring scouts pose for a photograph taken at an unknown location. They posed for another photograph (left) at a later date. The scouts assisted US troops in their war against the Modocs. Two Warm Springs Indians were killed at the Battle of Dry Lake on May 1, 1873. According to Modoc legend, when the different tribes were created by Gmukamps, he told the Warm Springs, "You will be brave warriors, too."

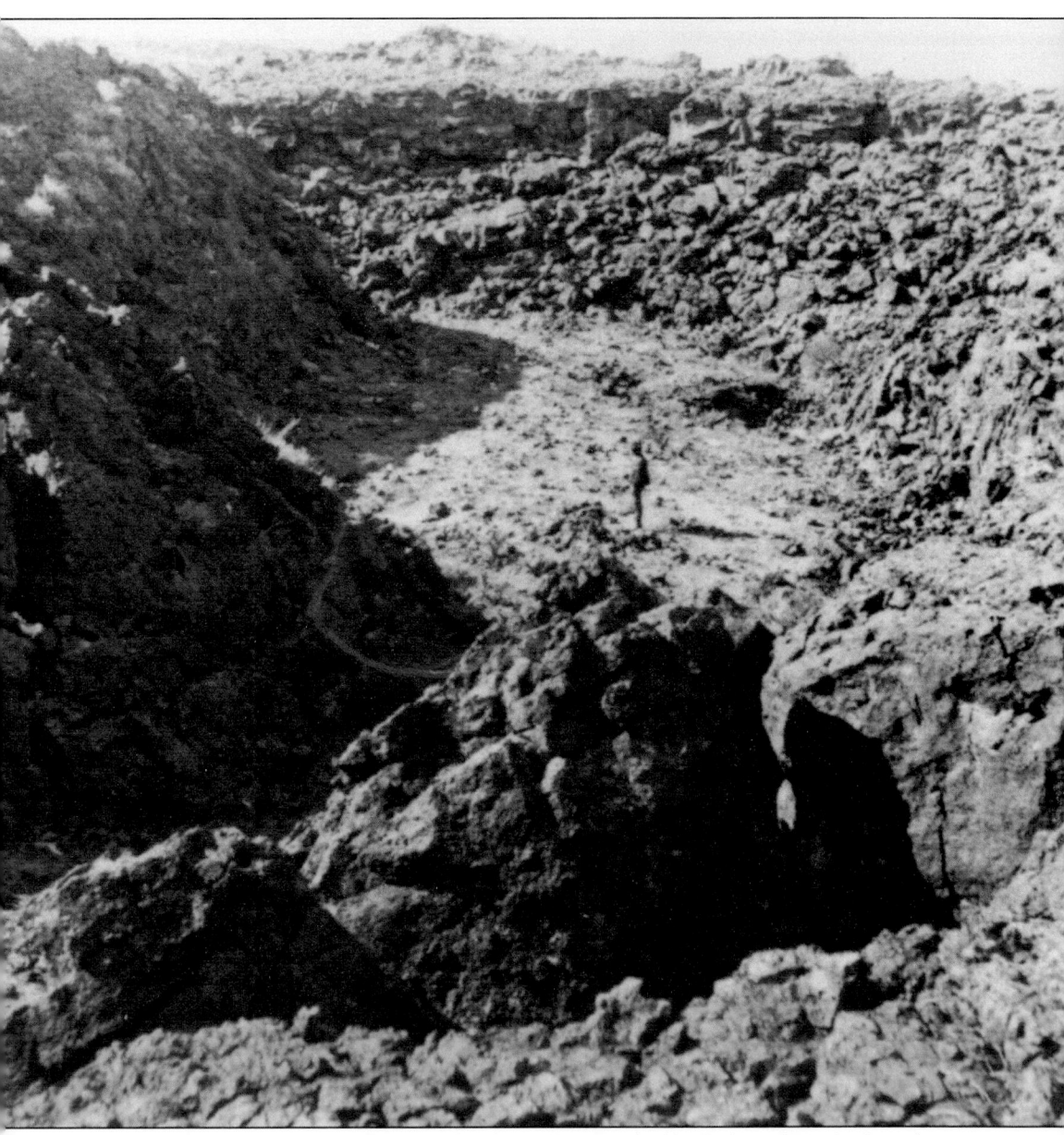

This large crevice in Captain Jack's Stronghold was photographed by Eadweard Muybridge, who was hired by the US government to photograph the area. Government officials hoped his photographs would help investigators understand why the Modoc War was so costly. Muybridge included a person in this photograph in an attempt to show the scale and Lava Beds' rugged terrain. It is believed that Muybridge arrived on May 2, 1873, and completed his work around May 12, 1873. The photographs were included in a May 23, 1873, report by Capt. G.J. Lydecker.

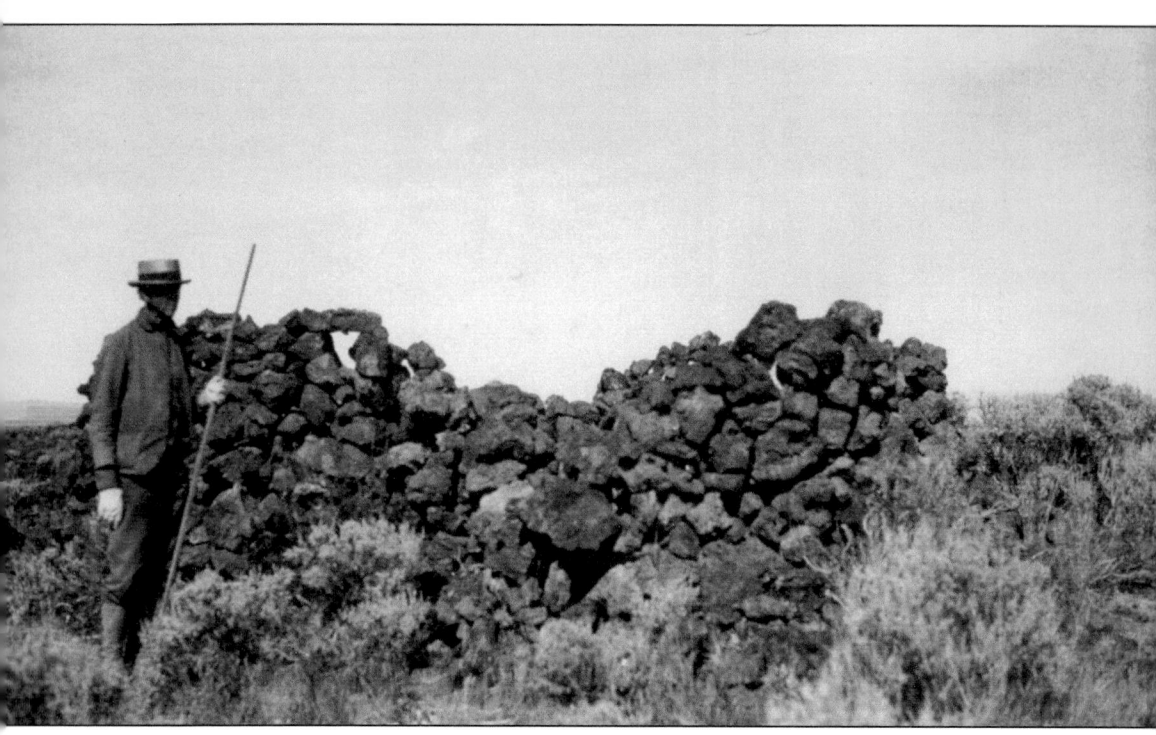

The caption on the back of this undated photograph says, "Old fort on Modoc battlefields. Col. Thompson, veteran of the war." The Modocs used the plentiful rocks to create defensive positions, although they typically kept fortifications low and closer to the natural terrain, while Army troops built taller structures. A series of fortifications can be found within the current Lava Beds National Monument boundaries and areas south of the monument managed by the Modoc National Forest.

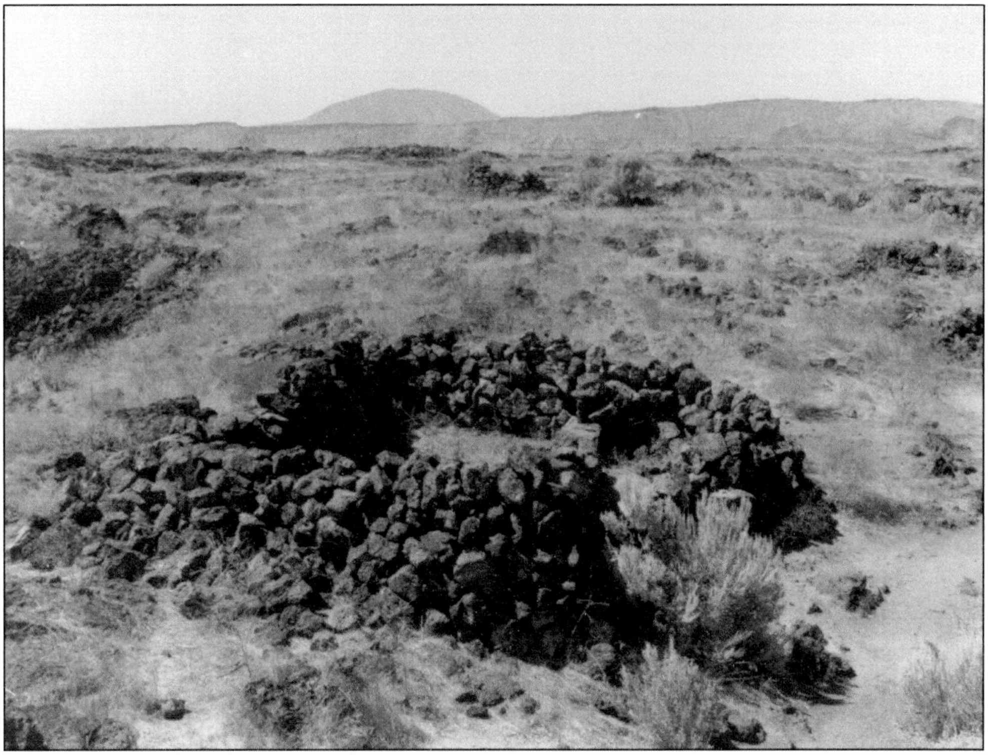

Modoc Indians and US Army troops used lava rocks to build outposts in and outside the stronghold, especially on slightly higher overlooks. Many of the outposts feature openings where a rifle could be placed while the shooter remained in the relative protection of the rocky fortress. The outposts can be seen in Captain Jack's Stronghold, especially on the long trail that loops around the southern end of the Modocs' place of refuge.

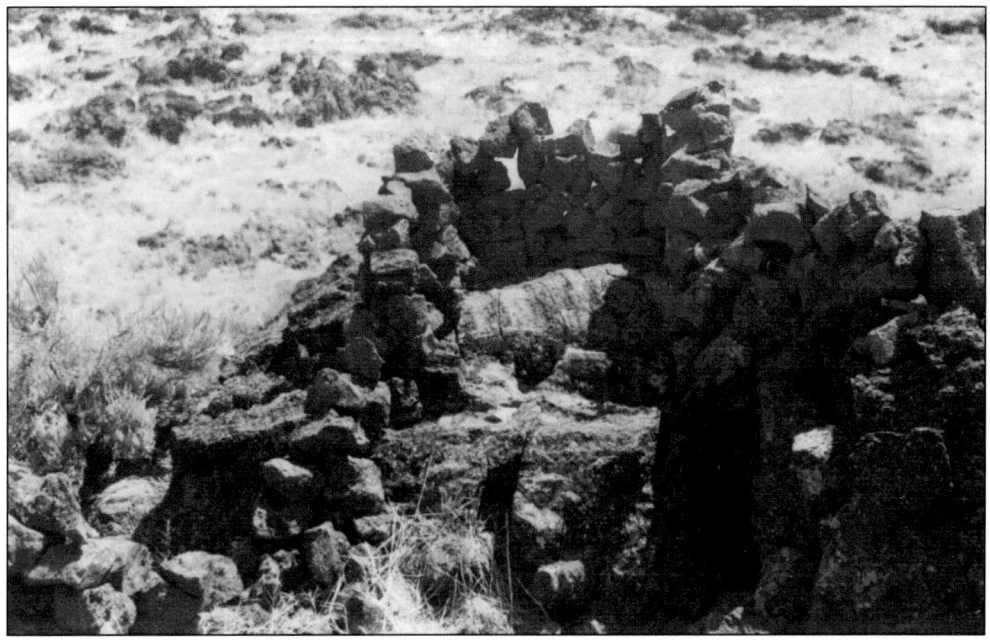

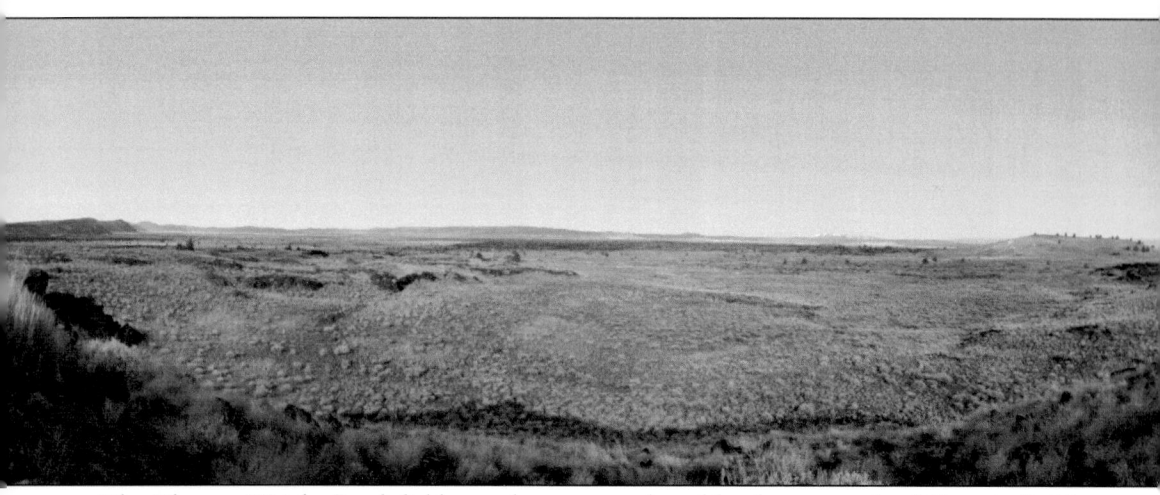

The Thomas-Wright Battlefield stretches across a broad landscape south of Captain Jack's Stronghold. The Modocs used the topography to monitor the movement of US troops. One of the war's major battles was fought northwest of a large butte now known as Hardin Butte. When the troops stopped for lunch, and before a group of soldiers moved up the butte for reconnaissance, waiting Modocs opened fire. Scarface Charley, the Modoc leader, supposedly yelled, "All you fellows that ain't dead yet had better go home. We don't want to kill you all in one day."

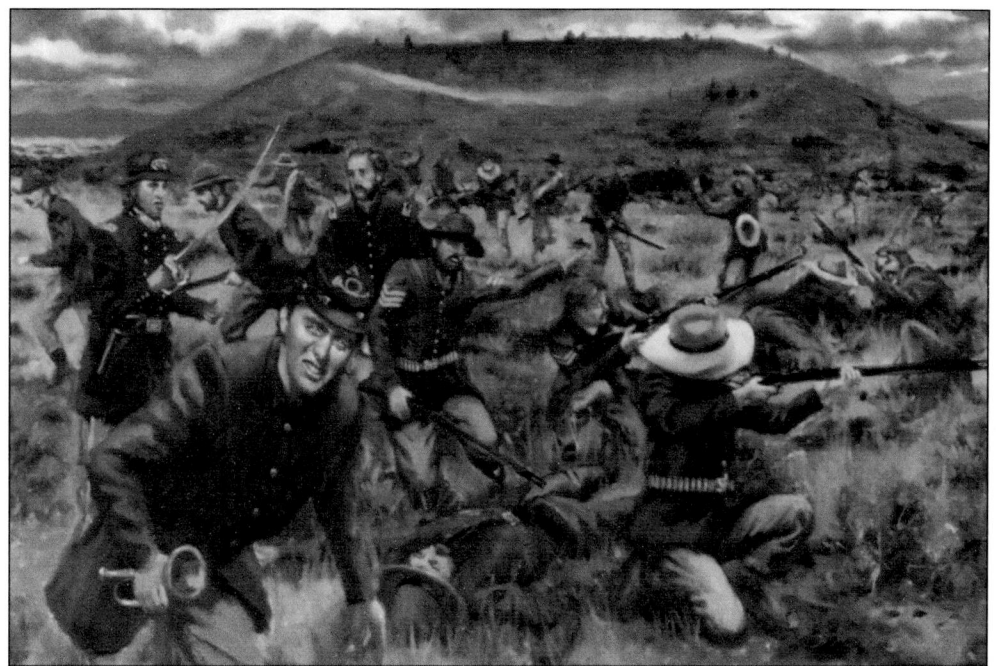

This painting by Mitch Caster shows Army troops confused and frightened while under attack at the Thomas-Wright Battlefield. The battle was a decisive victory for the Modocs.

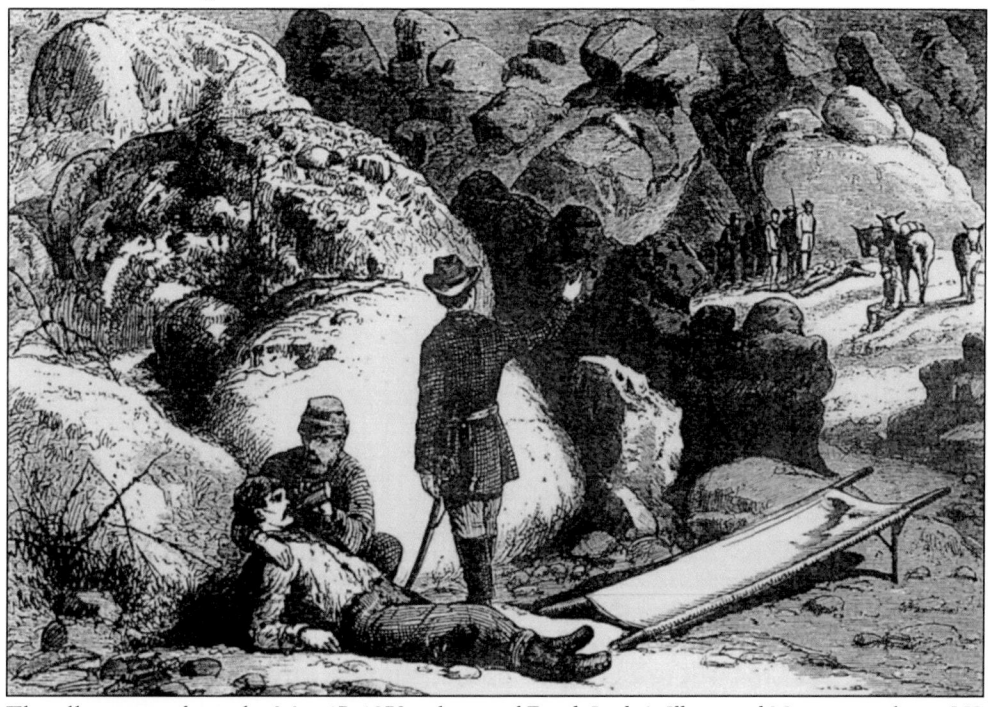

This illustration from the May 17, 1873, edition of *Frank Leslie's Illustrated Newspaper* shows US Army soldiers wounded in the Thomas-Wright Battle. The image, which was probably not based on a photograph, had a caption that read, "Oregon—The Modoc War—Bringing Back to Camp the U.S. Soldiers Wounded in the Ambuscade in the Lava Beds."

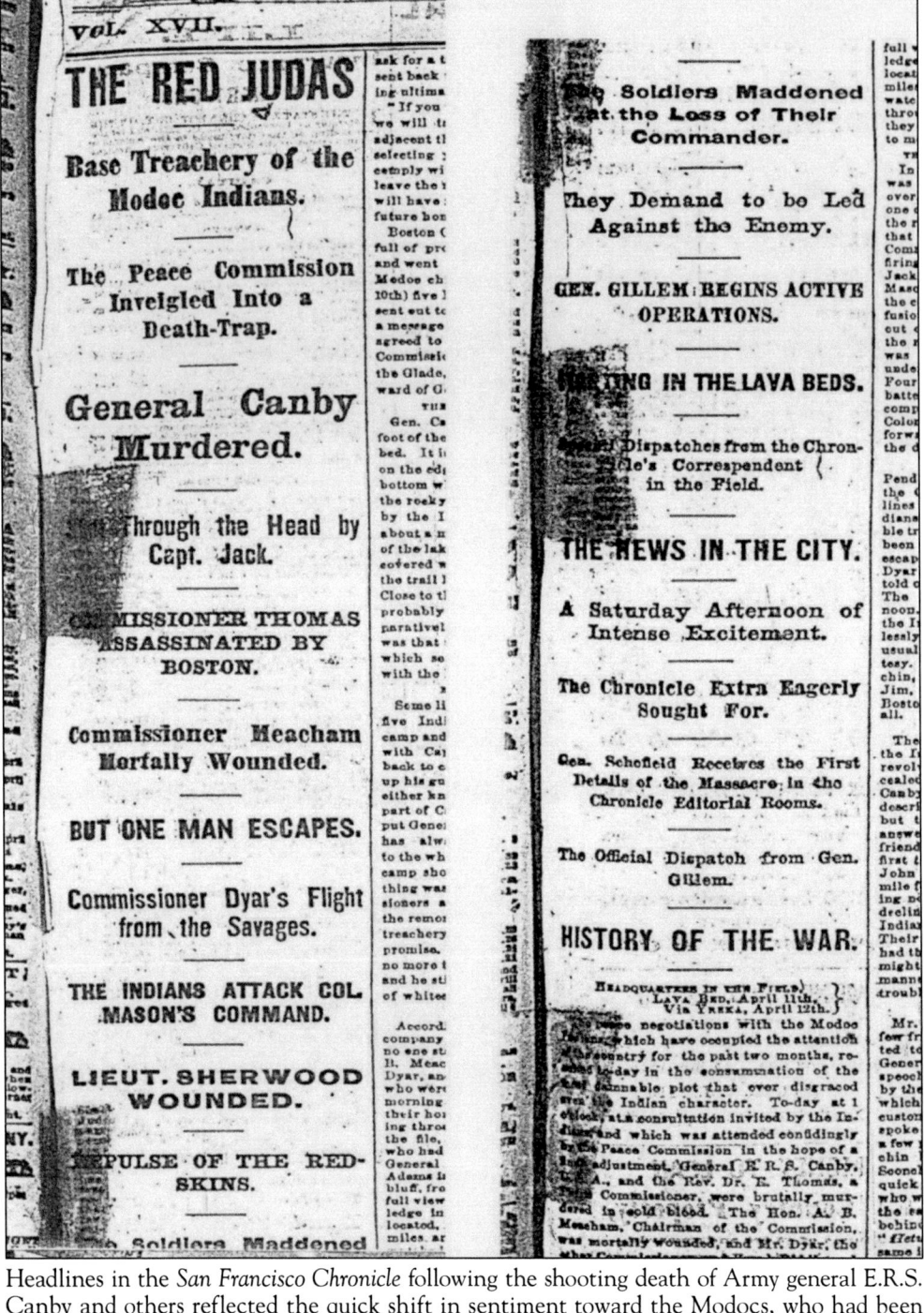

Headlines in the *San Francisco Chronicle* following the shooting death of Army general E.R.S. Canby and others reflected the quick shift in sentiment toward the Modocs, who had been portrayed sympathetically in earlier reports. The headlines preceded the story by Robert D. Bogart and appeared two days after the killing.

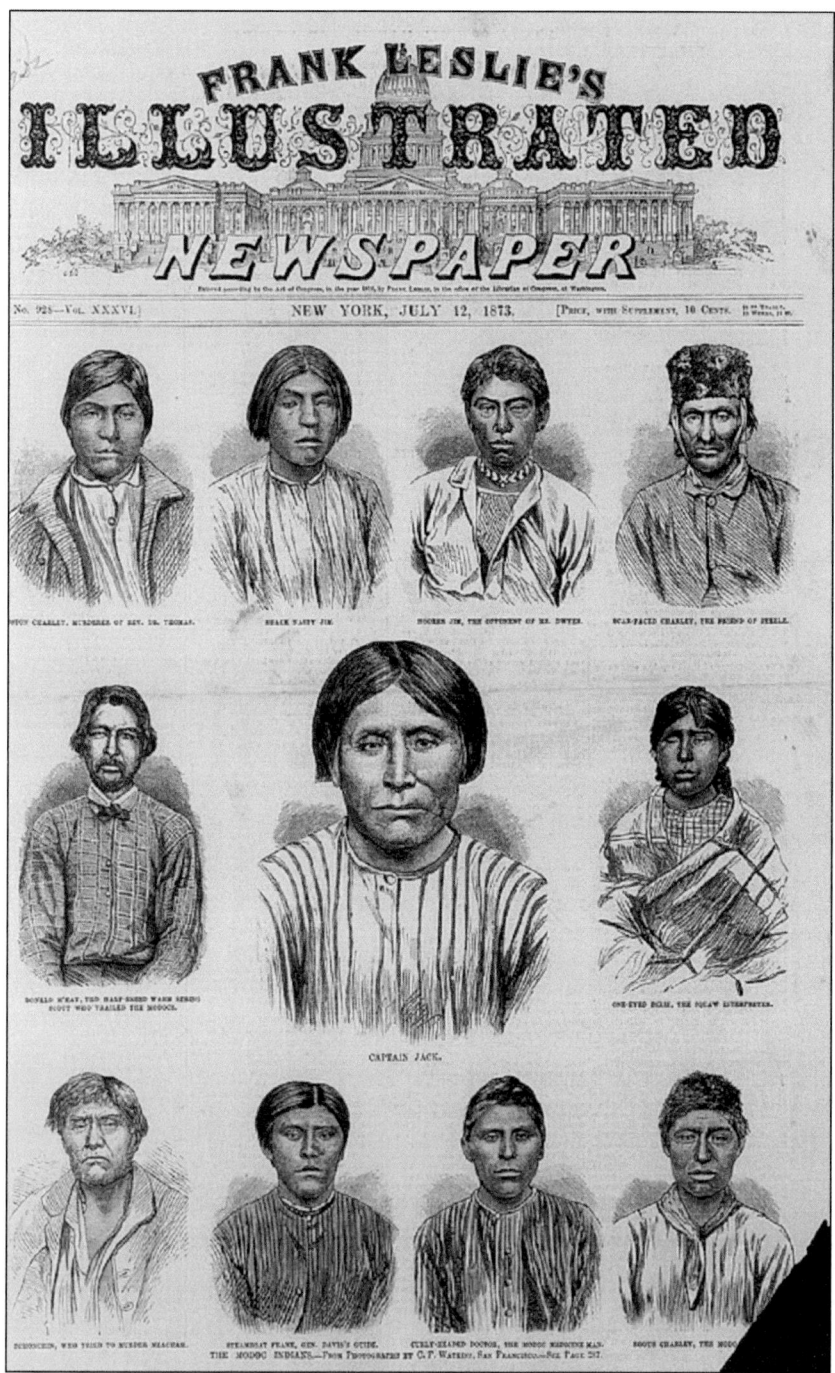

The cover of the July 12, 1873, issue of *Frank Leslie's Illustrated Newspaper*, published in New York, featured drawings of Captain Jack, in the center, and other Modocs; Donald McKay, a Warm Springs scout, and One-Eyed Dixie, an Army interpreter, are shown flanking Jack. Other notable Modocs include Scarface Charley (upper right), Schonchin (lower left), and Curly-Headed Doctor, (third from left on the bottom row). The drawings, based on photographs by Louis Heller, provided readers with the first photograph-based images of the Modoc warriors.

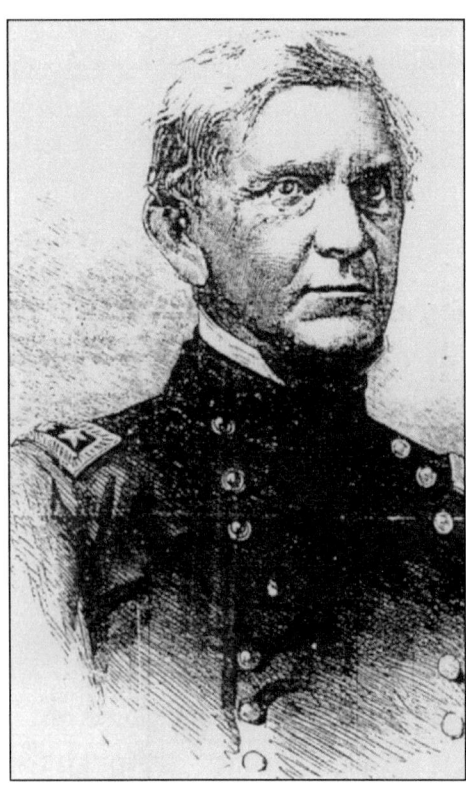

Shown here is Gen. Edward R.S. Canby as portrayed in the April 26, 1873, *Harper's Weekly* after he was shot to death during peace negotiations on April 11. The engraving was based on a photograph, much like one on the following page. His killing angered many, including his troops.

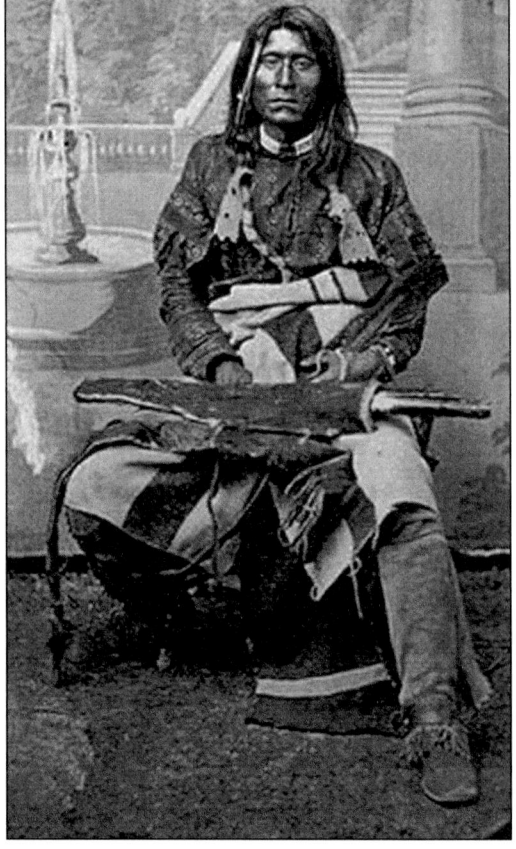

Captain Jack, or Keint-poos, is pictured here in 1864, about the time he became the leader of the Lost River band of the Modocs. He later led efforts to allow his band to live in the Lost River or, as an alternative, the Lava Beds region because of their unhappiness with living on the Klamath tribes' reservation.

Captain Jack, left, and Schonchin John were photographed after they were captured and taken to Fort Klamath, where they were held until both were found guilty of murder and hanged. Both had their hair cut short while in captivity.

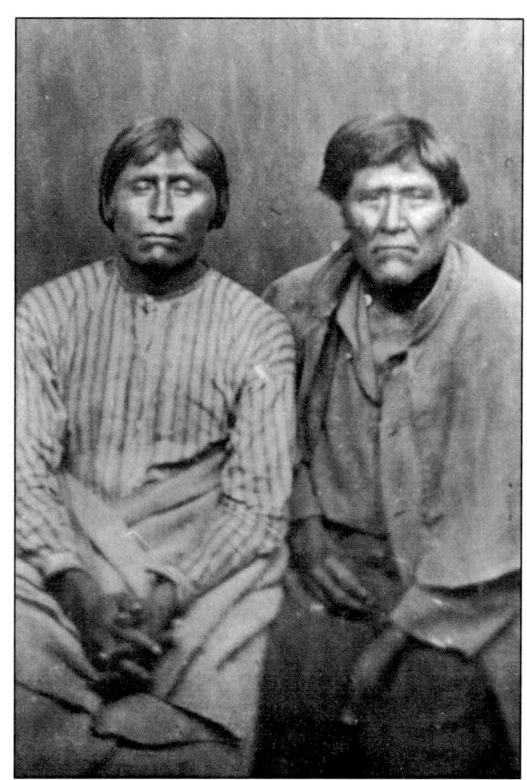

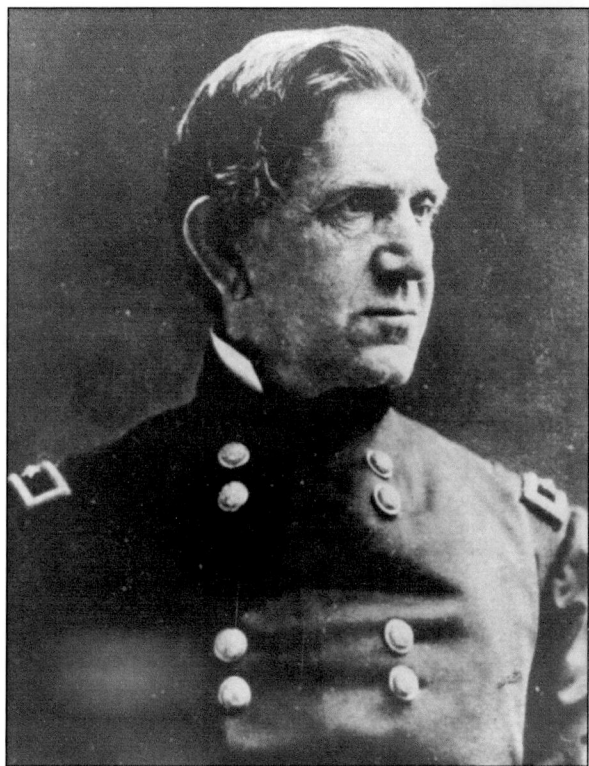

Army general Edward R.S. Canby is shown in a photograph probably taken in 1873, before he was killed during peace negotiations on April 11 of that year. He is the only Army general who was killed in an Indian war. His shooting death led to the Army increasing its attacks against the Modocs.

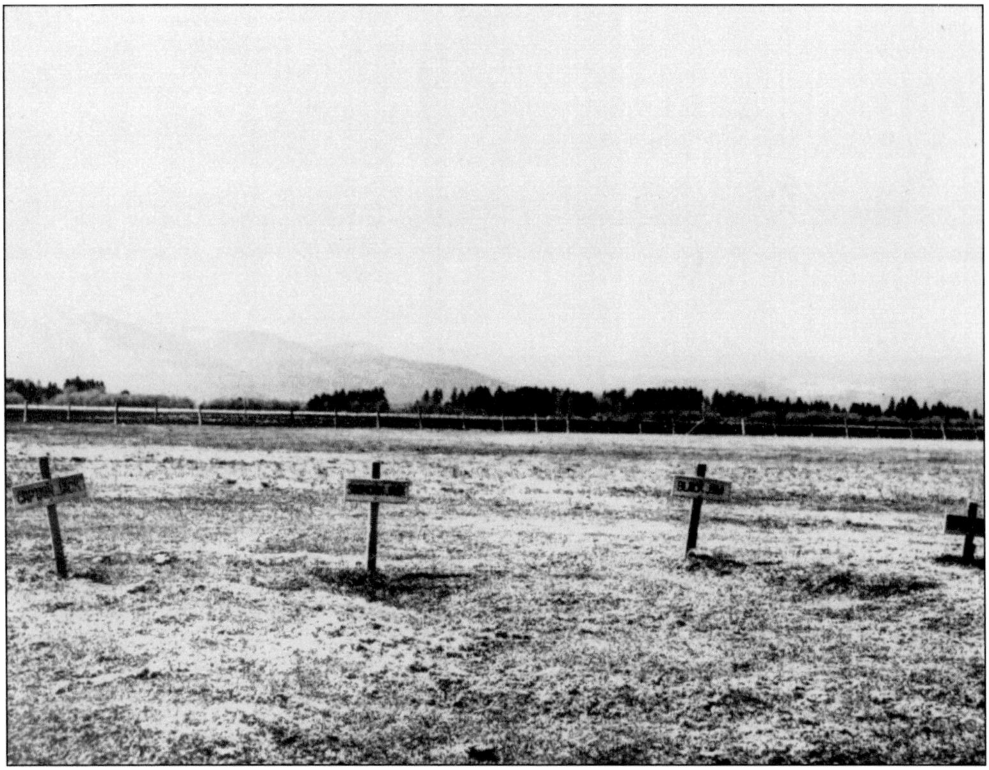

The four Modocs who were hanged for the deaths of Gen. Edward R.S. Canby and Rev. Eleazar Thomas were buried at Fort Klamath. It was later learned that the skulls of the four Modocs were removed after they were executed and shipped to the Army Medical Museum in Washington, DC, and later transferred to the Smithsonian Museum. The skulls were returned to a descendant of Captain Jack's cousin in 1984.

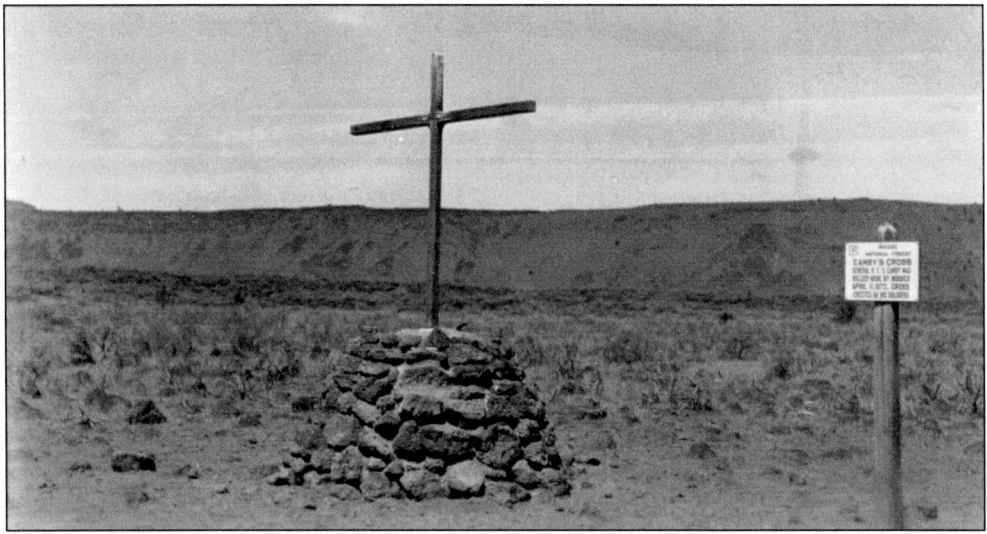

Canby's Cross was erected at the site where Army general Edward R.S. Canby was killed during peace negotiations on April 11, 1873. In 1882, Army lieutenant John S. Parke created this cross of timber "about six inches square, twelve feet high, with arms of four feet."

Four

AFTER THE MODOC WAR

The first non-Natives, originally fur traders, began visiting the Lava Beds region in the early 1820s. Peter Skene Ogden was the first white visitor to write about seeing the area. John C. Fremont explored the region in 1846, the same year Jesse and Lindsay Applegate created the Applegate Trail. The discovery of gold at Sutter's Mill, in California, in 1848 led to an influx of settlers and the creation of white settlements, including Yreka, 80 miles west of Lava Beds; Linkville (later renamed Klamath Falls), 30 miles northeast; and Alturas, 60 miles southeast. Conflicts over land followed as the white settlers created roads that traveled through Modoc lands and developed cattle ranches in the area. In the years before the war, Modocs adopted English names: Keint-poos became "Captain Jack," Cho-ocks became "Curly-Headed Doctor," and Chikchikam became "Scarfaced Charley."

A treaty between the federal government and three tribes—the Modocs, a larger group of Klamaths, and a small band of Paiutes—was signed in 1864, with the Modocs ceding all their land in exchange for 15 years of payments. These Native groups were all forced onto a reservation in Oregon, and dissension between the Modocs and Klamaths caused many Modocs, under the leadership of Captain Jack, to leave the reservation. This was a factor in events that resulted in the Modoc War.

The war made Lava Beds notorious, not only because of newspaper reports during the war, but also through "dime novels," usually with wildly fictional accounts of the battles and Captain Jack. After the war, the region became a travel destination, luring conservationist John Muir, who described the landscape as "forbidding and mysterious." Hunters were attracted by deer and bighorn sheep and a seemingly endless population of waterfowl. Ranchers and homesteaders ran sheep, cattle, and horses, and grew potatoes and other crops. During Prohibition, moonshiners used the ice caves to distill whiskey. Western writer Zane Grey used Lava Beds as the setting for his novel *Forlorn River*. The automobile allowed the Lava Beds region, with its war sites and caves, to become an easily visited tourism destination. In the early 1910s, motorists were able to make day visits from Klamath Falls and Alturas, which led to demands for improved roads.

Residents of the area—some wanting to lure more tourists and some seeking to protect the landscape and its historic sites—spurred efforts to have the area federally managed, originally by the US Forest Service, and, later, by the National Park Service. Over the years, Lava Beds, a formerly isolated region, has become a destination for hikers, spelunkers, and history buffs.

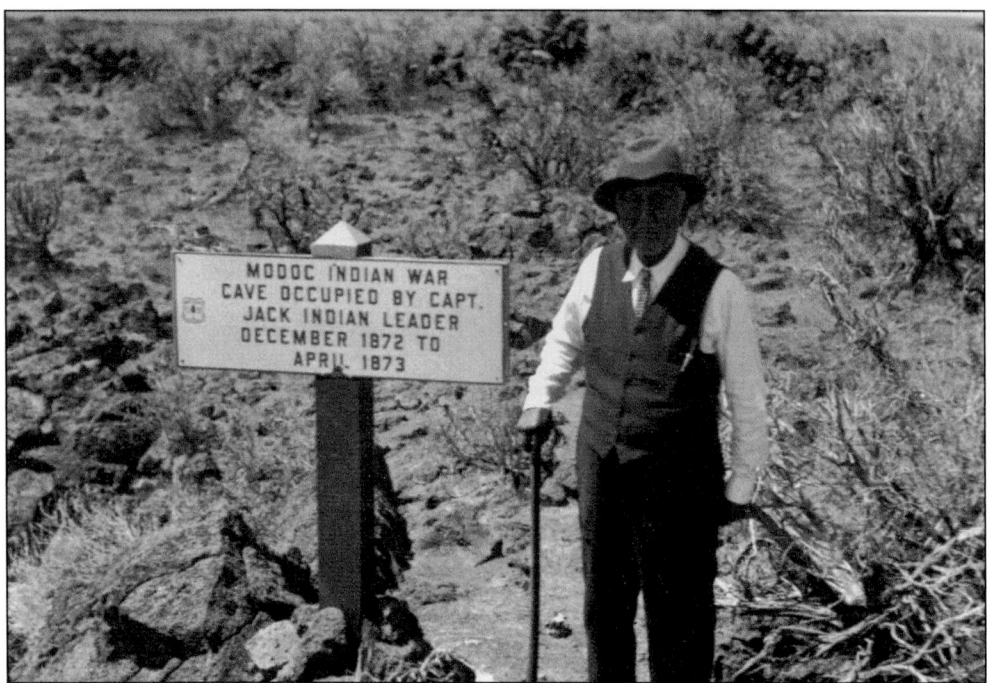

Peter Schonchin, who had been a young warrior during the Modoc War, revisited what was known as Captain Jack's Cave in the Stronghold, now known as Captain Jack's Stronghold. Schonchin also visited war sites with J.D. Howard.

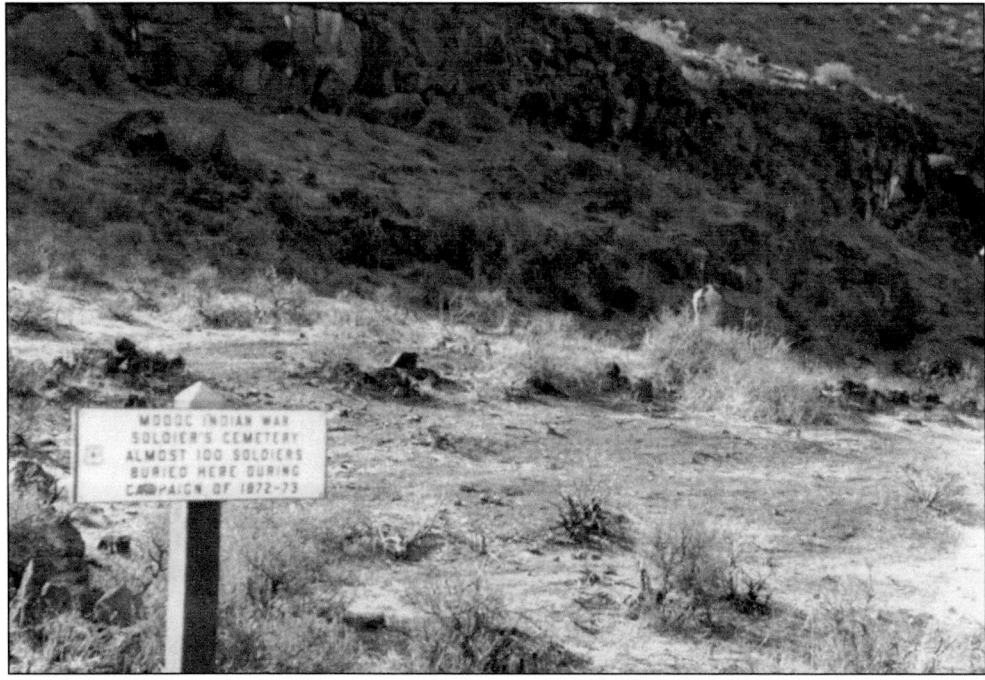

Shown here is Gillems Cemetery as it looked in 1934. More than 100 soldiers were buried at the cemetery near the US Army headquarters at Gillems Camp. Naturalist John Muir was among those who visited the graveyard in 1874, shortly after the Modoc War ended.

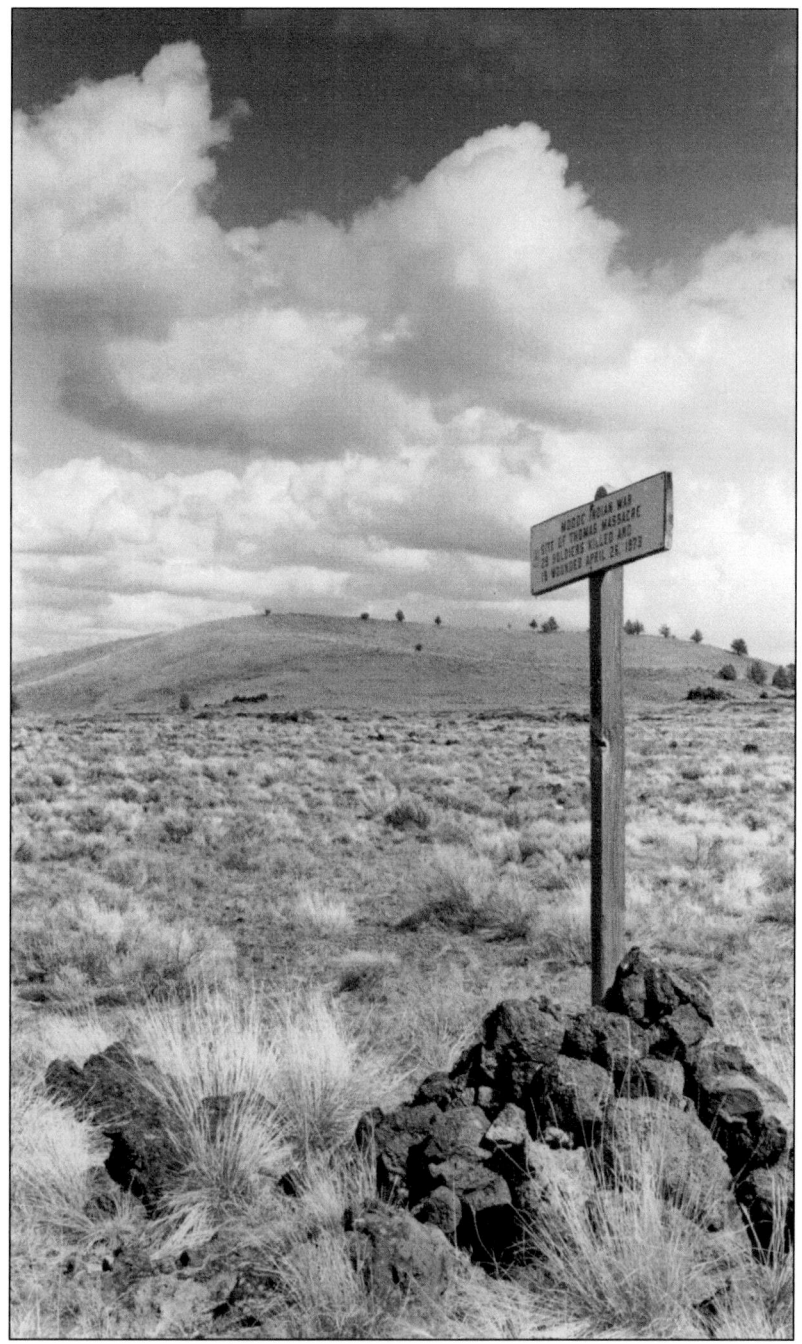

For many years, the site of the Thomas-Wright Battle was known as the Thomas-Wright Massacre Site. In the 1970s, its name was changed to the Thomas-Wright Battlefield, and it was added to the National Register of Historic Places in 1978. The battle took place on April 26, 1873, when Capt. Evan Thomas, four other officers, and 59 enlisted men were sent to investigate fires spotted in the Schonchin Flow. When the group stopped for lunch, Modoc warriors opened fire. By the day's end, 3 officers and 20 enlisted men were dead, and 16 were wounded. The Modocs suffered only a single death.

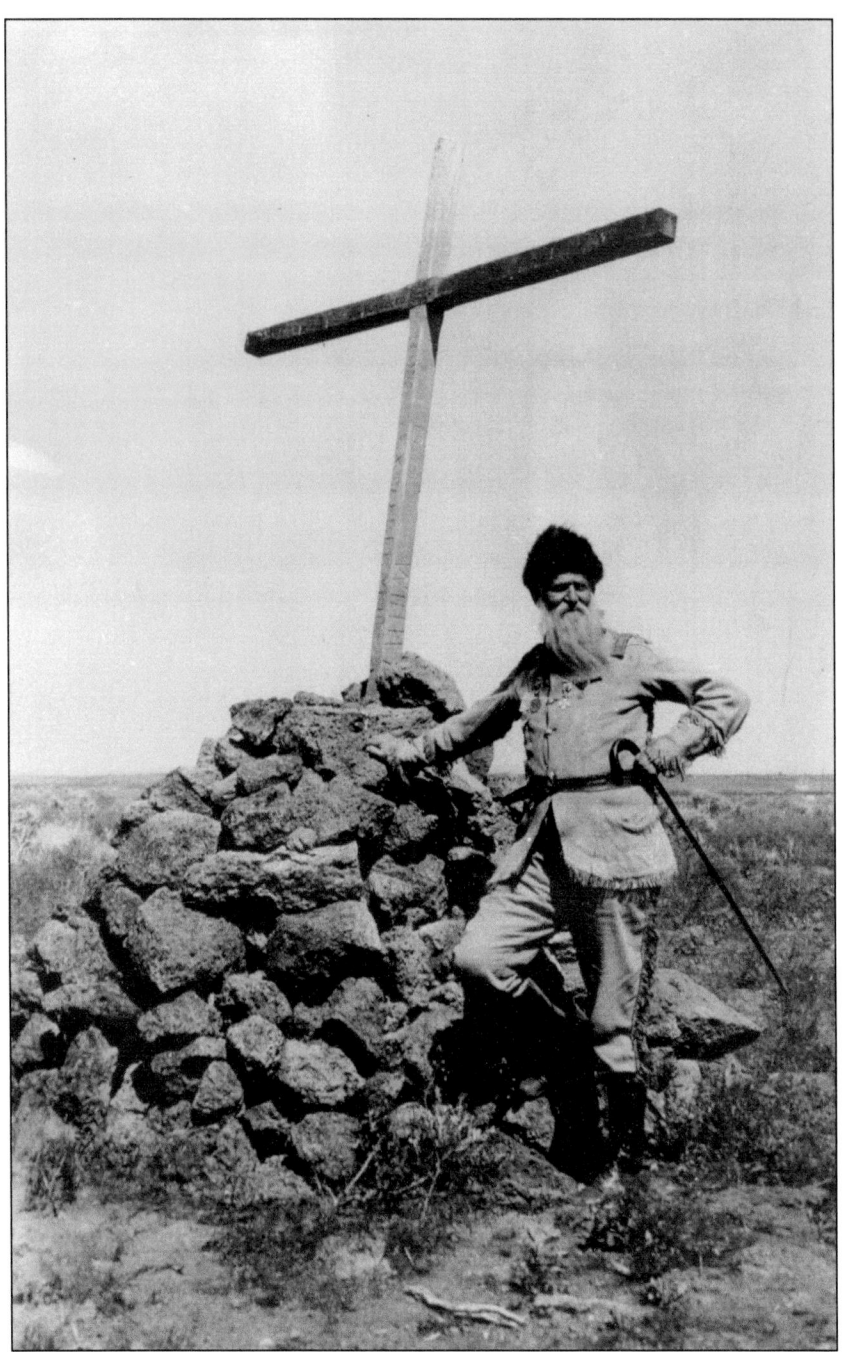

Oliver C. Applegate is shown posing in front of Canby's Cross. Applegate served in the Modoc War as an Oregon volunteer. Applegate was the son of Lindsay Applegate, a prominent early settler. He led a group of 68 volunteers, mostly composed of Klamath Indians from the Klamath Reservation, during the buildup to the first attack on the Modocs' stronghold. After the war, Applegate worked with J.D. Howard and others to enact protection for Lava Beds. Applegate wrote a letter sometime before 1920 suggesting the area "should perhaps be placed under government control and improved as a national park."

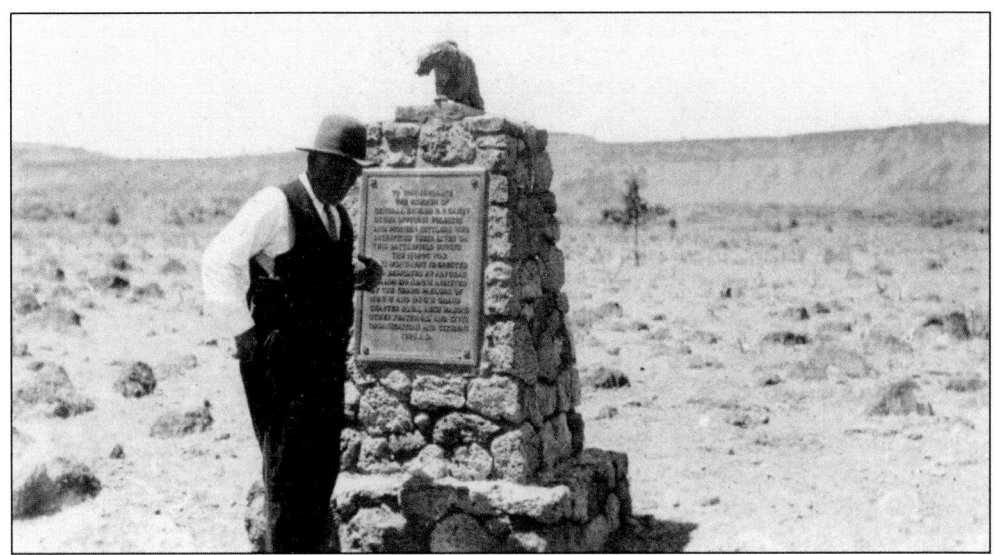

Peter Schonchin was among those who attended dedication ceremonies for the Canby Monument when it was unveiled on June 13, 1926. The monument featured a golden bear wounded by Indian arrows and a plaque honoring Gen. Edward R.S. Canby.

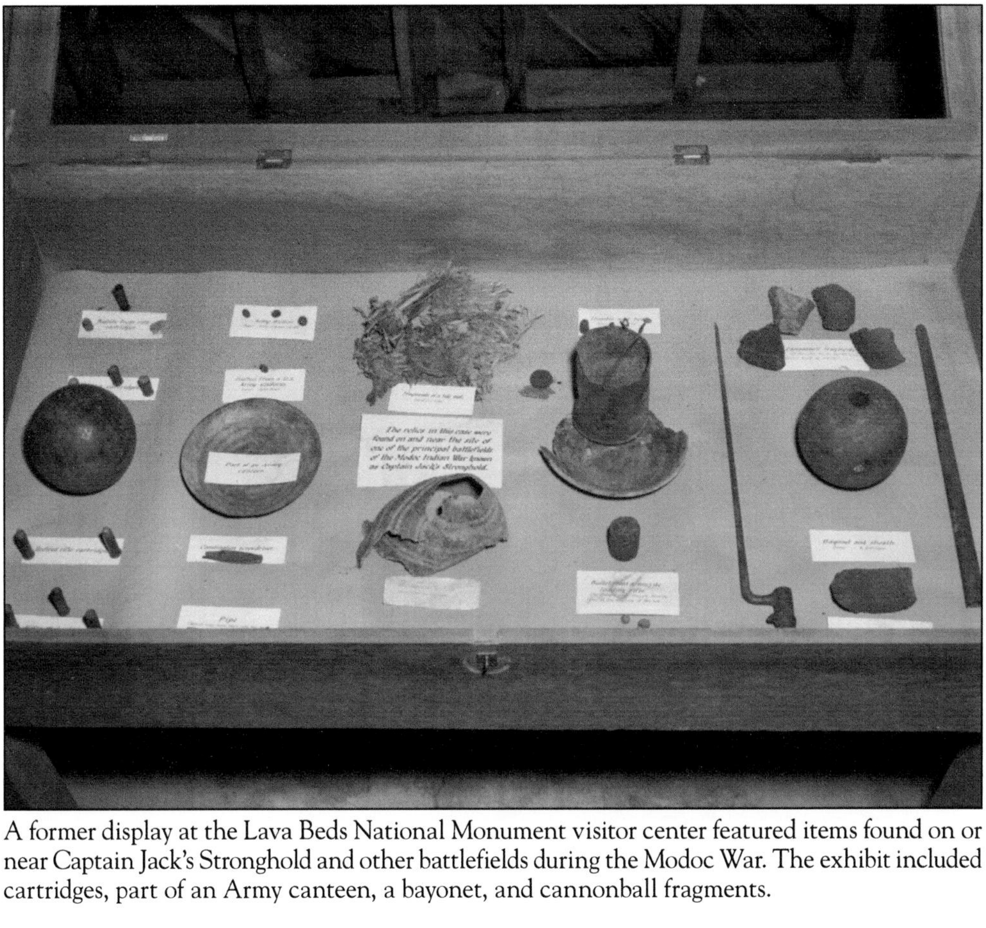

A former display at the Lava Beds National Monument visitor center featured items found on or near Captain Jack's Stronghold and other battlefields during the Modoc War. The exhibit included cartridges, part of an Army canteen, a bayonet, and cannonball fragments.

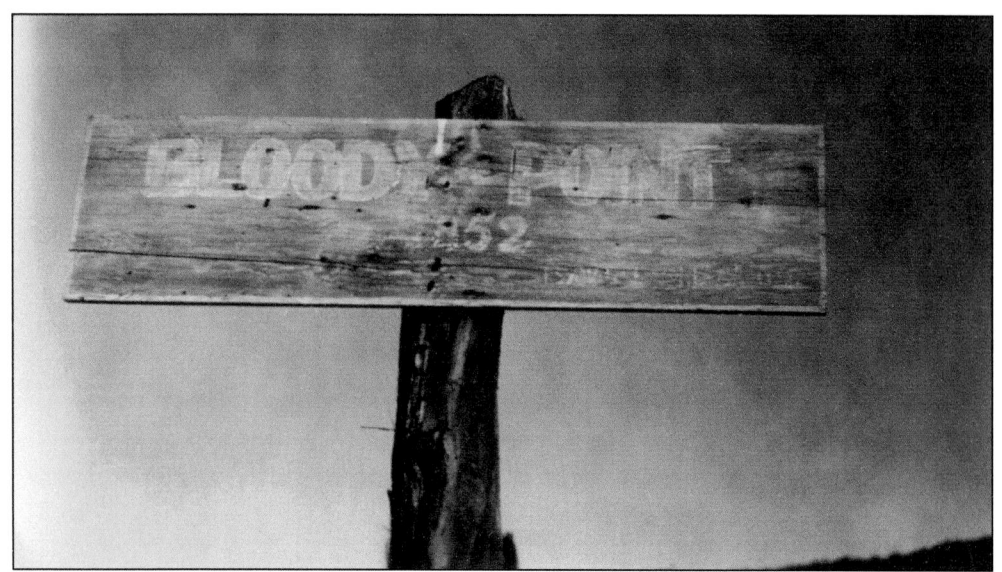

This sign marked the location of Bloody Point, so named because several white settlers were killed by Modocs there in 1849. The area, located near Tule Lake, was often used as an overnight camp by travelers. Modocs hid in the nearby boulders before attacking. Historian Keith A. Murray described the site as "possibly the grimmest spot in the history of emigrant travel."

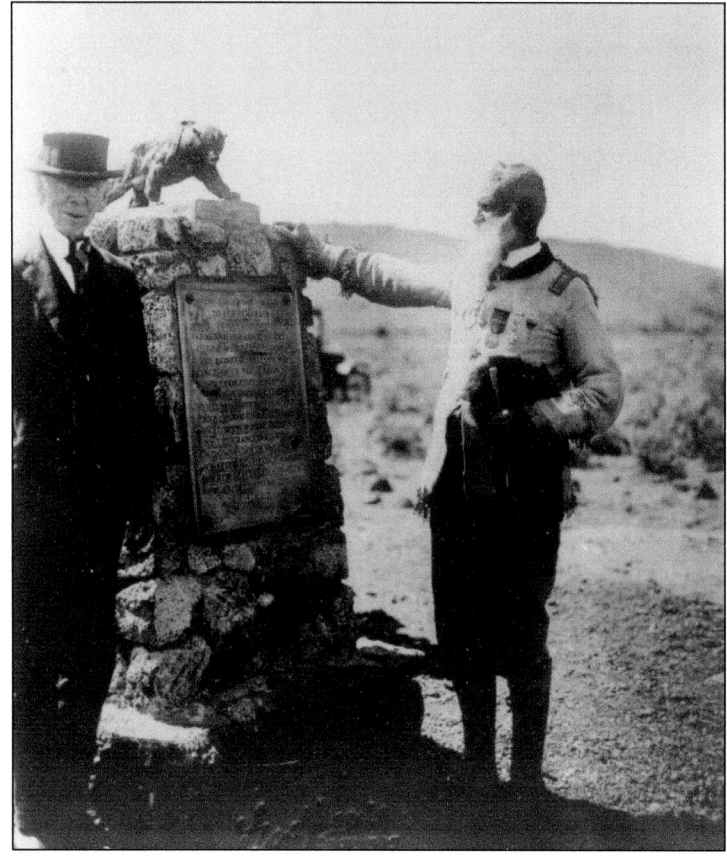

Oliver C. Applegate (right) was outfitted in his uniform during the June 13, 1926, dedication of the Canby Monument. At left is Col. William Thompson. More than 1,000 people, in 175 cars, attended the ceremony to celebrate the event that, according to organizers, "helped pass on to future generations the spirit of progress and advancement" by commemorating Gen. Edward R.S. Canby's service.

Five

Cave Discoverers

Each year, thousands of visitors explore some of the 700-plus lave tube caves at Lava Beds National Monument. For some of the earliest discoverers, the caves served practical purposes. Charles Caldwell and Anna Lauer, who later became his wife, ran horses at Lava Beds and used what is now called Caldwell Ice Cave to provide water for themselves, their workers, and their horses and mules in the early 1900s. During the Prohibition era, moonshiners used some caves to house their stills. A resort was developed at Bearpaw Cave, now known as Merrill Ice Cave.

Other early settlers, including Ernest Heppe, who ran sheep, used ice caves for water and, with friends, including Judson Dean ("J.D." or "Judd") Howard, explored and located new caves. Heppe and Howard discovered Heppe Cave, Silver Cave, and Bertha's Cupboard, which, at Heppe's request, was named for his wife. Members of the Cox family, herdsmen who arrived in 1901, used Cox Ice Cave for water.

It is Howard who is best remembered for his early explorations and persistent efforts to have Lava Beds designated as a national monument. He arrived in the Klamath Basin in 1916 and began his explorations almost immediately. Howard, who spent two winters camped in a tent at Lava Beds, shared with the public his fascination with the region's geology and cultural history, especially Indian petroglyphs.

Howard is known for locating, naming, mapping, and photographing many caves. He painted cave names near the entrances, and those names are still visible in dozens of caves. Howard, who died in 1961, said he "found 123 caves, 75 chimneys, and 50 natural bridges and one tree cast." Because of his efforts in helping to create Lava Beds National Monument, he is called the "Father of Lava Beds." In 1994, a brass plaque purchased by his friends was embedded on a rock across from the entrance to Mushpot Cave.

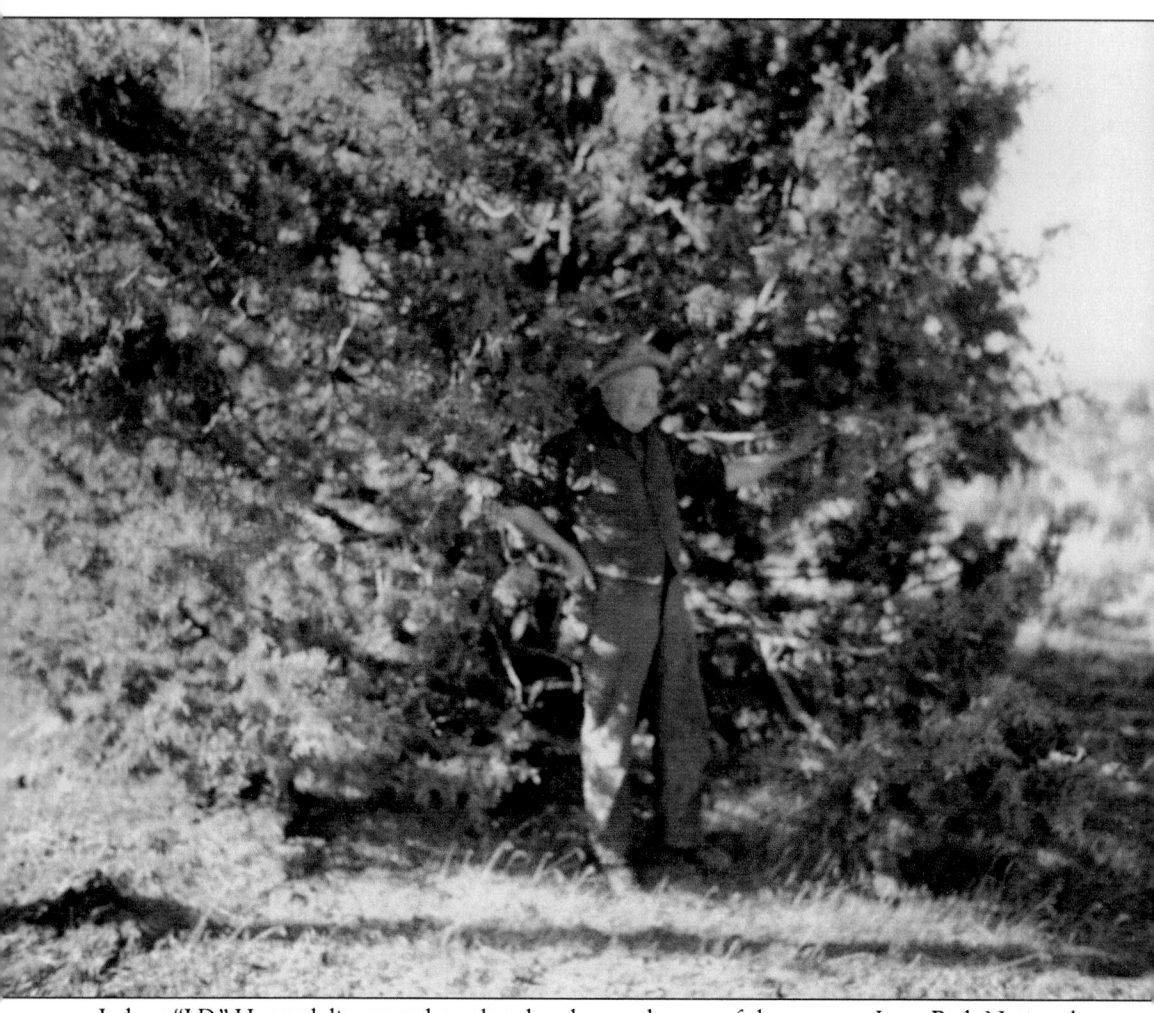

Judson "J.D." Howard discovered, explored and named many of the caves at Lava Beds National Monument. He frequently took friends on tours of the area and was among those who lobbied to have the area designated as a national park. Although he photographed numerous geological features and visitors, he appears in only two photographs. A miller by trade, he moved to Klamath Falls, Oregon, in 1916 and made his first visit to Lava Beds later that year. He spent many of the following 20 years exploring the region, even living in a tent at Lava Beds during some winters.

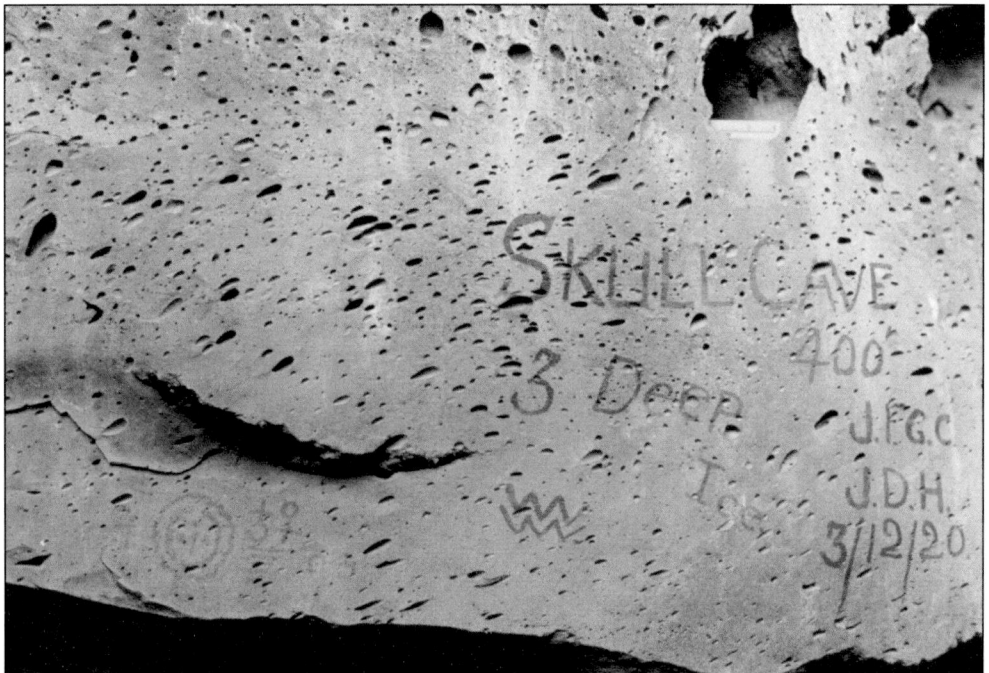

Along with naming many of the caves, J.D. Howard was known for recording their basic information, usually near the entrances. He left this information at Skull Cave on March 12, 1920.

Howard's extensive explorations included his discovery of the multilevel Crystal Cave. He named the cave after the large ice formations usually found there in winter. For a time, the cave was used by Jim Howard (not related to J.D.) to make moonshine. Because the heat from the still destroyed the ice, J.D. advised Jim to move his operation.

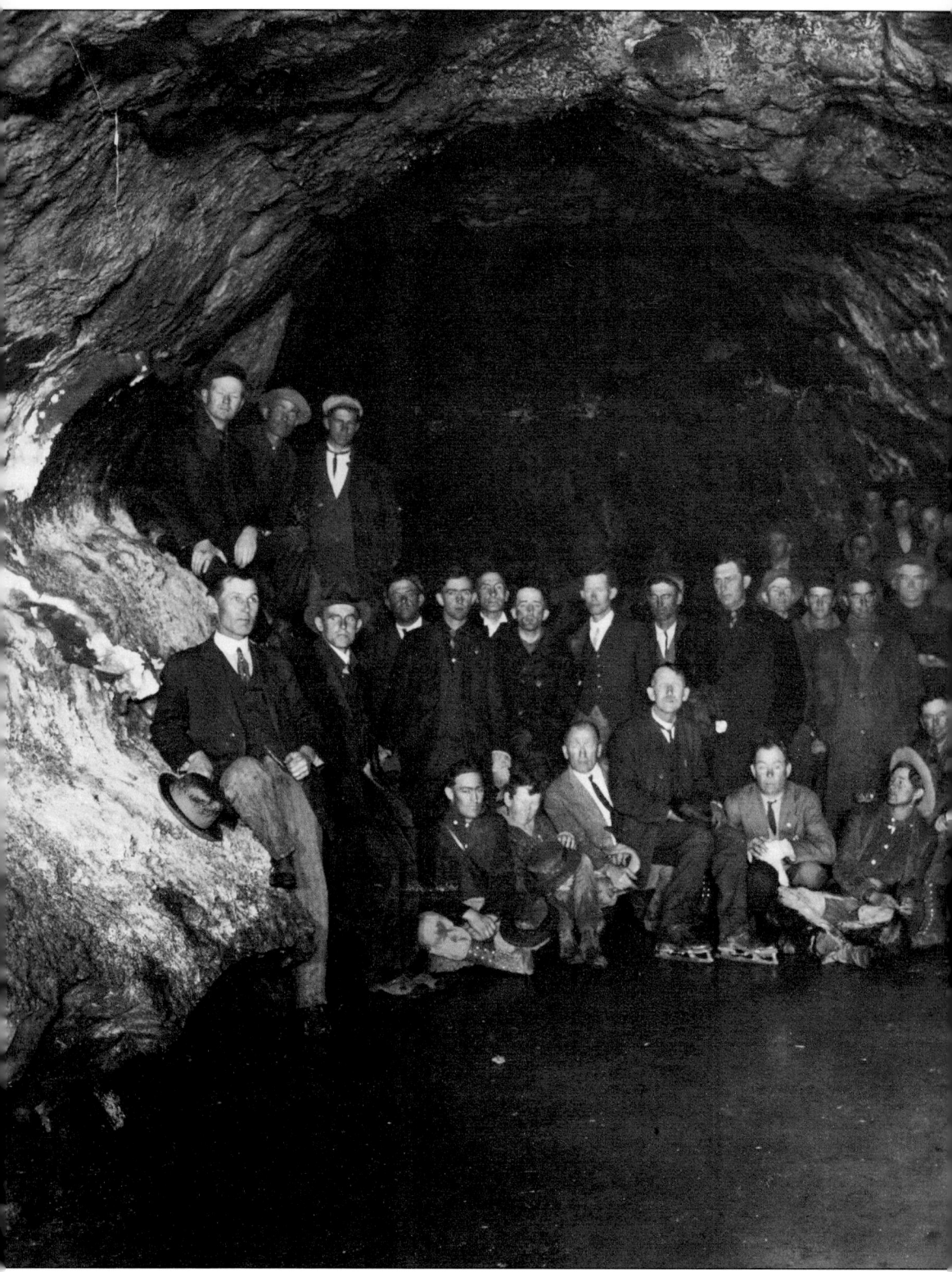

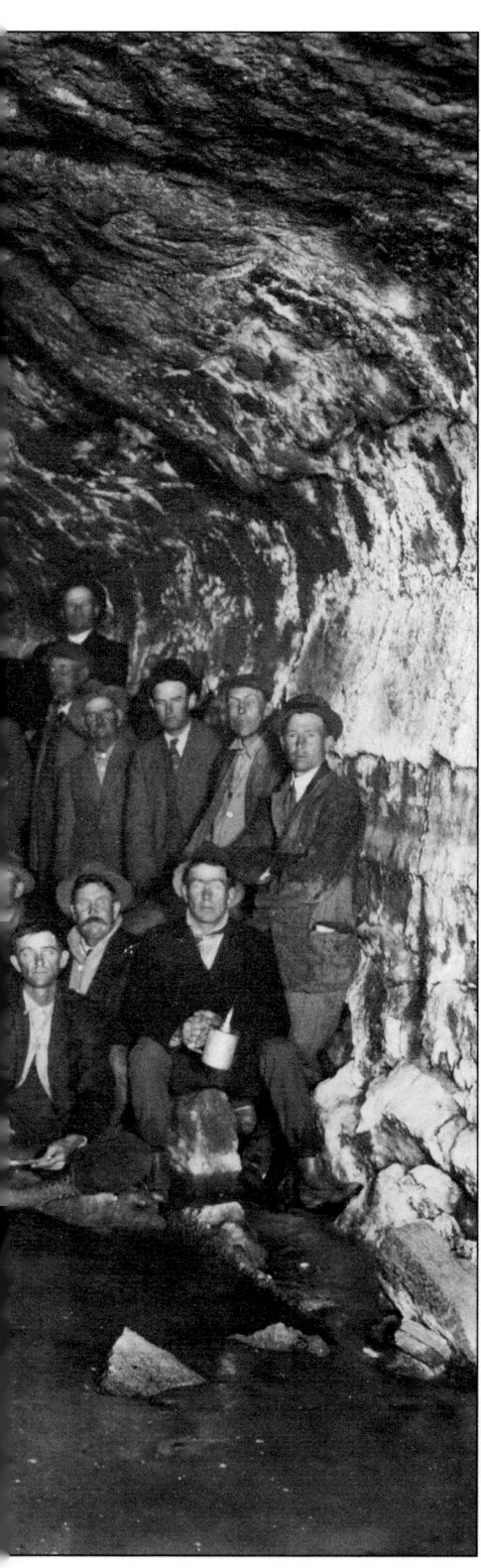

The introduction of the automobile increased travel throughout the United States, including to the Lava Beds region. The Merrill family, who had a sheep and horse operation, apparently began using the area around what was originally known as Bearpaw Cave as a winter camp for their horses. After building a road to the cave, Charles H. Merrill began efforts to buy 160 acres near the cave in 1916. By 1923, his son Guy had opened the Bearpaw Resort, which drew visitors, including the large group in this undated photograph. One of the men in the front row is wearing ice skates.

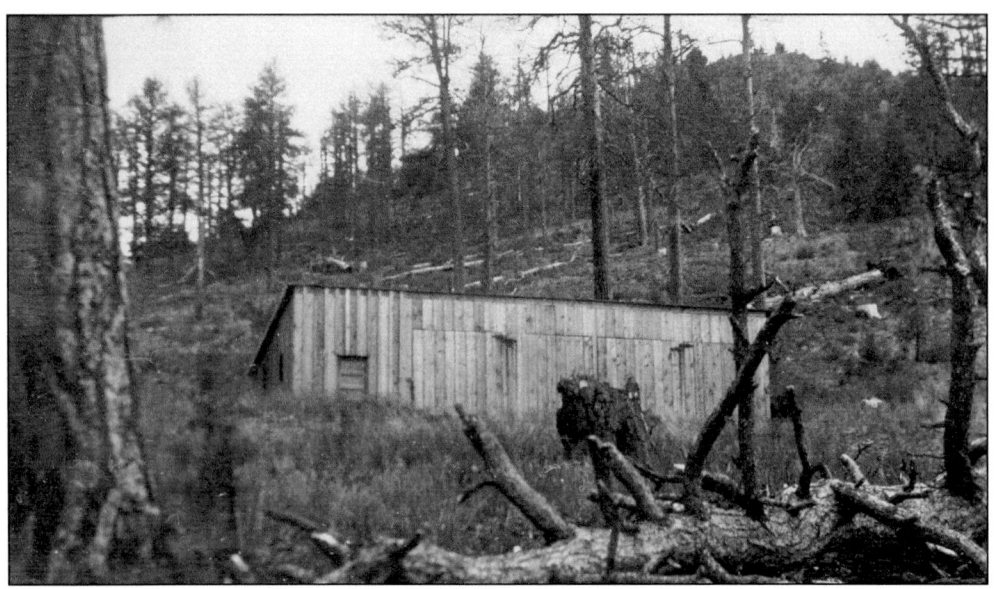

The Bearpaw Resort briefly served as a popular area resort in the 1920s. The resort hosted dances and reportedly served moonshine whiskey during the Prohibition years. The above photograph shows the resort's dance platform, with Bearpaw Butte in the background, in 1934, after it closed. The 1934 photograph below shows the Bearpaw dining hall, which was part of the resort. The resort was developed by Guy Merrill and opened in 1923. The resort complex included a restaurant, hotel, and dance hall. It closed in 1927.

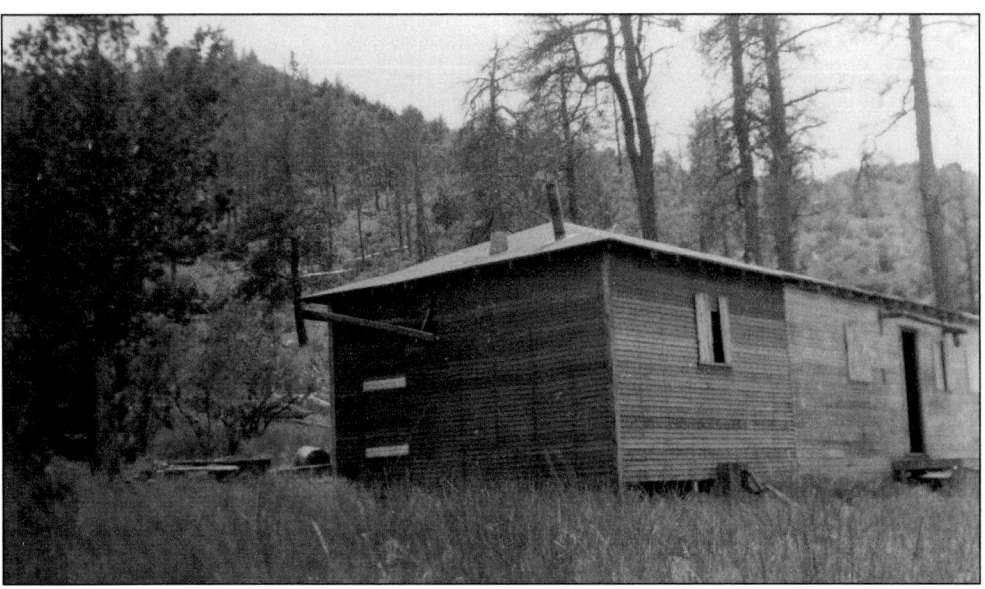

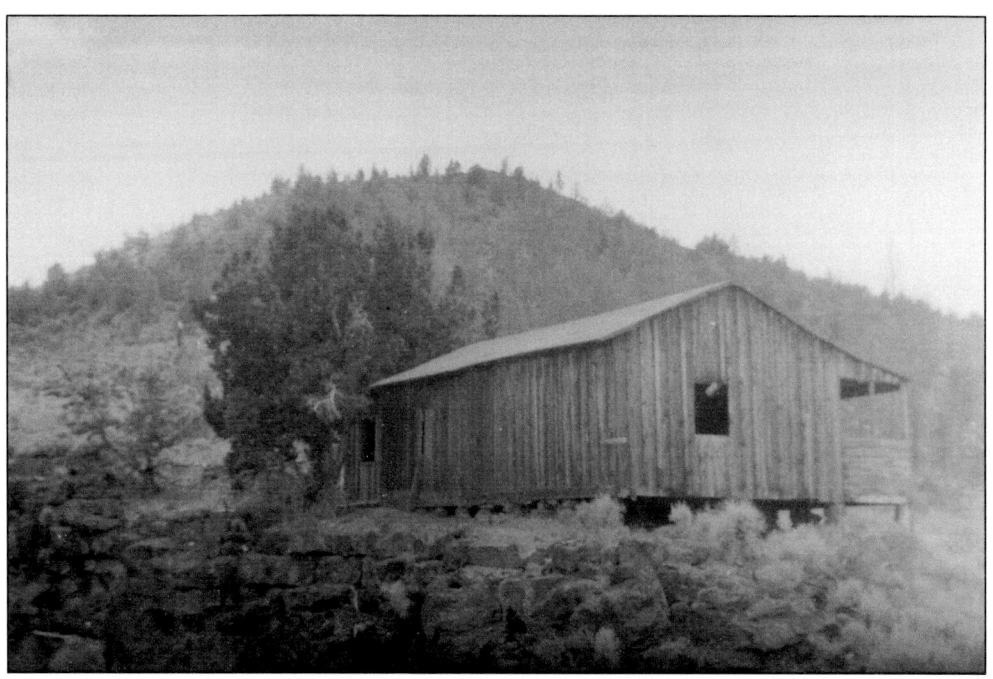

The 1934 image above shows the Bearpaw Resort dining room as photographed from another angle. Little was written about the resort, although it is believed the leftover mash from making moonshine was fed to hogs owned by the Merrill family. There are brief references to a "private summer resort" in a 1920s US Forest Service brochure. A map in the 1926 *Alturas Plaindealer* newspaper showed the "Barefoot Resort" next to "Bearfoot Cave." The below photograph shows the building from its more attractive front entrance.

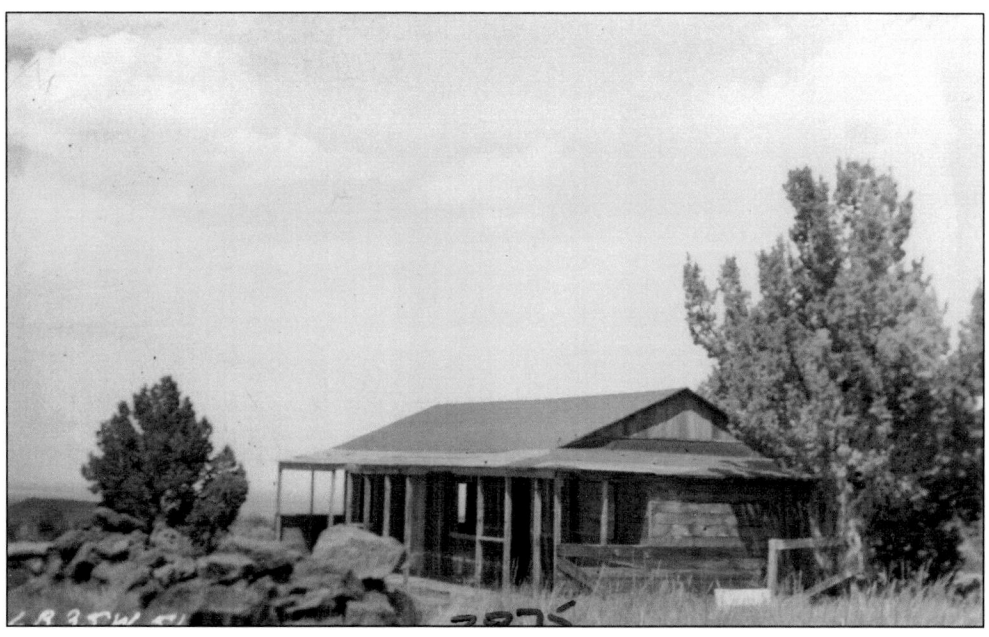

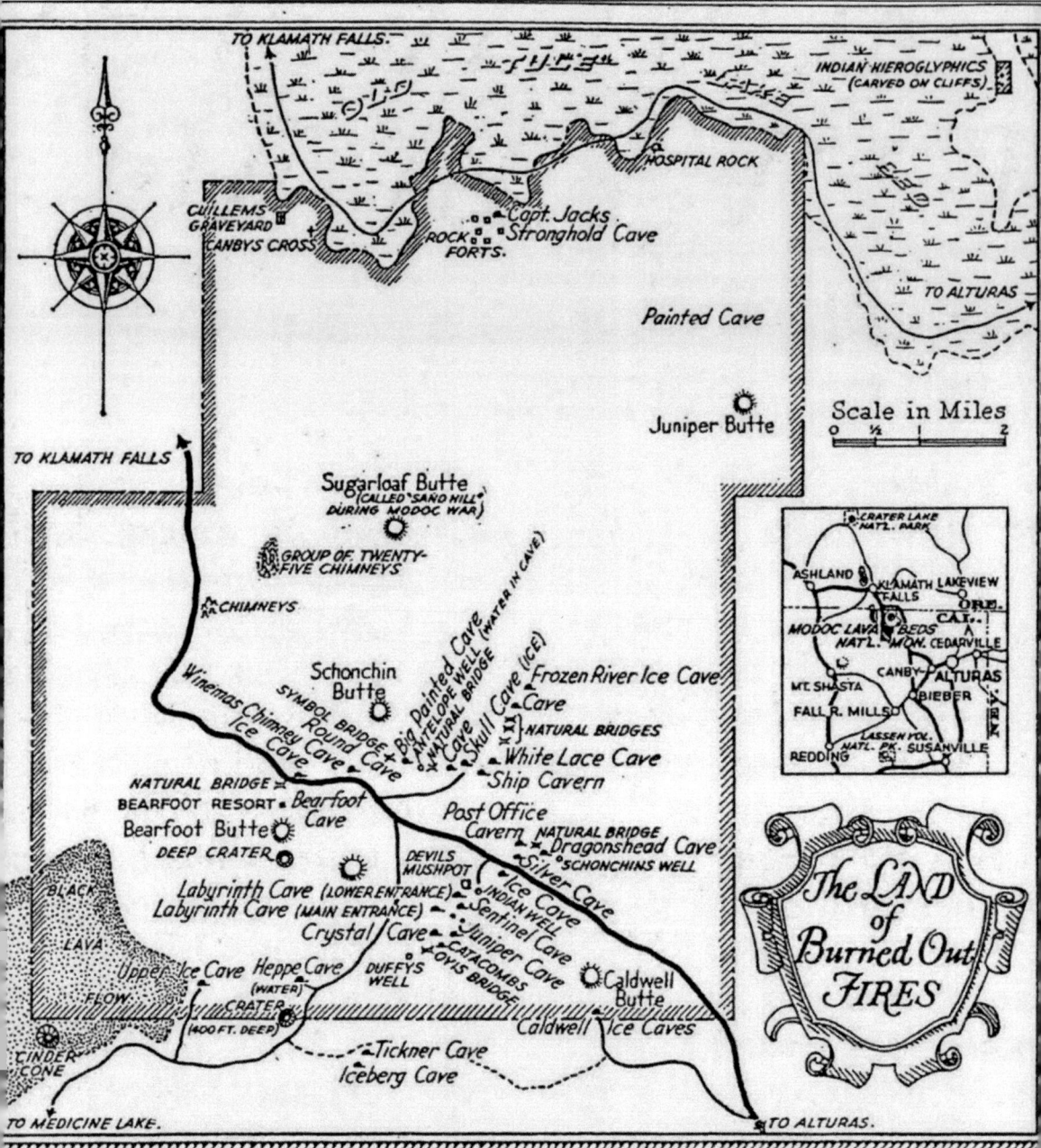

A 1927 map of Lava Beds National Monument, the "Land of Burnt Out Fires," from the magazine *Touring Topics*, provides a good perspective of the monument's many features. The Bearfoot Resort, also known as the Bearpaw Resort, is shown near Bearpaw Butte in the lower left of the map. The map does not show the Lyons Road and the main road from the Bearpaw area to Gillems Camp. It does show significant sites from the Modoc War, including Gillems graveyard, Canby's Cross, Captain Jack's Stronghold, and the Hospital, all at the far north end of the monument. Many of the popular caves still visited today, including Catacombs, Crystal, and Sentinel, are indicated.

Large sheep operations were located in and near Lava Beds before and after it became a national monument. This 1941 photograph shows Pat Brown working sheep, owned by Hugh and Dennis O'Connor, through a counting gate. In 1916, the *Dorris Times* reported that 60,000 sheep were grazing in Lava Beds.

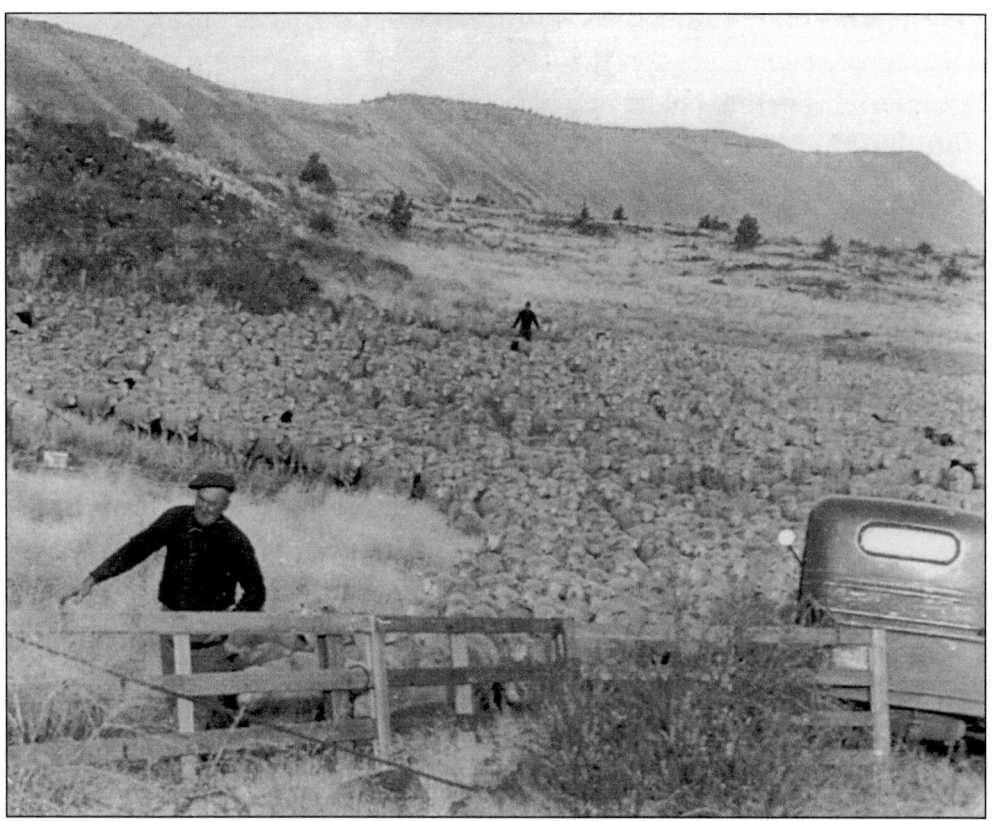

Charles Caldwell and his crews ran horses in Lava Beds and built a cabin near Caldwell Cave. They used the terrain to toughen the hooves of their horses, which were often sold in the San Francisco Bay area. His future wife, Anna Lauer, obtained land near what is now Caldwell Cave in 1904. Remains of the cabin are still visible.

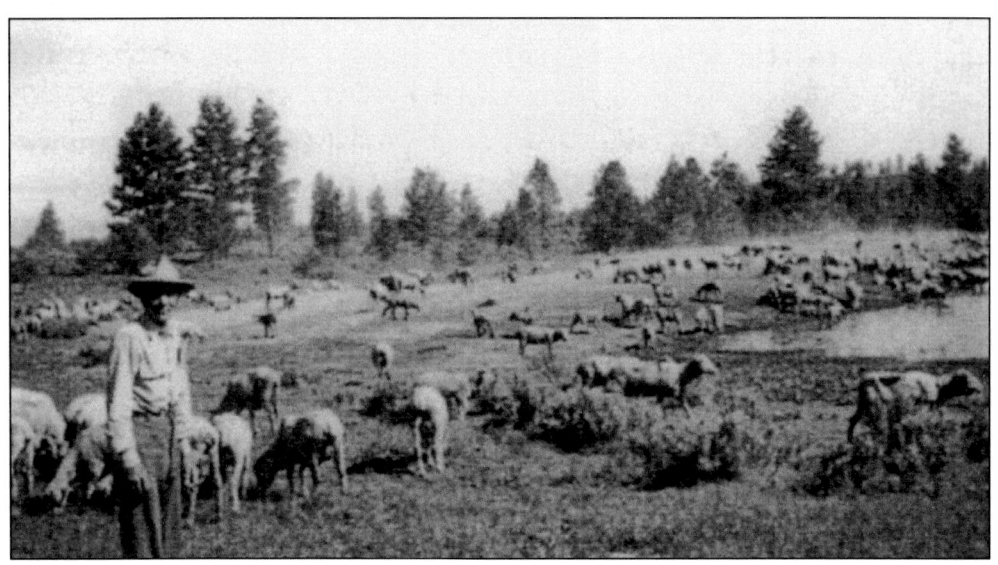

The Cox family arrived in the Tulelake Basin in 1901 and soon started a sheep operation based in Lava Beds. Family members had a camp in a juniper grove south of Schonchin Butte. In this photograph, Charles Cox is shown with sheep near Perez, outside the monument, prior to World War I.

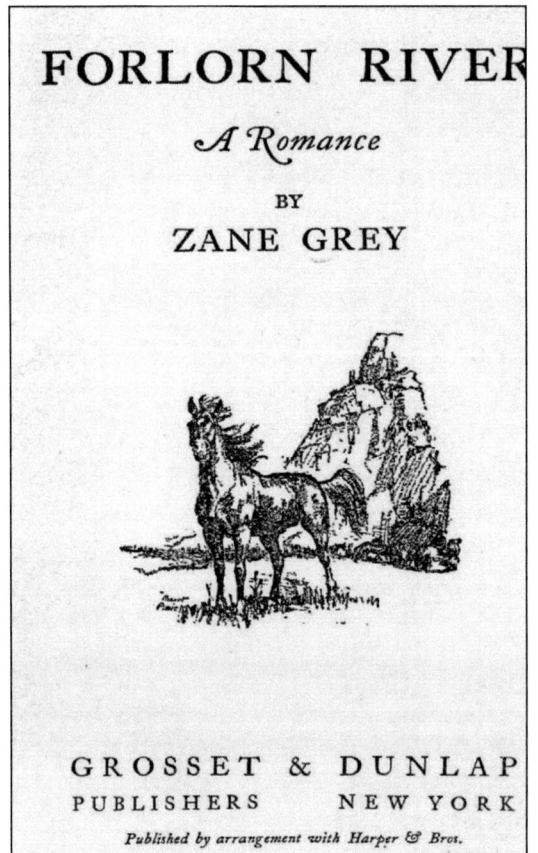

Lava Beds provided some of the setting for Zane Grey's western romance *Forlorn River*, published in 1927. Grey lived in Klamath Falls and visited with Tulelake Basin ranchers while researching the book. The book provides an accurate description of Lava Beds and neighboring areas.

Six

THE CCC INFLUENCE

Several agencies were instrumental in helping to develop roads, trails, structures and other facilities at Lava Beds National Monument. Relief workers started improvement projects in 1932, a year before newly elected Pres. Franklin D. Roosevelt transferred management responsibilities from the US Forest Service (USFS) to the National Park Service and two years before the actual transfer.

In June 1932, Pres. Herbert Hoover signed legislation establishing public works programs with the Emergency Relief and Construction Act. Public Works Administration crews began arriving that fall. Under the direction of the USFS, they built roads and constructed trails in some of the caves. In a relatively short time, crews did extensive work during the winter of 1933–1934, helping to improve the monument's water system, installing trails and ladders in 32 caves, and building trails to Mammoth Crater and the Thomas-Wright Battlefield.

The 1933 establishment of the Civilian Conservation Corps (CCC), under President Roosevelt's New Deal program, had a greater impact. CCC workers lived and worked at Lava Beds from late 1933 until 1942. More than 1,000 young men were stationed at Lava Beds—about 130 at a time for six-month periods. Most were from Florida, Georgia, Alabama, Kentucky, Texas, Ohio, Wyoming, and Colorado. Infrastructure improvements by the CCC were substantial. Working with National Park Service architects, crews constructed several rustic architecture buildings, including several that are still in use, such as the superintendent's residence, garage and shop building, and operations building. Using native stone from the monument and cedar logs from Oregon caves, crews also built picnic tables with benches and the Schonchin Butte Lookout, which is still seasonally used. Other CCC projects included telephone and power lines, water systems, and participation in firefighting, fire fuel abatement work, surveying, and various road and trail maintenance projects.

The last CCC workers left the monument in 1942, when the federal government shut down the program because of World War II. The legacy of the CCC and Public Works Administration crews remains alive and visible.

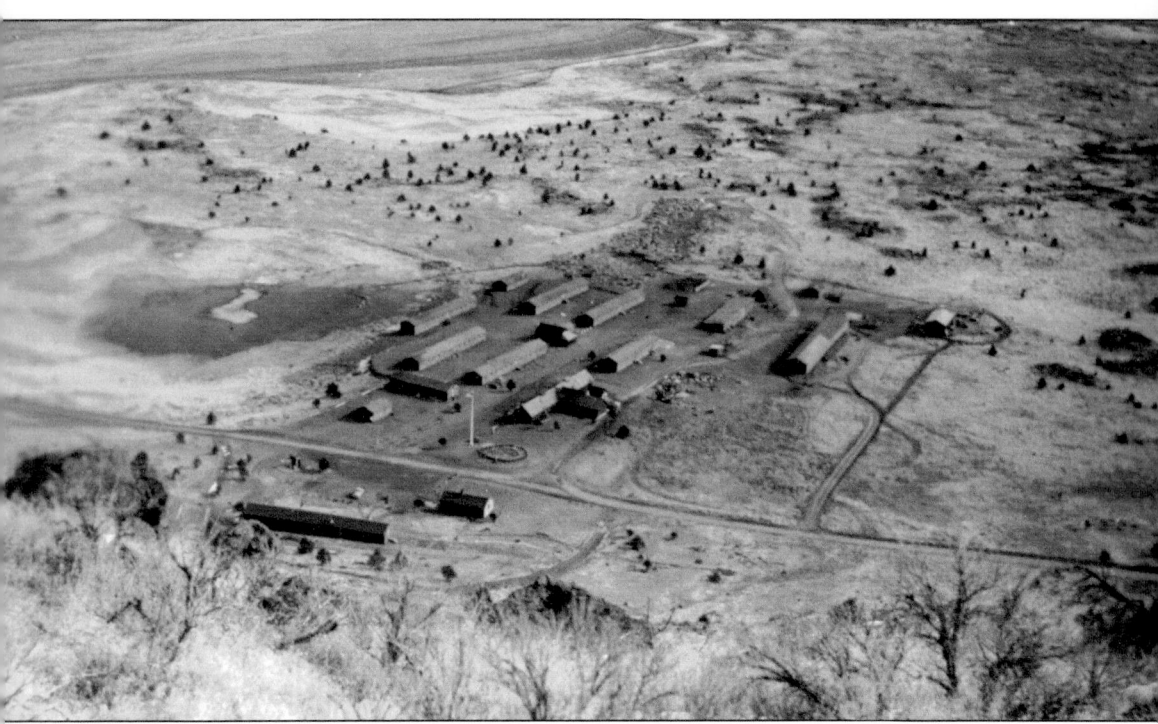

The Civilian Conservation Corps camp at Lava Beds housed men participating in a Depression-era work program that resulted in significant improvements to areas around the nation and to the fledgling Lava Beds National Monument. More than 1,000 young men participated in programs at Lava Beds. The CCC camp was established at Gillems Camp, which had been the US Army headquarters during the Modoc War, and began as a tent camp that operated only in the warmer months. The year-round camp, pictured here in a photograph taken between 1937 and 1942, shows various structures that mitigated living conditions at the camp.

This CCC work crew is pictured with their truck in an undated photograph. CCC crews worked on a variety of projects, including building trails, roads, and other infrastructure such as telephone and power lines and water systems.

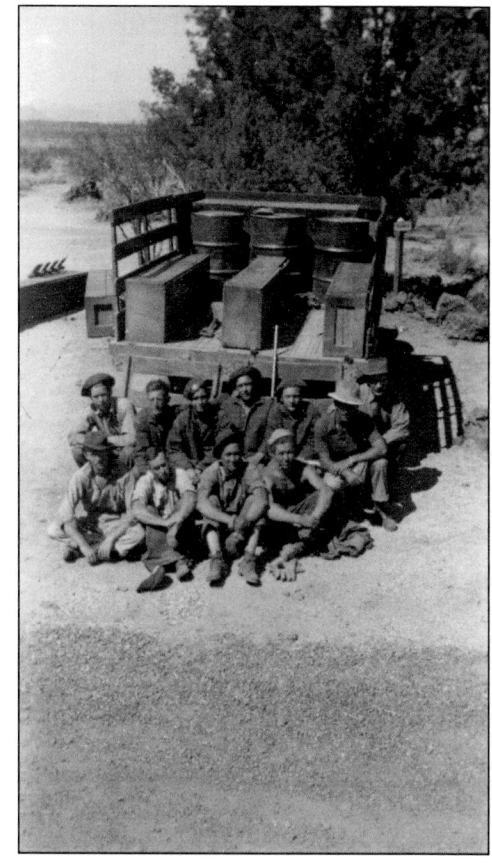

One of the tasks taken on by CCC crews during their years at Lava Beds was loading cinder used in road construction, as shown in this undated photograph. The results of the CCC crews' work is still evident throughout the monument, from trails to several park buildings, including the stone building known as the superintendent's house.

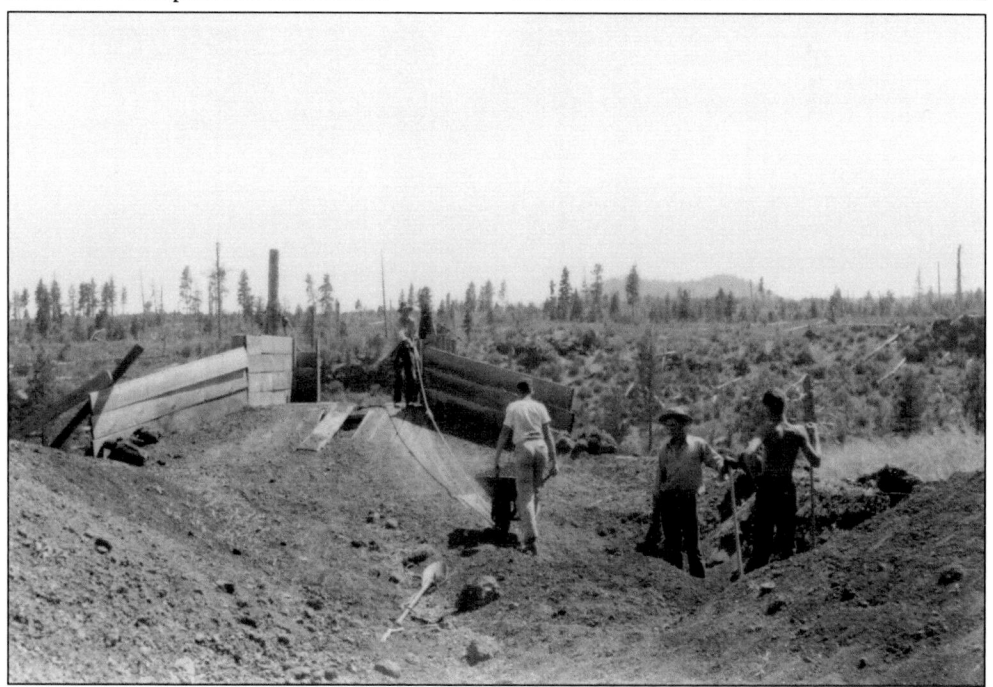

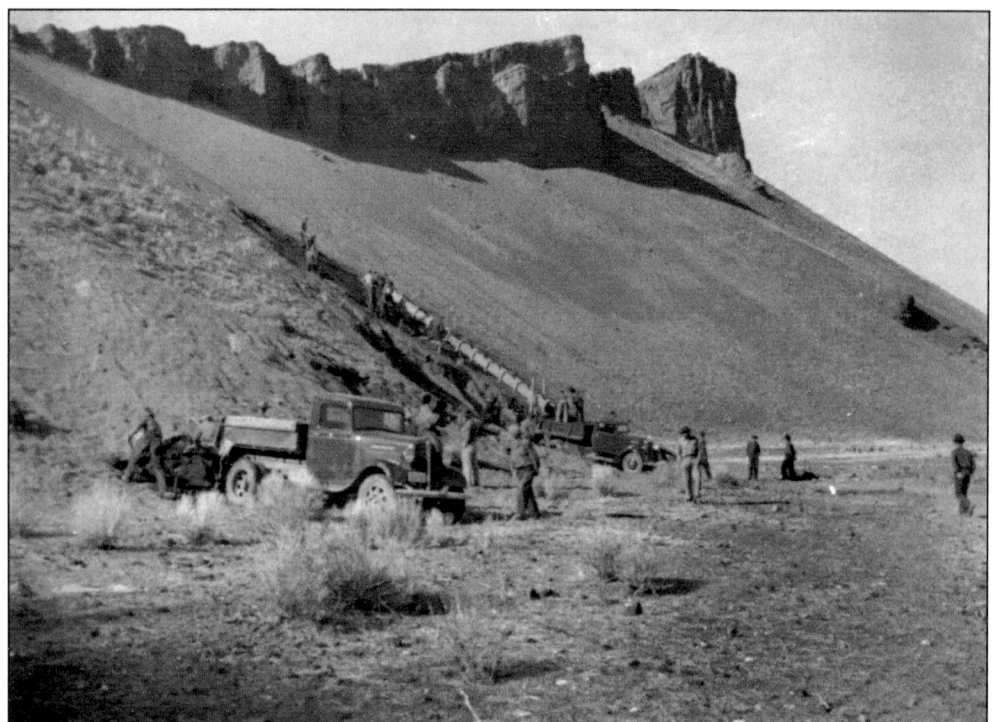

CCC crews worked on a variety of projects around the monument, including building roads and fences along with other projects that greatly expanded park infrastructure. The CCC program also offered opportunities for education.

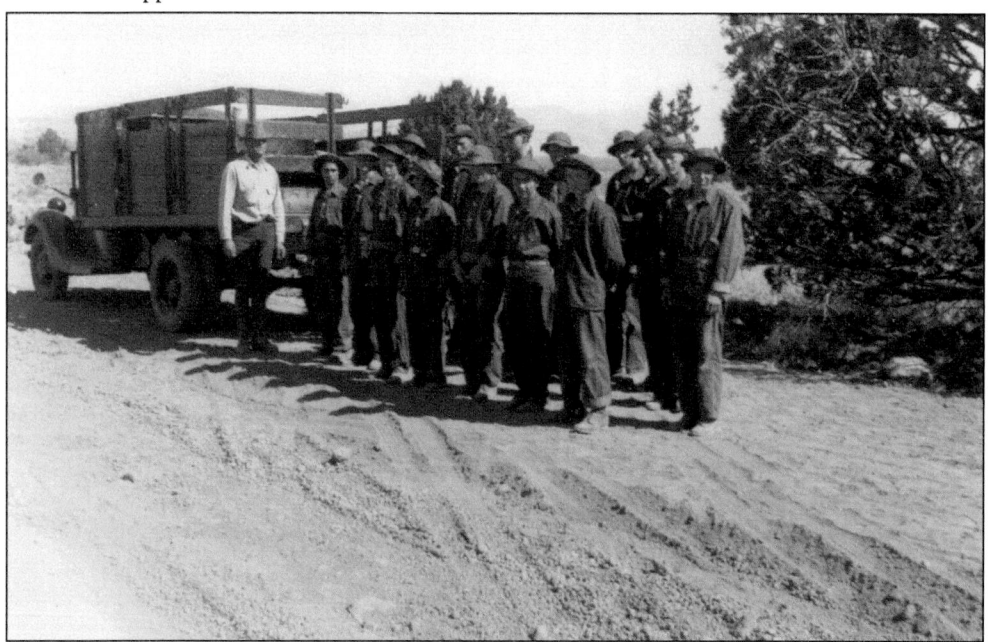

A crew of young CCC enrollees, dressed in their uniforms, is pictured in this undated image before heading out to work. Records indicate crews worked on access trails, cave trails, ladders, and other improvements for several caves, including Skull, Fern, Valentine, Catacombs, and Indian Well.

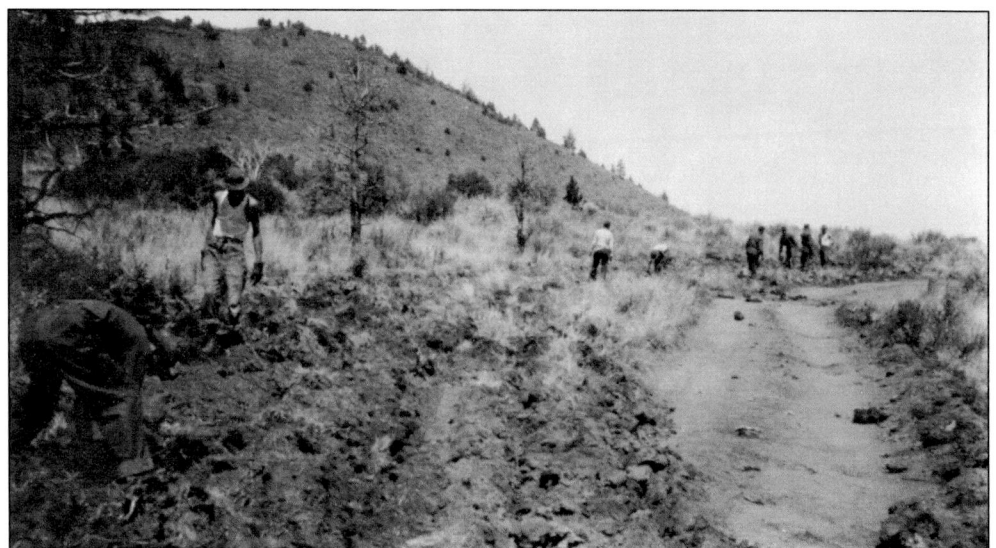

Most of the jobs tackled by CCC crews required them to be outdoors during the chilly winters to the hot summers. One of the projects was the construction of the main road from Gillems Camp to Indian Well. The crews widened the road from 12 to 22 feet and made slight changes in its alignment.

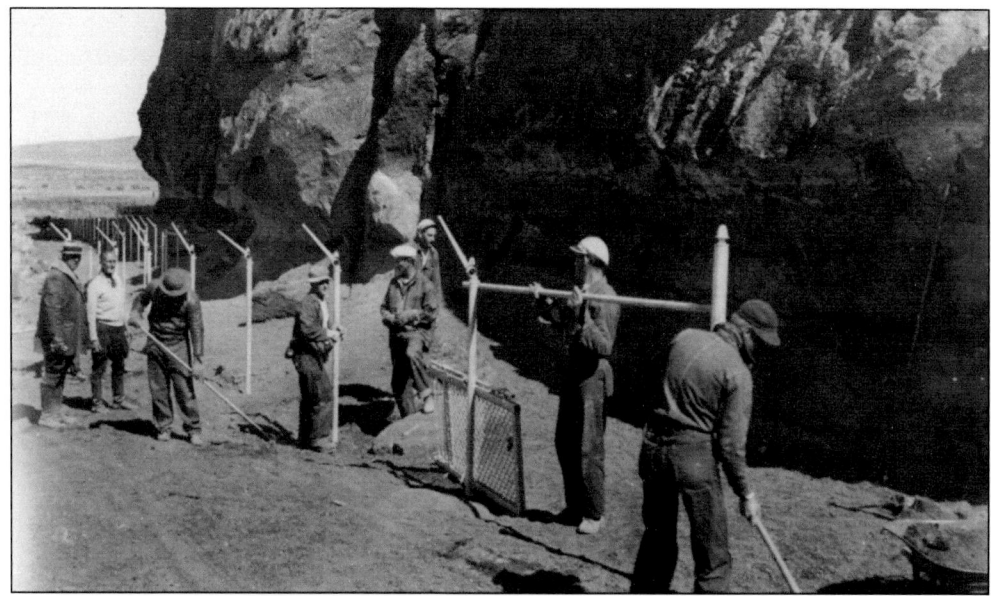

Petroglyph Point was among the areas improved by CCC crews; they erected fences there in 1936 to try to protect the images painted onto and etched into the rock walls. The original fence has since been replaced. Several other noticeable CCC projects, including the superintendent's residence, are still standing in the monument.

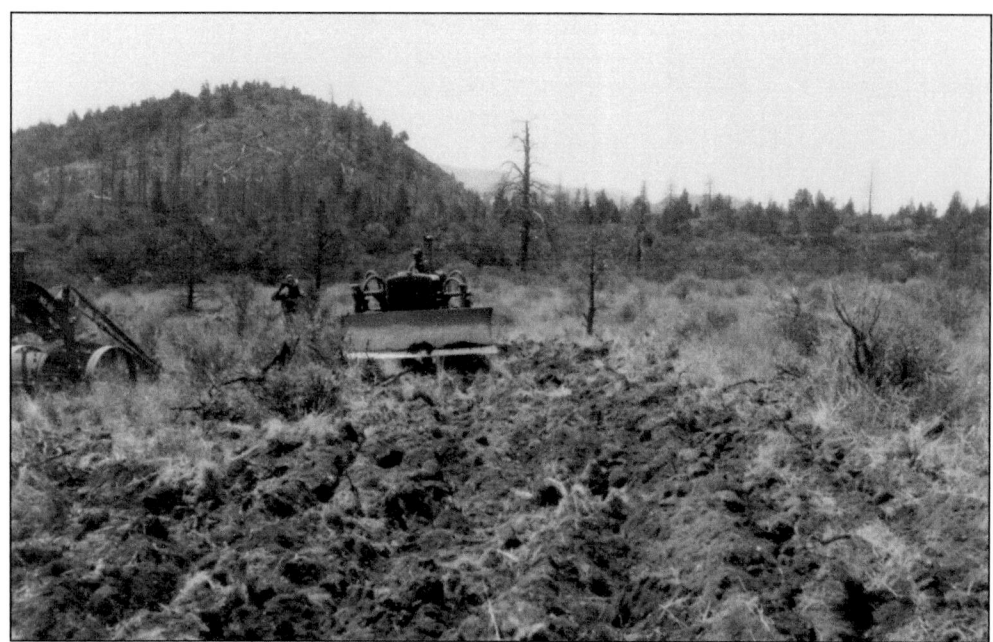
A tractor carves out a future road near Schonchin Butte in this undated photograph. One of the road projects involved improving and realigning the North Boundary Road, which had been entirely outside the monument's boundary and followed the old Tule Lake shoreline.

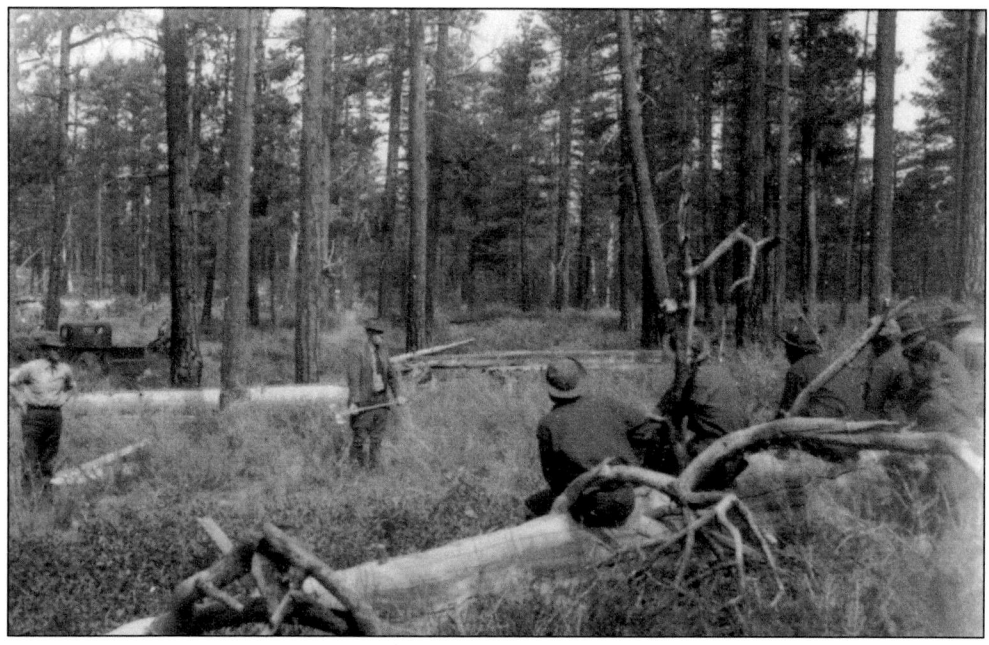
Training sessions were part of camp life at the Lava Beds National Monument and neighboring CCC camps. The young men in the program often lacked work skills, so along with learning construction-related skills, they were coached on how to apply for and keep a job.

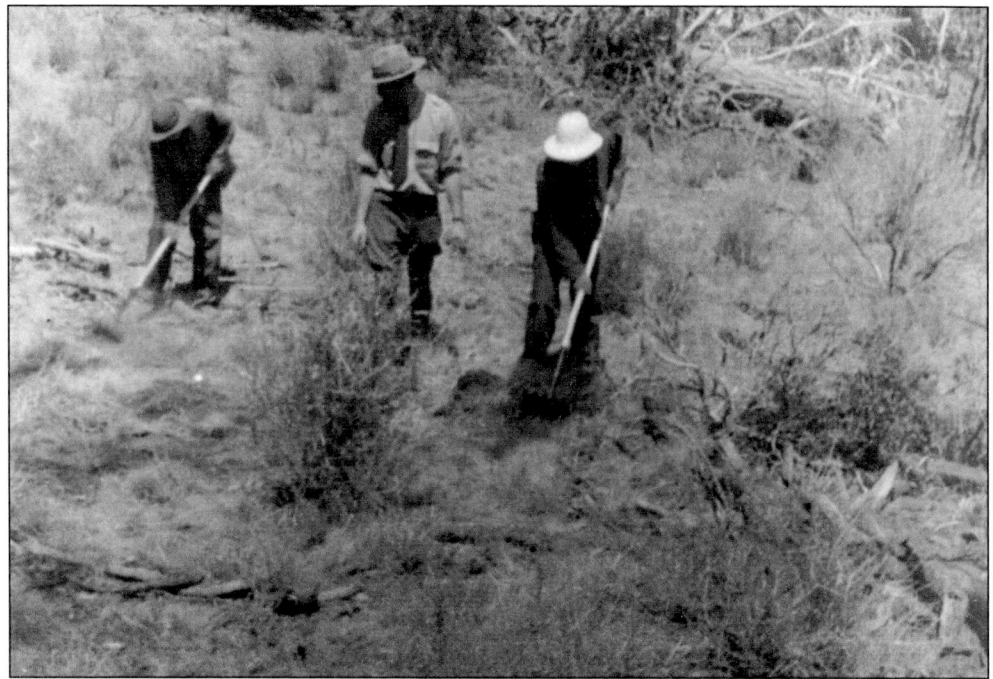
Hand labor was part of the routine for CCC enrollees, from helping to build roads to carving hiking trails. One of the goals of the camp was to help participants learn life skills that they could use after leaving the program.

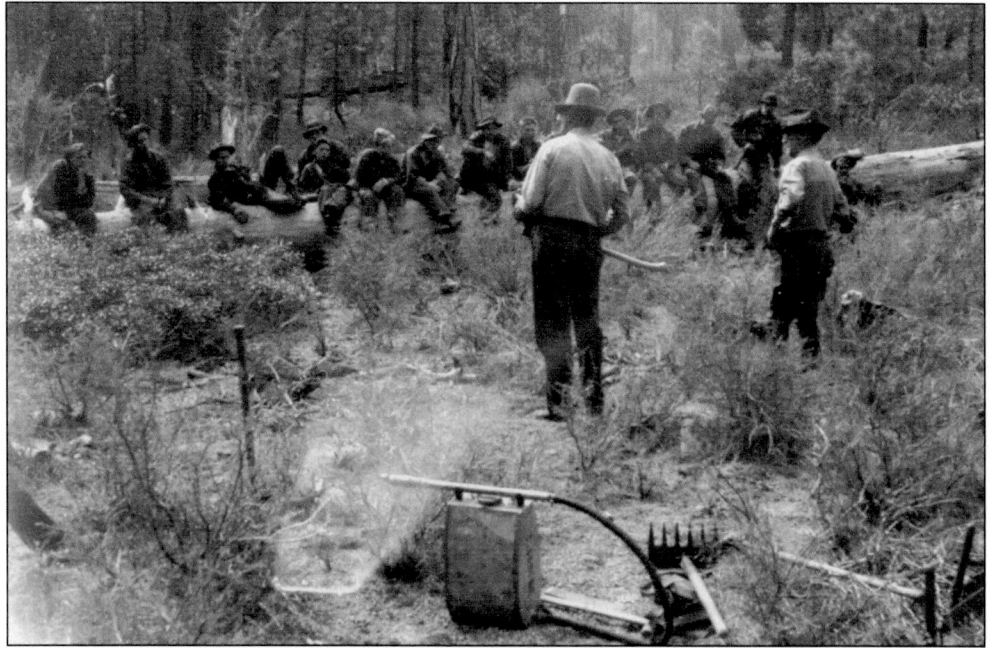
Classes in a variety of subjects, from using specialized tools for building trails to sessions focusing on life skills, were emphasized by CCC camp directors. Correspondence courses were also offered, with the most popular offering being mechanics. These CCC men are pictured at a fire-training class.

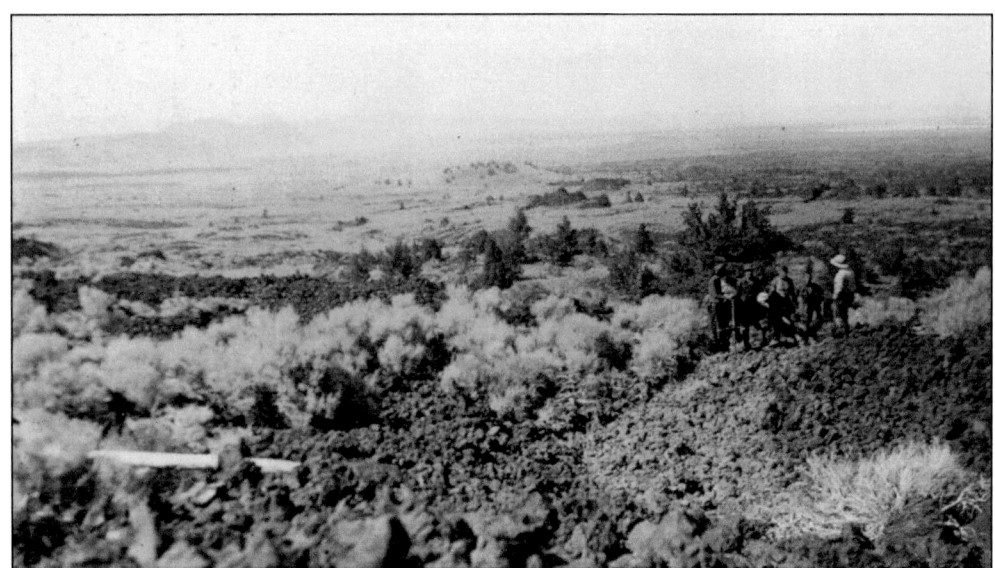

A crew of CCC workers is shown taking a work break at an unknown lava flow. Some of the tasks completed by CCC workers included improving parking areas and access roads to Catacombs, Frozen River, Fleener Chimneys, Valentine Cave, Schonchin Butte, and Petroglyph Point.

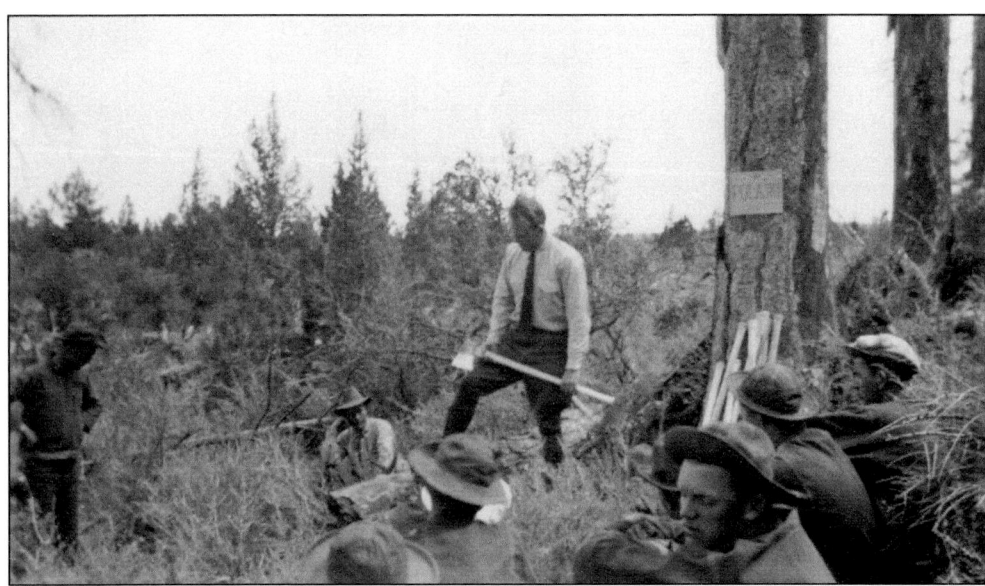

Instruction in the proper use of handling an ax was among the skills taught to youthful crews, which largely consisted of young men with no or limited practical work experience. By July 1933, within a few months of the creation of the CCC, crews were stationed and working at Lava Beds.

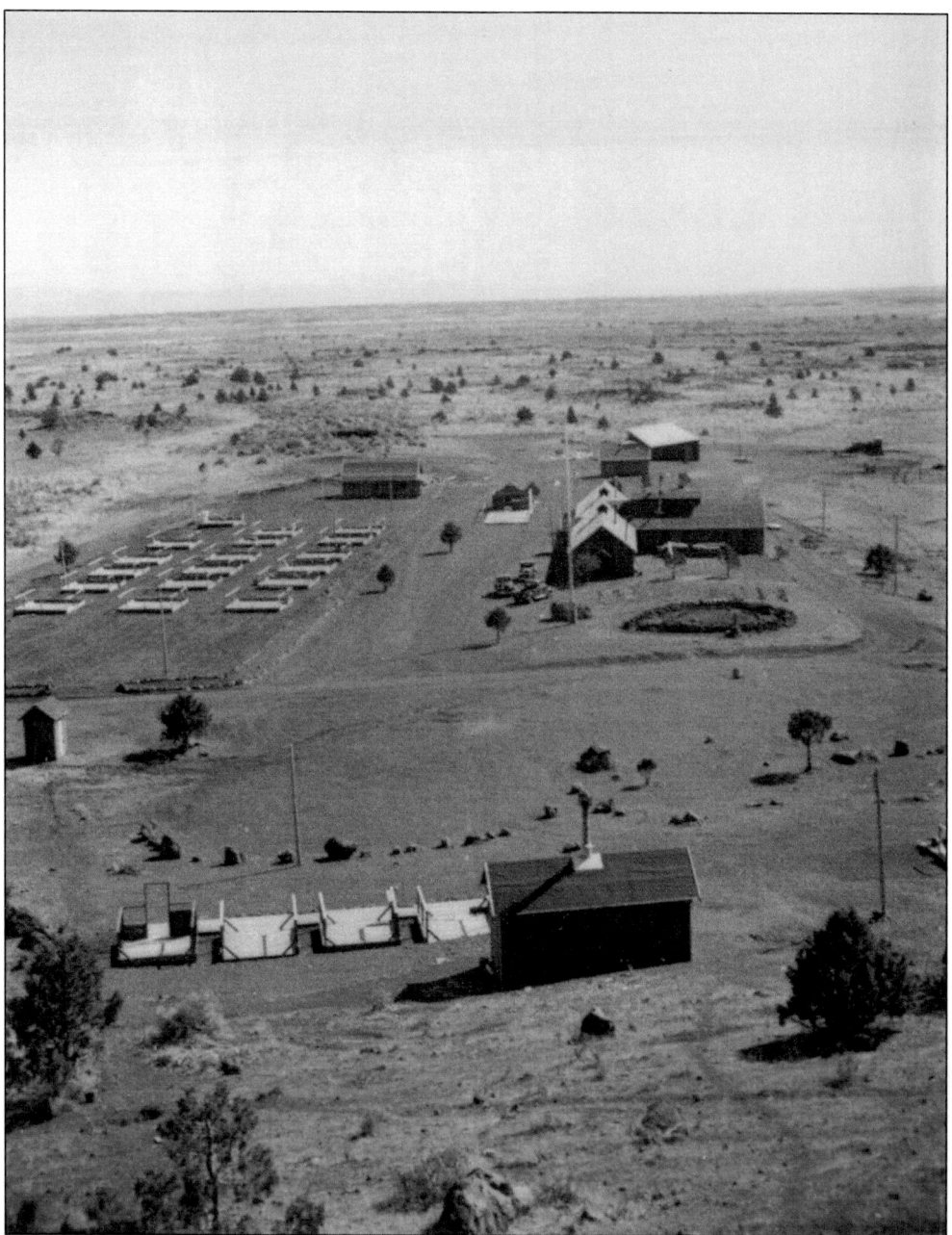

The CCC camp at Lava Beds was established at the former Gillems Camp. Although it was initially a tent camp used in the warmer months, it expanded and within a few years had 40 tents, a large mess hall, six long buildings (probably used as barracks), and six smaller buildings. The site also included a headquarters building for the camp commander and technical offices for the National Park Service superintendent, along with an infirmary, recreation hall, bathhouse, equipment shed, powder house, lumber shed, and supply house. The crews worked on a variety of projects, building everything from picnic tables to parking lots to the ranger's residence, later called the superintendent's house, which features native stones. The CCC crews also constructed other buildings in what is now the park's headquarters area.

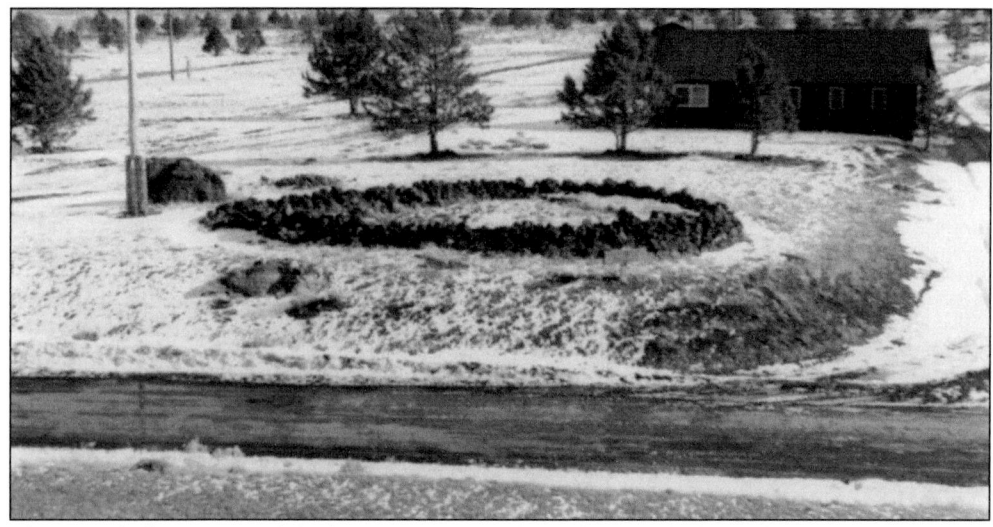
The mess hall was part of the larger CCC complex. Along with physical labor, enrollees were encouraged to advantage of educational programs. In a September 1935 camp newspaper, a listing of available classes included history, first aid, typing, algebra, music, citizenship, spelling, motor transportation, psychology, and bookkeeping.

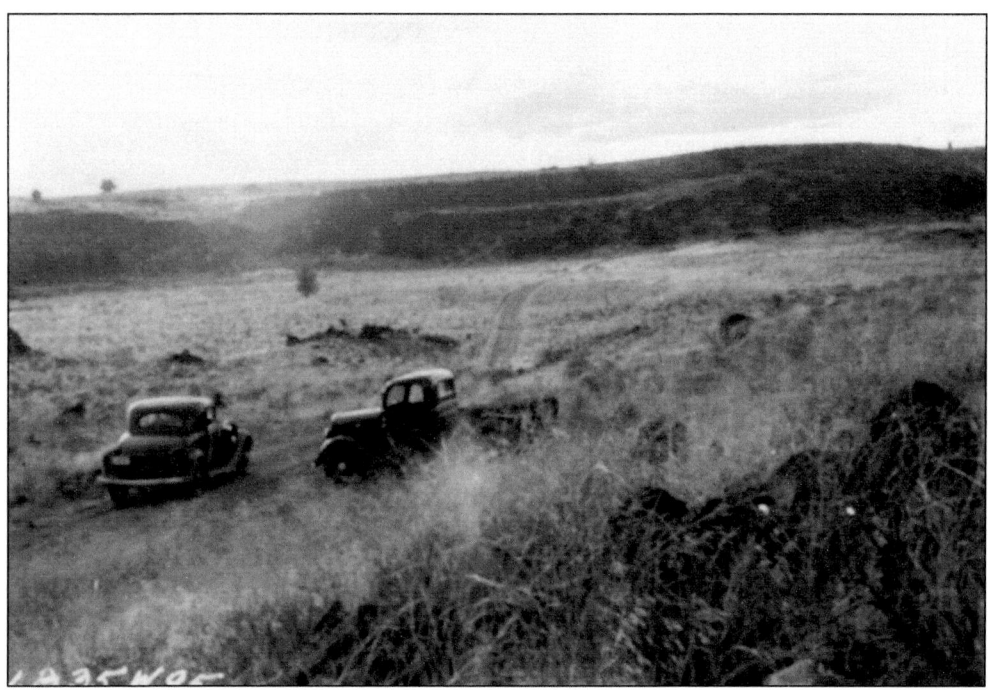
CCC crews were sent on work details throughout Lava Beds, often to build new roads and do other infrastructure improvements. One of their tasks was improving the road from Gillems Camp to Indian Well.

Seven

Development of a National Monument

When Pres. Calvin Coolidge created Lava Beds National Monument on November 21, 1925, under authority of the Antiquities Act of 1906, which allows presidents to establish national monuments by executive order, it culminated years-long efforts by a coalition of groups. The US Forest Service (USFS), which had recommended making Lava Beds a national park because of its historic interest and unusual cave features, took over management responsibilities.

The first known request to designate Lava Beds as a national monument was made by J.S. Diller of the Geologic Survey in a letter to Oliver C. Applegate in 1910. In 1914, California congressman John E. Raker, at the urging of Applegate and others, lobbied for a special designation as part of an effort to promote tourism in far northern California. In 1923, J.D. Howard sent letters to the California Highway Commission and *Sacramento Bee* seeking national monument status for Lava Beds. Several newspapers and organizations, including the Alturas chapter of the Native Daughters of the Golden West, supported the efforts.

Even before its designation as a national park, Lava Beds had become accessible through a network of roads that connected historic sites such as Gillems Camp, Canby's Cross, Captain Jack's Stronghold, and Hospital Rock with the lava tubes. The early roads were built by Howard and others, with the USFS gradually taking control of road-building and signage.

Howard, who discovered many caves, installed ladders in some, but the national monument designation led to the USFS overseeing the development of visitor access to the caves.

The administration of national monuments, including Lava Beds, was transferred from the USFS to the National Park Service in 1933.

Don Fisher was assigned as the monument's temporary ranger in 1934. While the administration change did not seriously change management, it eventually reflected the National Park Service's philosophy of preserving the area "unimpaired for future generations."

Because of the Great Depression, Pres. Herbert Hoover launched public works programs, including one that led to road- and trail-building projects in 1932. Those efforts accelerated with the election of Pres. Franklin D. Roosevelt and his creation of the New Deal agencies, including the Civilian Conservation Corps (CCC). In July 1933, just months after the creation of the CCC, crews were working at and near Lava Beds, which resulted in substantial infrastructure improvements.

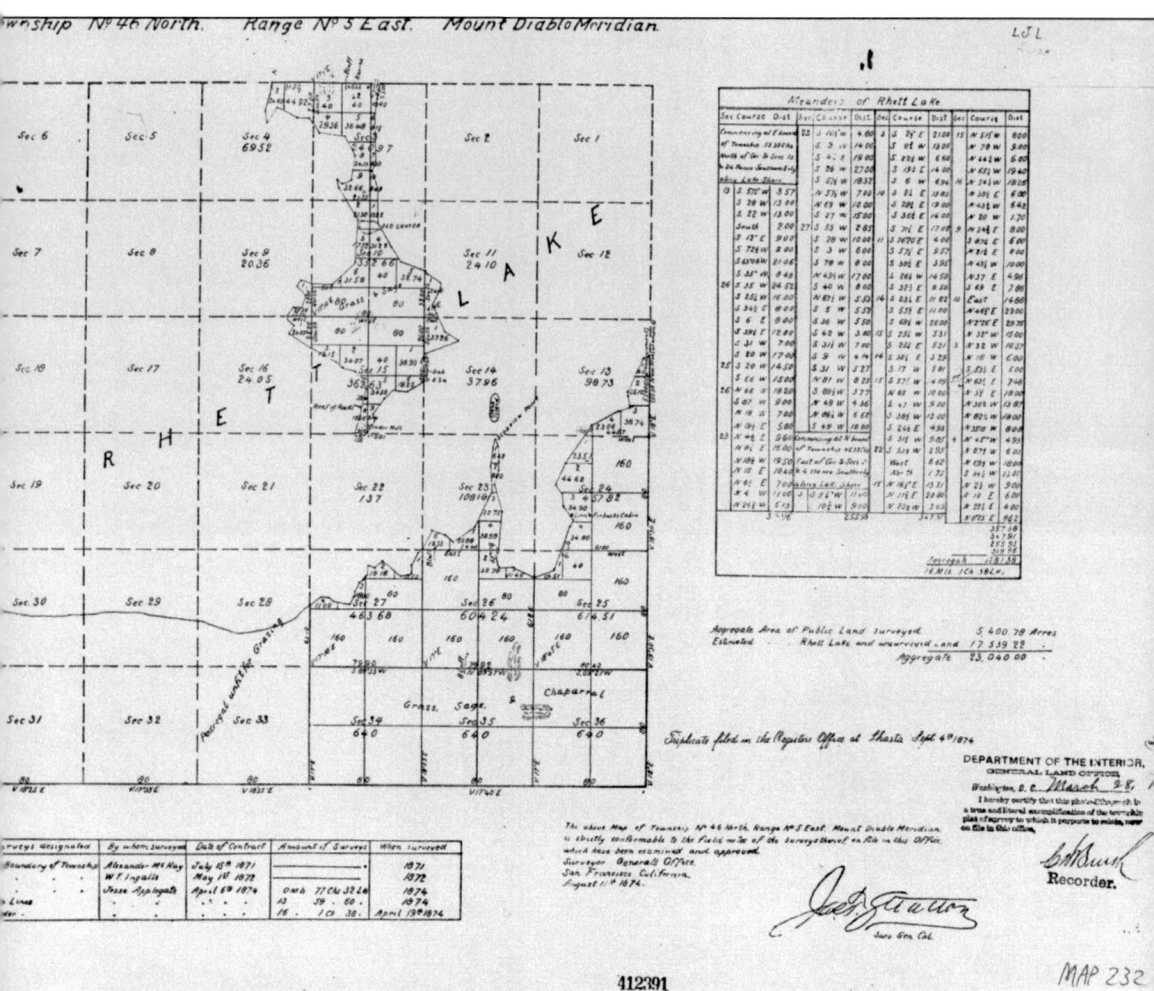

This map of Lava Beds National Monument was prepared by the US Department of the Interior's general land office in June 1943. The survey was prepared to define the monument's northern boundary. The southern boundary, then as now, is aligned with the Tule Lake National Wildlife Refuge. By this time, the National Park Service had taken over management of the monument, which had previously been administered by the US Forest Service, leading to an emphasis on resource protection.

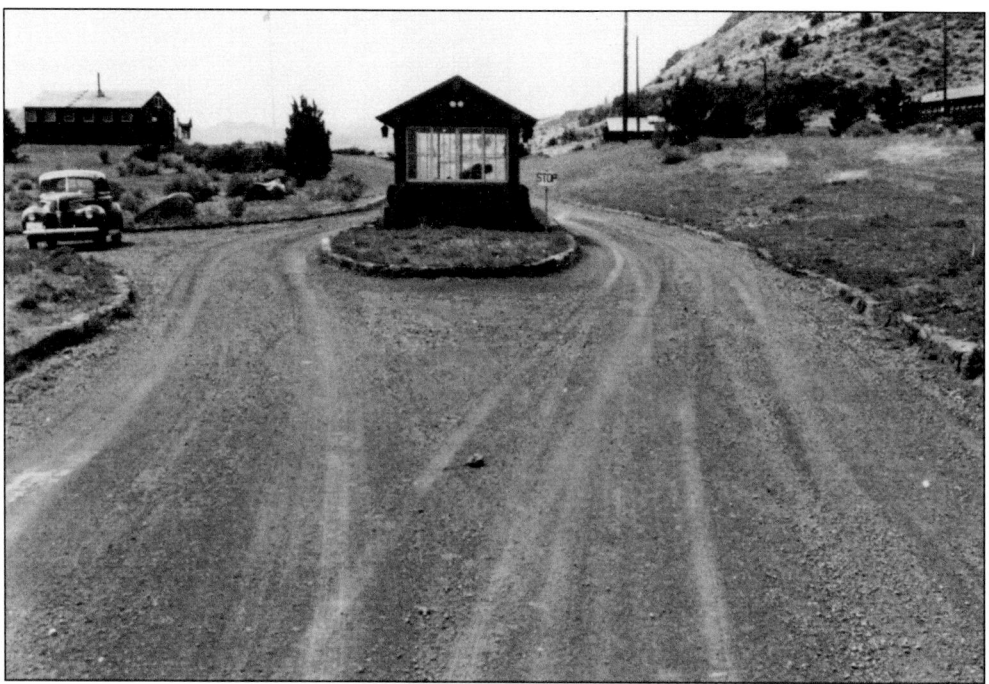

This entrance station was located near the monument's northwest boundary. Note the number of adjacent buildings in this undated photograph. The monument's main entrance station is located near Gillems Camp, where today's visitors can obtain information on recommended activities.

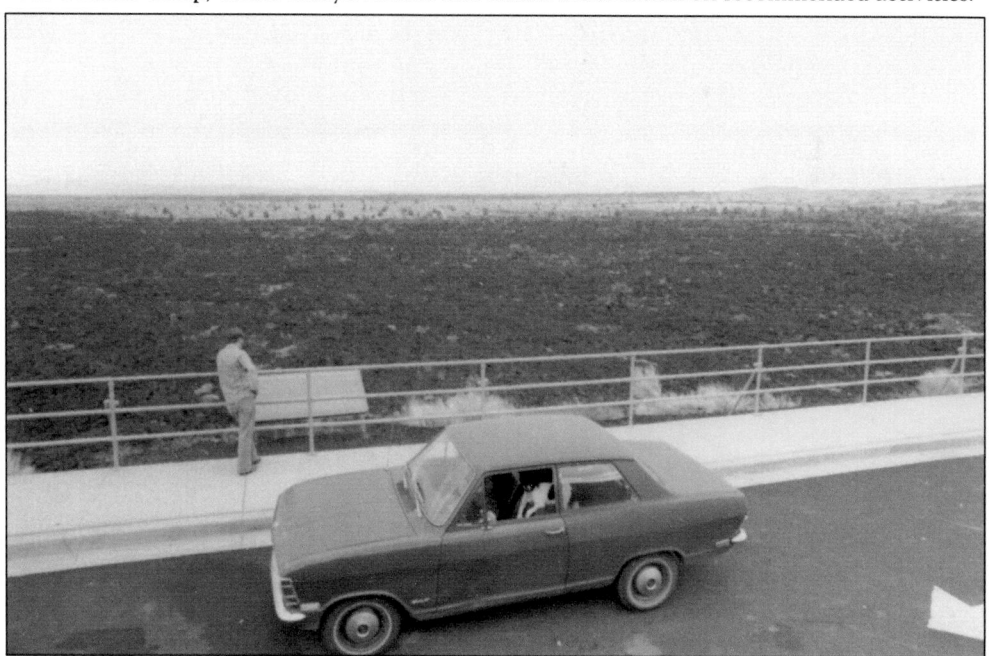

This overlook gives visitors a view of the Devils Homestead flow. The flow begins as a lava fan about a mile and a half south of Gillems Camp. The flow was created by volcanic activity from the neighboring Medicine Lake Highlands. The monument's main road skirts along the flow, providing visitors with expansive views of the foreboding terrain.

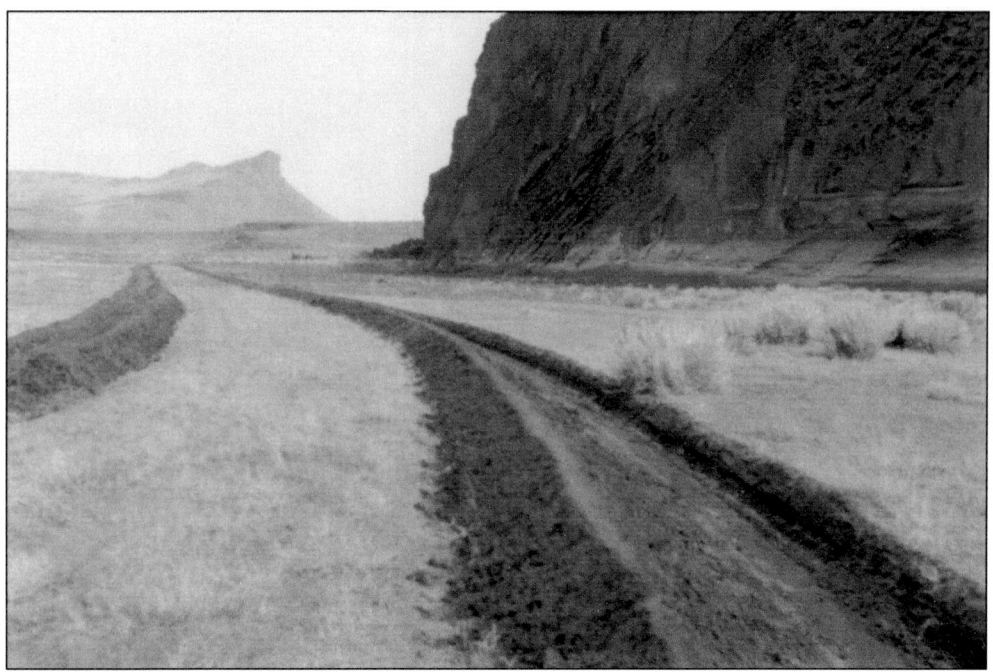

Building roads became a priority after Lava Beds came under the management of the National Park Service in 1933. Along with preserving the area's geological and cultural resources, one of the key goals of the NPS was to develop the region for visitor use and services.

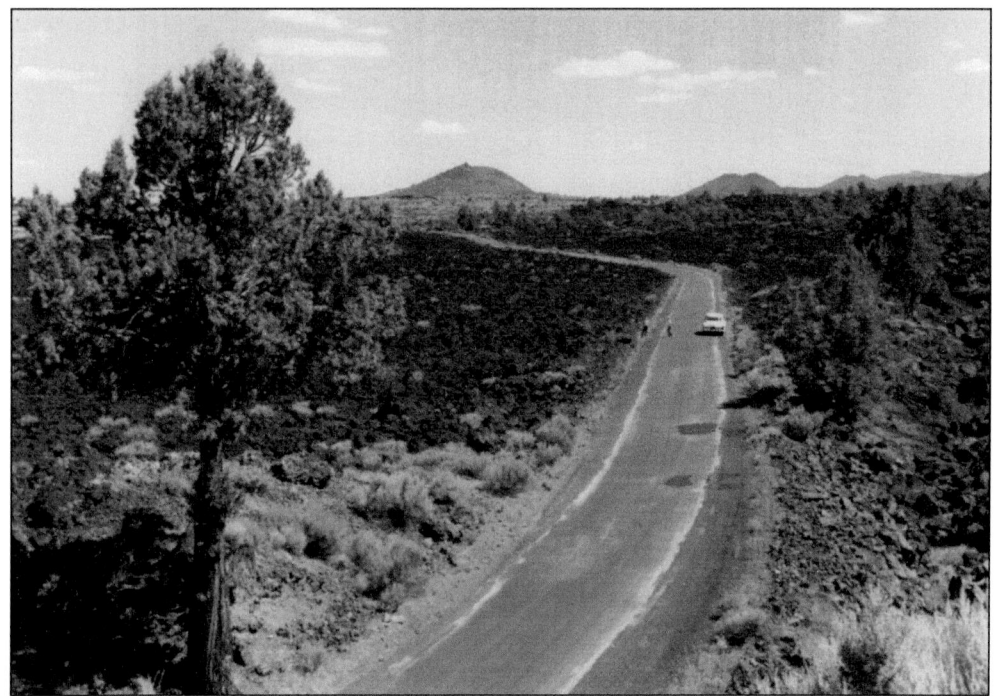

The main north-south road carves its way through the Devils Homestead flow, near the monument's north corner, which gives visitors a close look at the ragged aa lava flow. The mountain in the background is Schonchin Butte, one of the monument's most recognizable features.

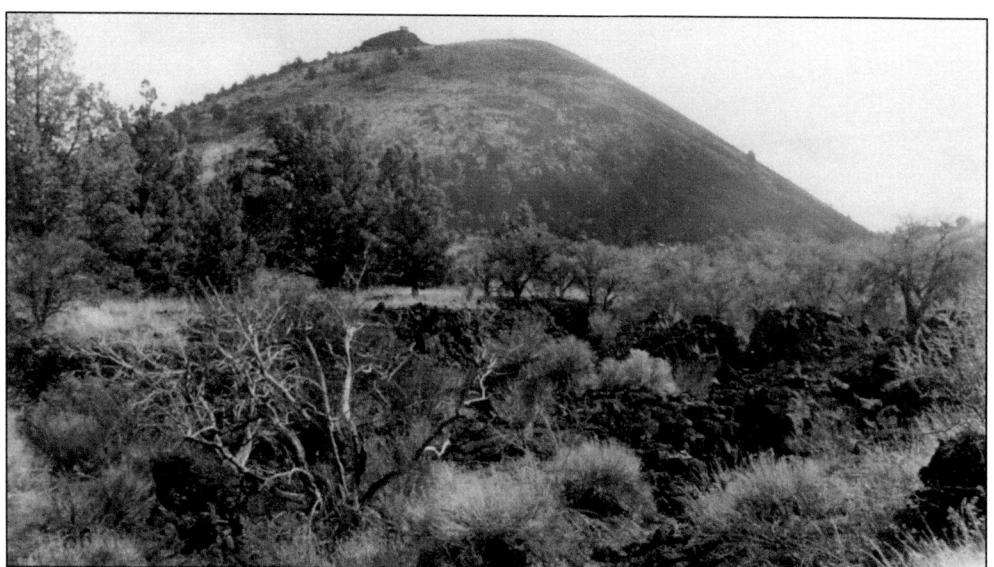

Schonchin Butte is among the most prominent peaks in the monument. CCC crews built a lookout at its summit in 1940 and 1941, beginning with the construction of a motorway to the base of the butte and a horse trail to its top.

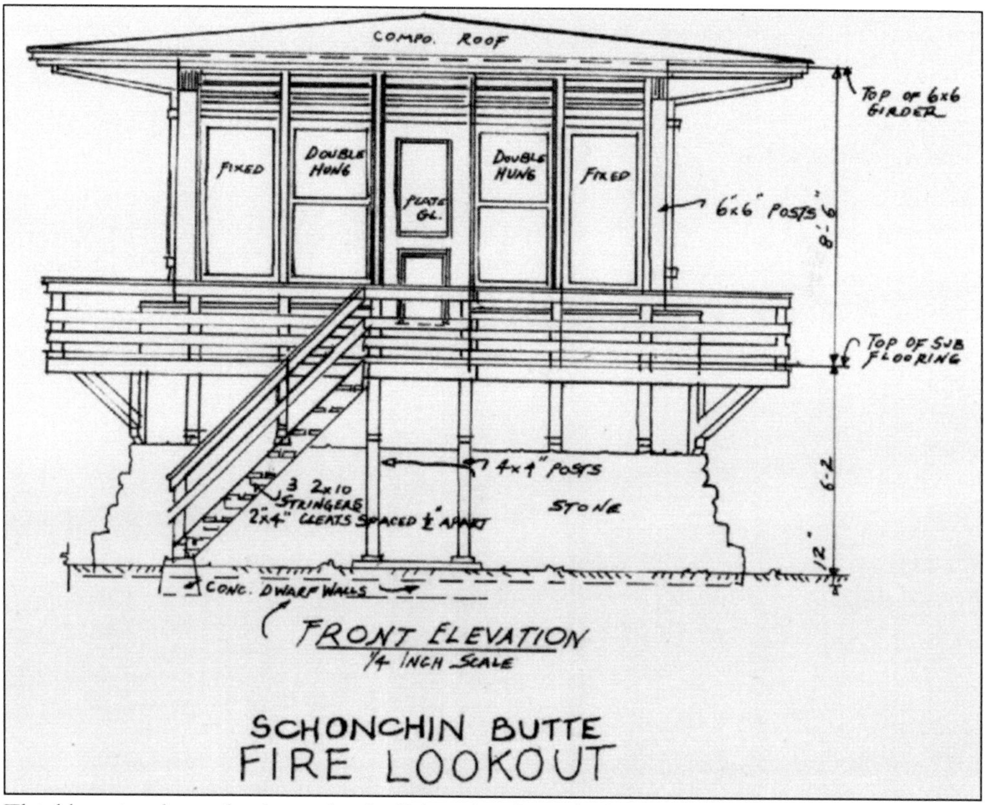

This blueprint shows the design for the Schonchin Butte lookout. Workers prefabricated ironwork and lumber at camp before constructing the lookout on the lava outcropping on top of the butte. Rocks were used for the foundation, but the lookout is a wood-frame structure.

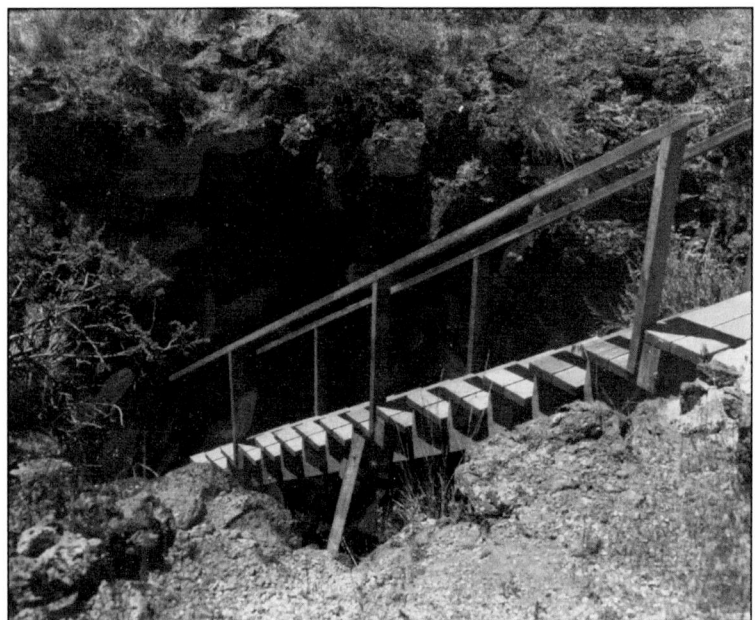

This wooden staircase was built to provide easier and safer access to Thunderbolt Cave, one of the lava tubes along Cave Loop Road. The 1,200-foot-long cave is slightly difficult to explore because crawling is required. It connects with the Labyrinth and Blue Grotto Caves.

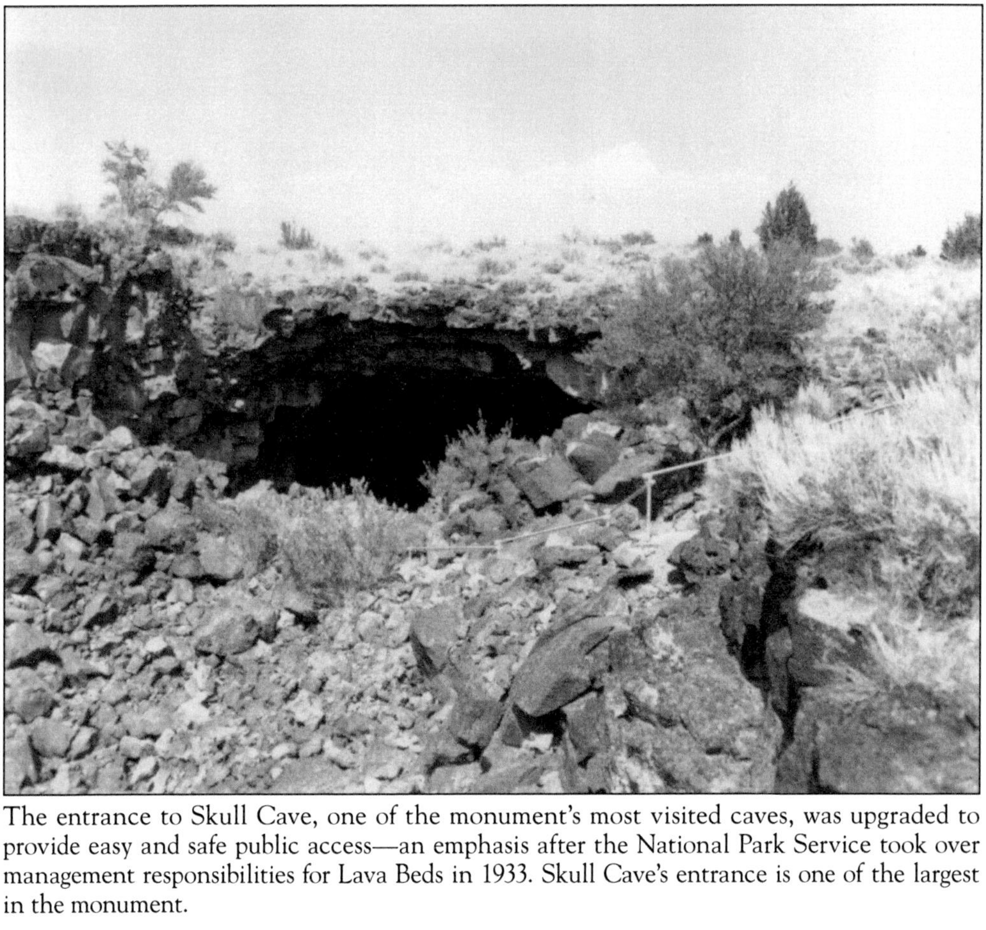

The entrance to Skull Cave, one of the monument's most visited caves, was upgraded to provide easy and safe public access—an emphasis after the National Park Service took over management responsibilities for Lava Beds in 1933. Skull Cave's entrance is one of the largest in the monument.

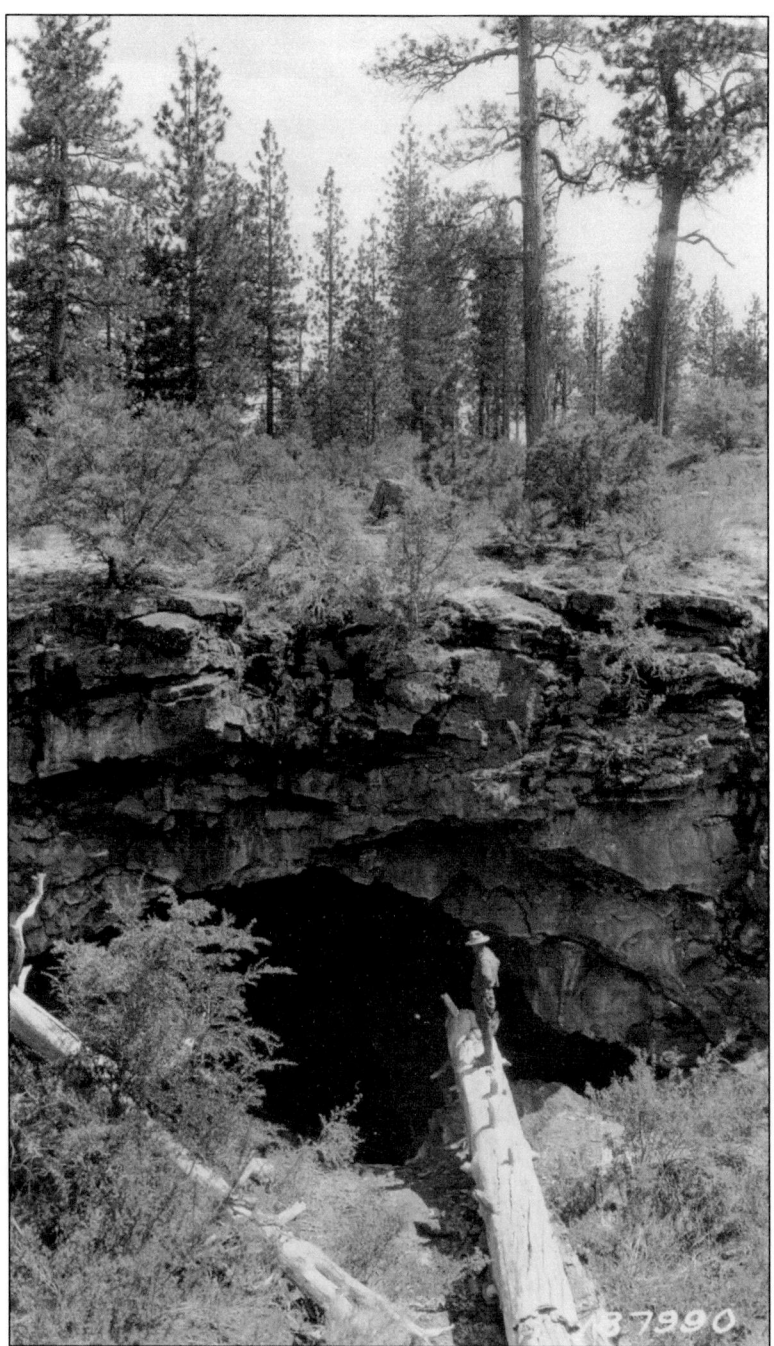

A visitor stands on a fallen log near the entrance to Caldwell Ice Cave. Along with being a fascinating multilevel cave, it also has a captivating cultural history. Charles Caldwell and Anna Lauer were among the few who owned land within Lava Beds. Lauer and Caldwell, who eventually married each other, raised Clydesdale horses that they sold in San Francisco and elsewhere. Along with raising horses, Caldwell also ran livestock. Remains of the Caldwell cabin are still visible near one of the cave's entrances. Lauer, who had worked to acquire lands before she and Caldwell were married, continued her involvement after Caldwell died and she remarried.

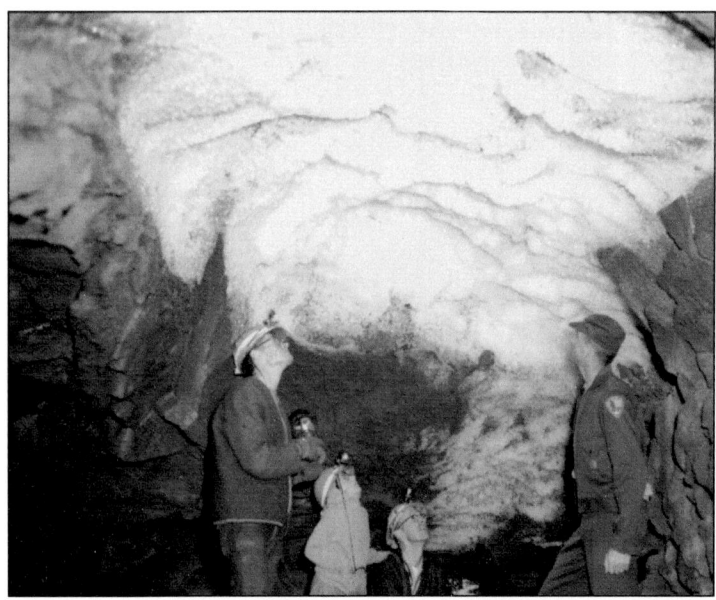

Ranger-led tours into various caves, including Crystal Cave, give visitors the opportunity to not only visit caves but to gain an understanding of their unique features. To protect the cave's fragile features, tours into Crystal Cave are restricted to a small number of visitors on a reservation basis during Saturdays in the winter.

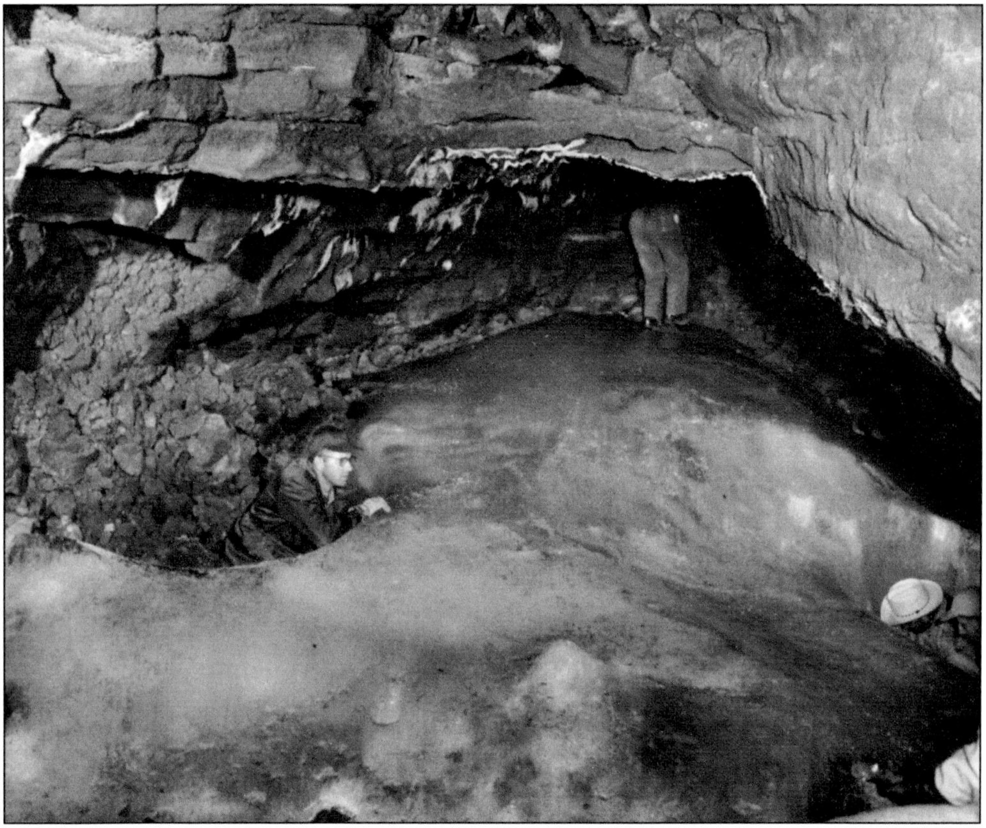

Visitors admire one of the solid ice formations in Crystal Cave, which is best known for its accumulations of ice. Jim Howard found the entrance, but it was J.D. Howard (no relation) who explored the cave and named it. Visiting the cave can be challenging because of its icy floors and narrow passages.

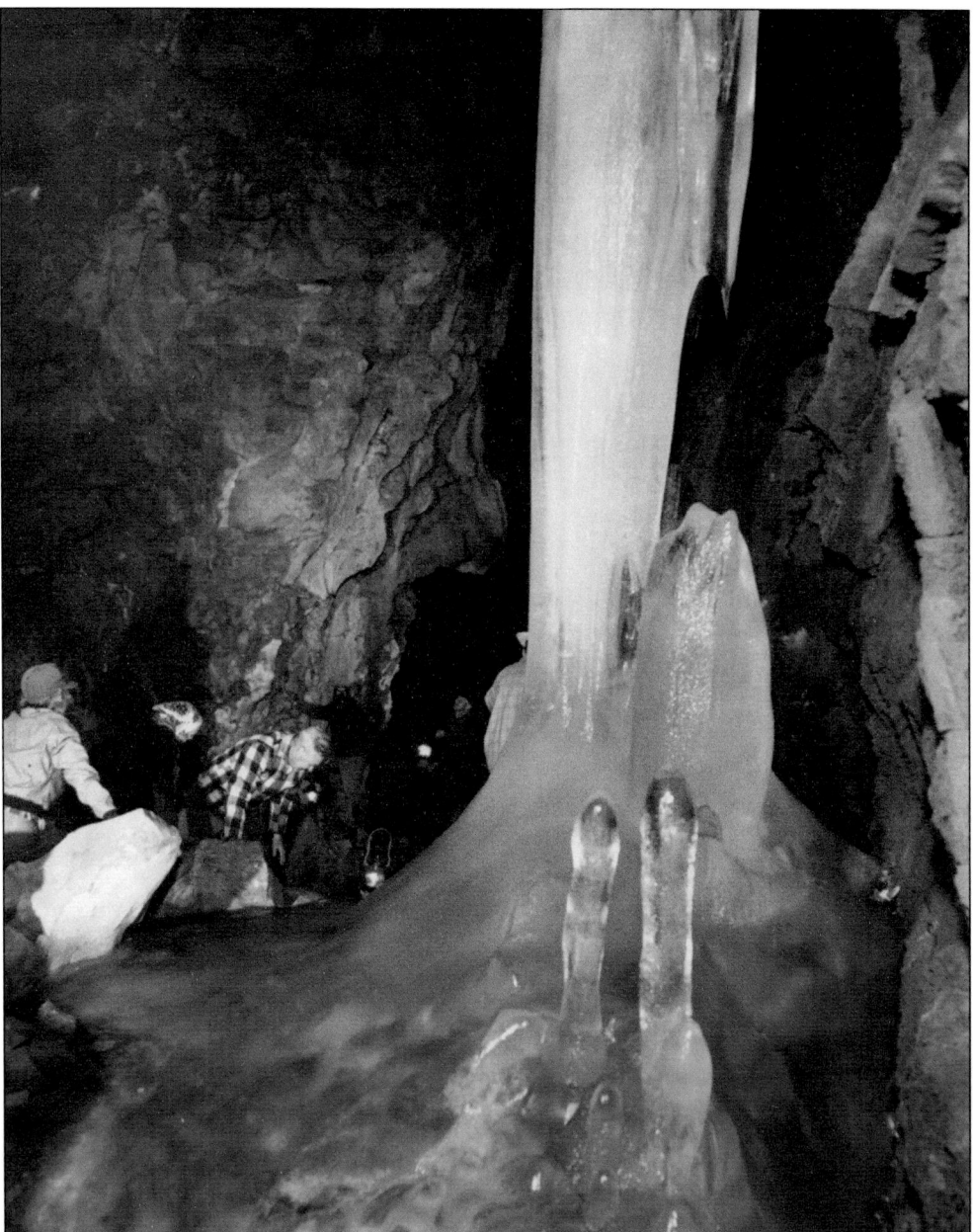
Towering ice formations are among the unique features in Crystal Cave. The multilevel cave drops about 150 feet below the surface, and its average width is about 30 feet. In Crystal Cave, as with other caves containing ice, perennial ice has been slowly receding. In the early 1970s, the National Park Service imposed visitor restrictions. In 1980, the NPS increased restrictions and added strict controls that greatly restrict visitation. Accessing the cave is challenging because of some tiny openings, necessary travel over ice, and narrow passages. Over the years, ice levels have changed, sometimes dramatically. One area that used to be open, the Crystal Room, has been closed for several decades because of changing ice conditions.

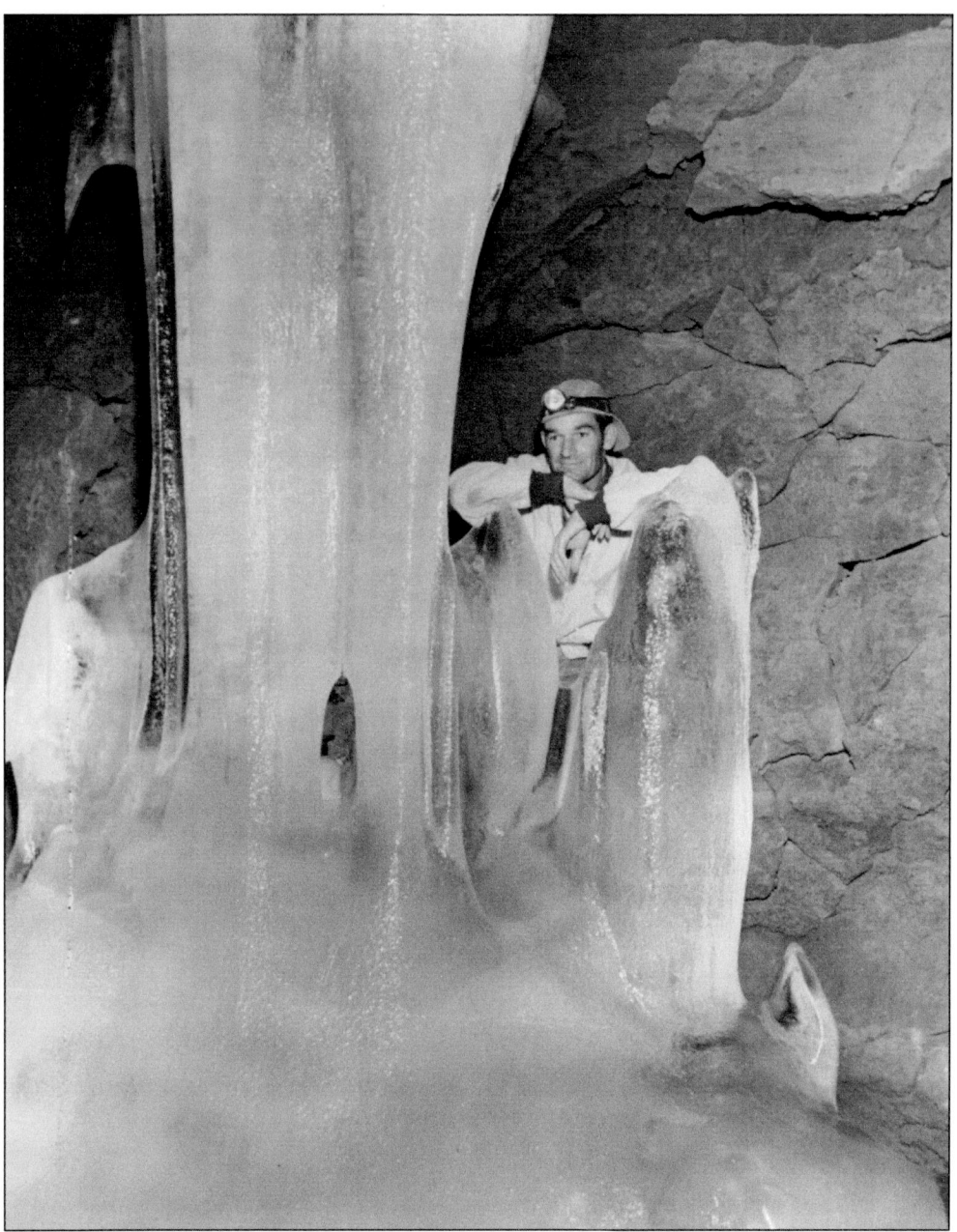

A US Forest Service employee is shown resting on an ice formation in Crystal Cave in this undated photograph. In 1931, when the monument was managed by the USFS, a brochure included photographs showing the crystals. Before and during the Prohibition era, various ice caves, including Crystal, were used by moonshiners who required large amounts of water to produce whiskey. Crystal and other caves, including Bearpaw (now Merrill), Mushpot, and Schonchin, were used because the operations could be easily concealed. The process for making the "hooch" involved "soaking the mash—a potent combination of corn and sugar—and putting the fermentable, starchy mixture over a fire."

Visitors, equipped with hard hats, kneepads, headlamps, and flashlights, crawl through a narrow passage in an unidentified cave. One of the attractions for many monument visitors is the opportunity to walk and wriggle through caves on their own. The National Park Service recommends that visitors get advice—and free flashlights—at the visitor center.

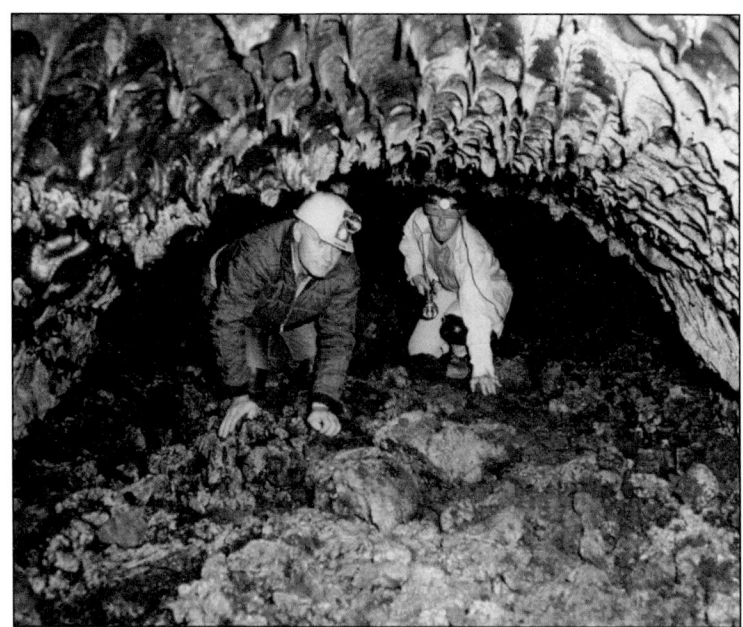

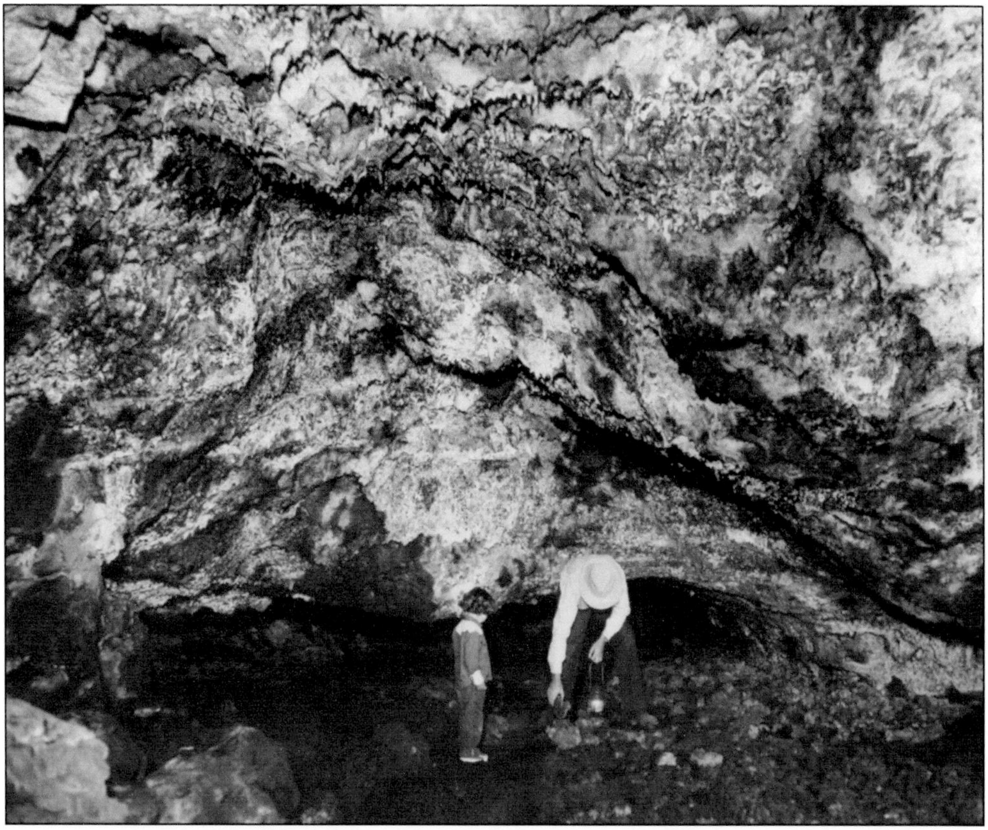

A visitor and a young child study cave features in one of the park's many lava tubes. The man is carrying a lantern, which the NPS used to issue to park visitors. Because of various concerns, they have long since been replaced with flashlights. The NPS also recommends hard hats.

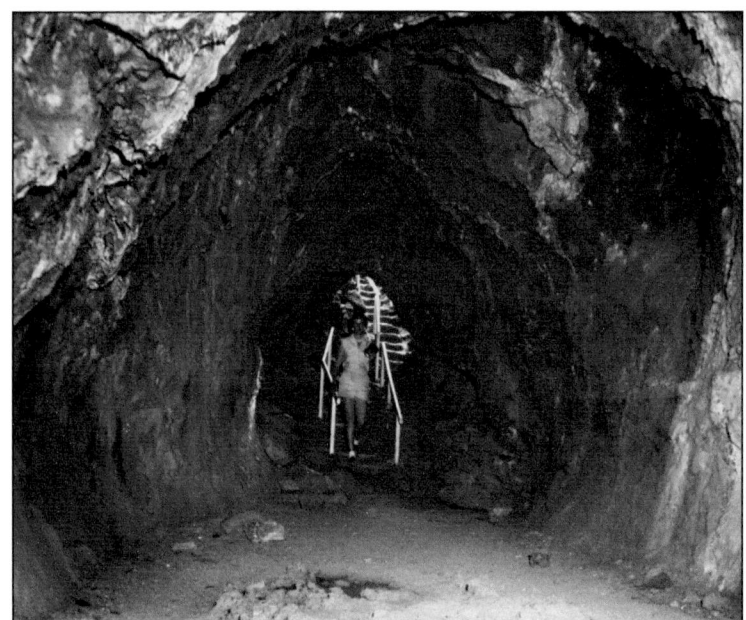

A lightly dressed woman exits a stairway into a cave. Because of cool temperatures and rugged features, visitors are advised to wear long pants, sturdy shoes, long-sleeved shirts, and helmets and to carry flashlights or wear headlamps to help navigate the caves.

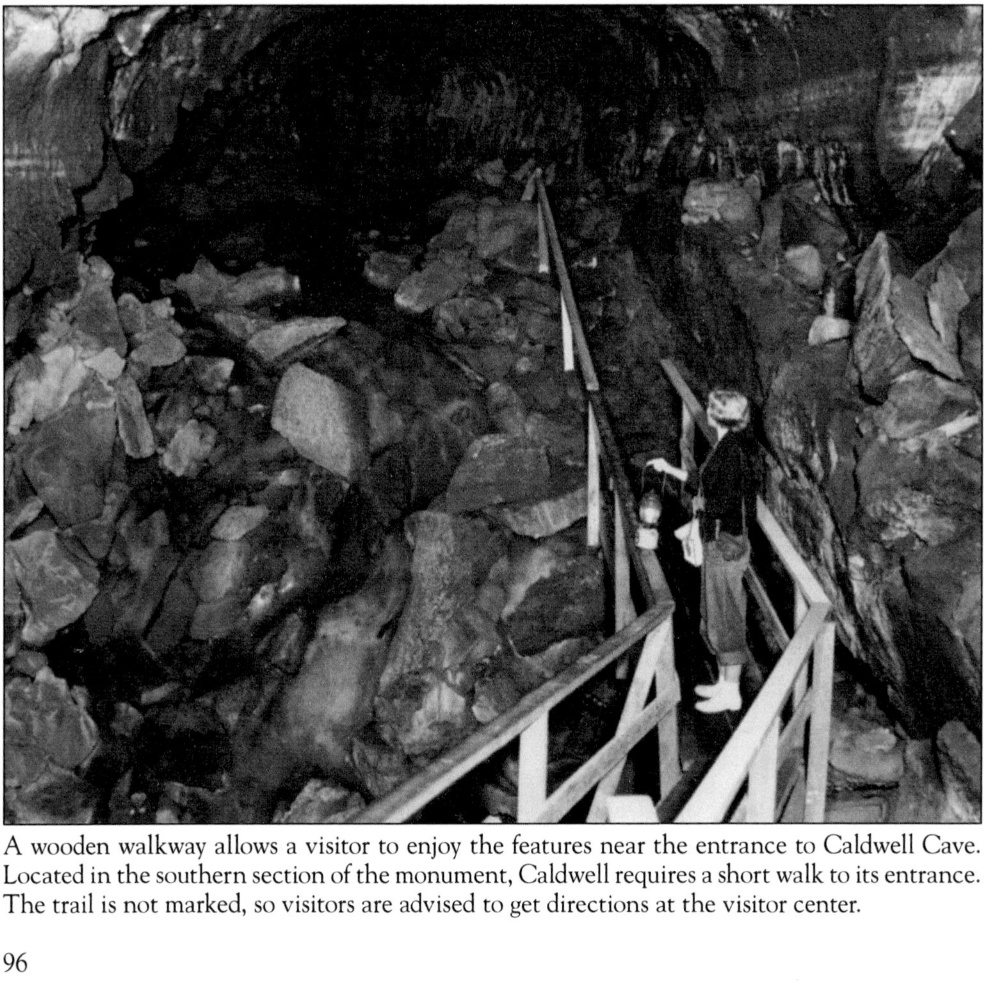

A wooden walkway allows a visitor to enjoy the features near the entrance to Caldwell Cave. Located in the southern section of the monument, Caldwell requires a short walk to its entrance. The trail is not marked, so visitors are advised to get directions at the visitor center.

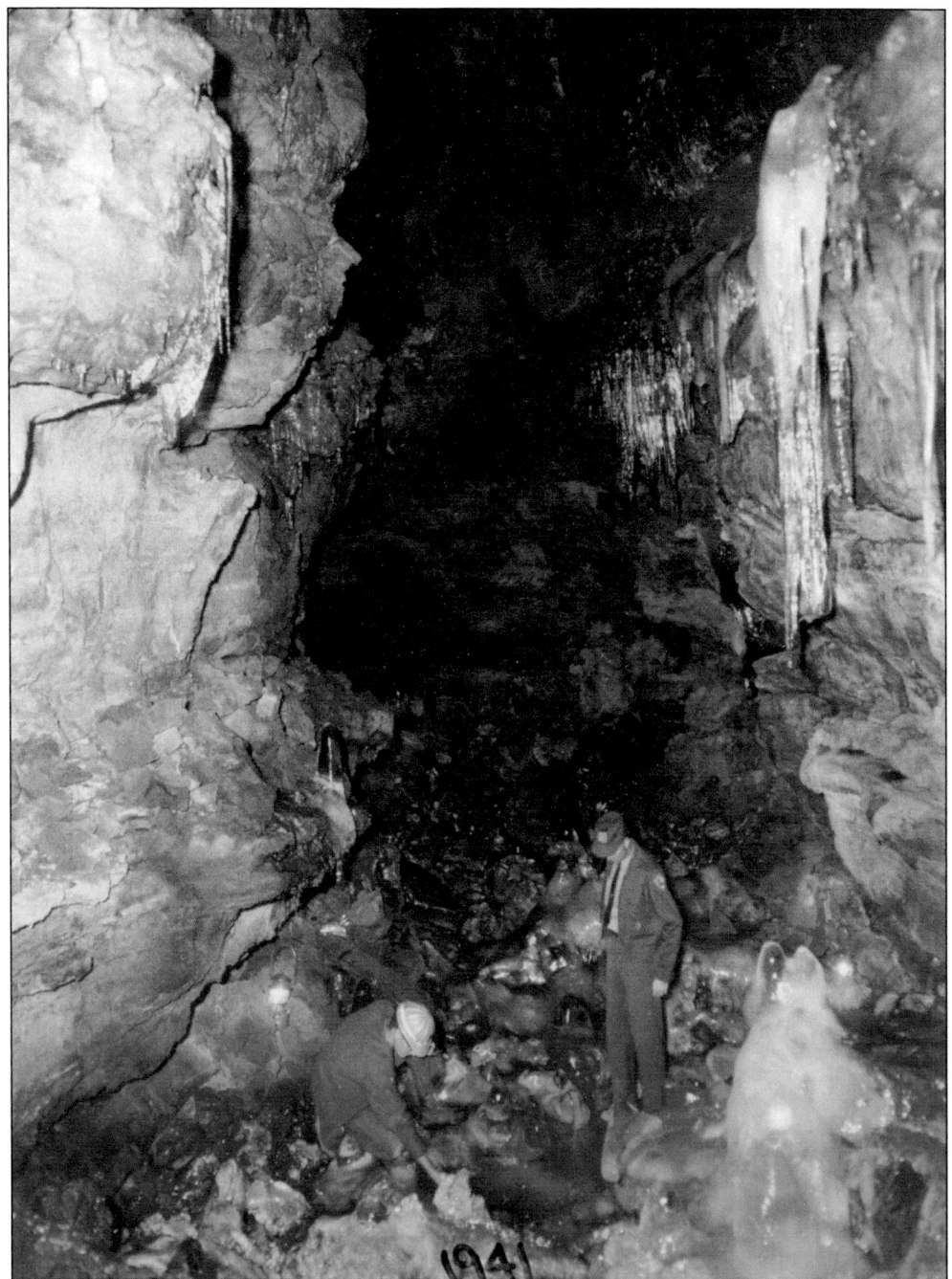

Ice formations in Crystal Cave have frequently been studied and appreciated by rangers and visitors. Stalactites and stalagmites are among the cave's many features. Stalactites are cylindrical or tapering formations that hang from a ceiling or overhanging surface. The word is from the Greek meaning "oozing out in drops." Stalagmites are deposits on a cave floor or ledge formed by the accumulation of material that dripped from above. The word is from the Greek meaning "that which drops." Both formations are also frequently seen in other monument caves, including the easy-to-access Indian Well.

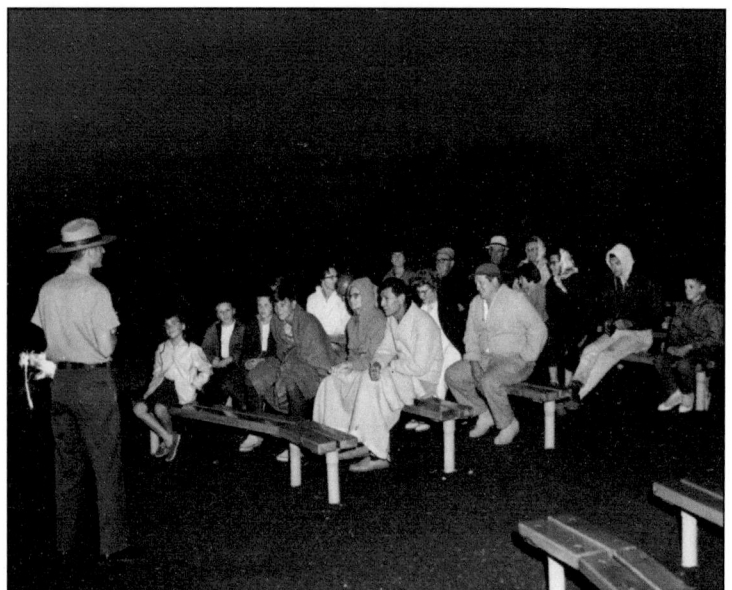

Campers staying at Indian Well Campground, the monument's only campground, wear warm jackets and wrap themselves in blankets while listening to a ranger speaking in the campground amphitheater. During the summer, rangers give free nightly programs on a variety of park-related topics.

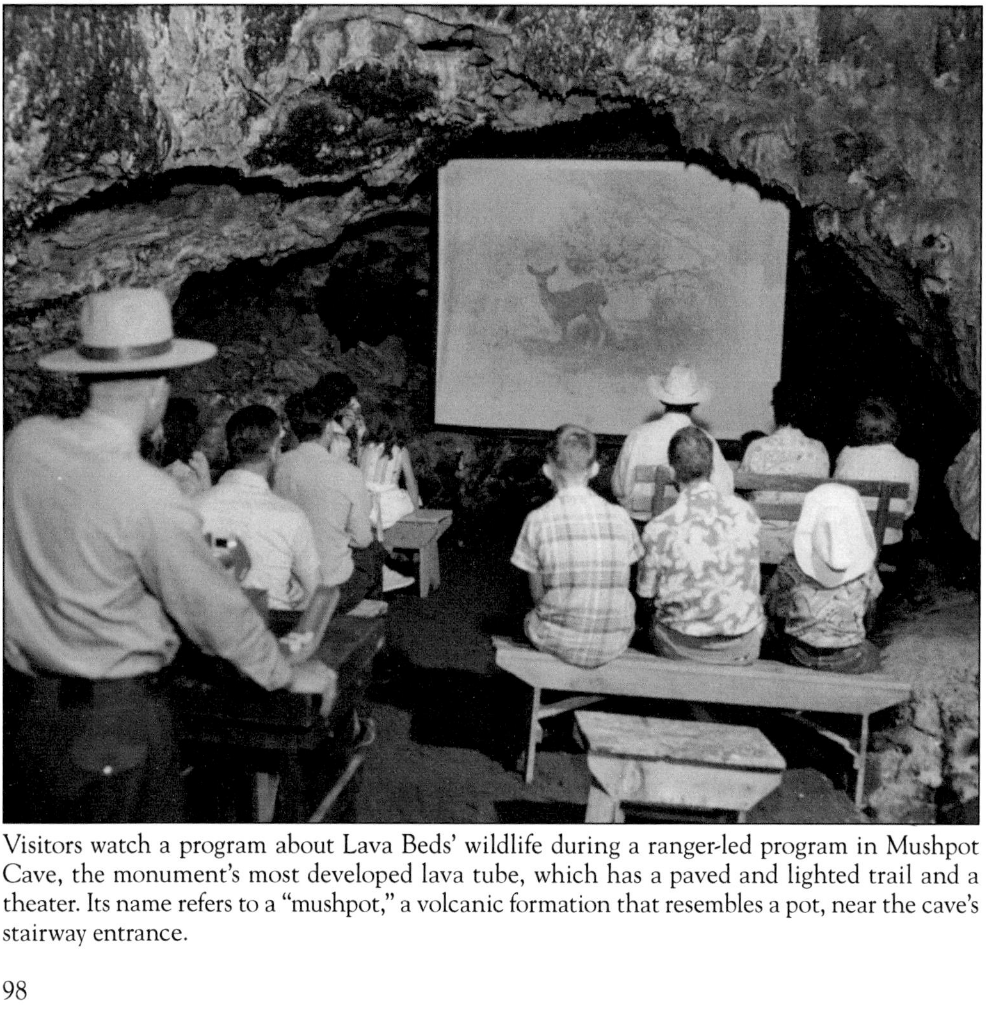

Visitors watch a program about Lava Beds' wildlife during a ranger-led program in Mushpot Cave, the monument's most developed lava tube, which has a paved and lighted trail and a theater. Its name refers to a "mushpot," a volcanic formation that resembles a pot, near the cave's stairway entrance.

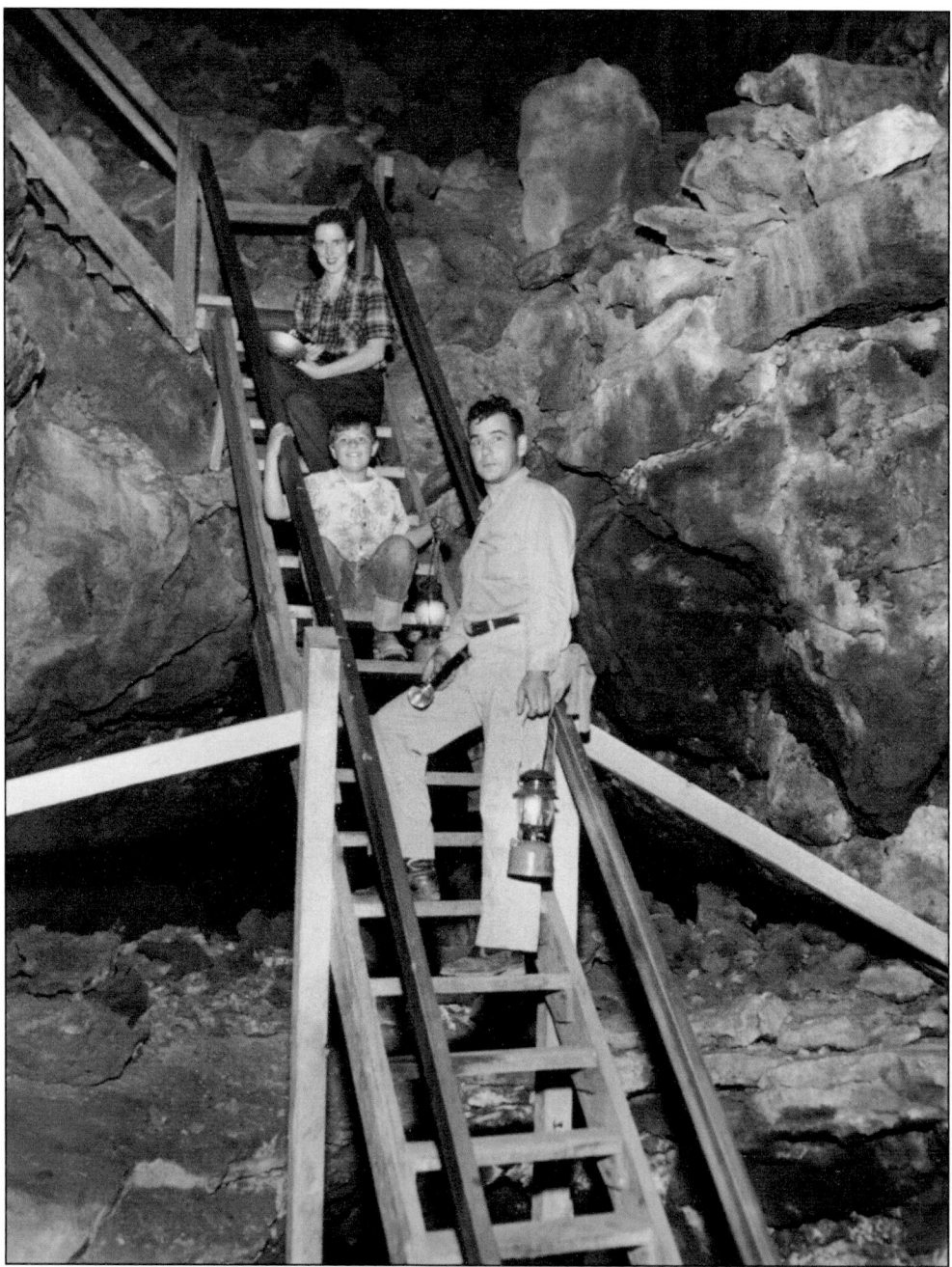

One of the park's the most popular caves is Skull Cave, a multilevel segment of the 10-mile-long Modoc Lava Tube System. Development of Lava Beds as a national monument led to the construction of ladders and other improvements in Skull and several other caves. This cave entrance is one of the largest in the monument, a collapse trench about 450 feet long. Note the man on the wooden staircase is carrying a flashlight and a lantern—the National Park Service loaned lanterns to visitors for several years, eventually replacing them with flashlights. Skull Cave was named by E.L. Hopkins after he and others found a large accumulation of bones there.

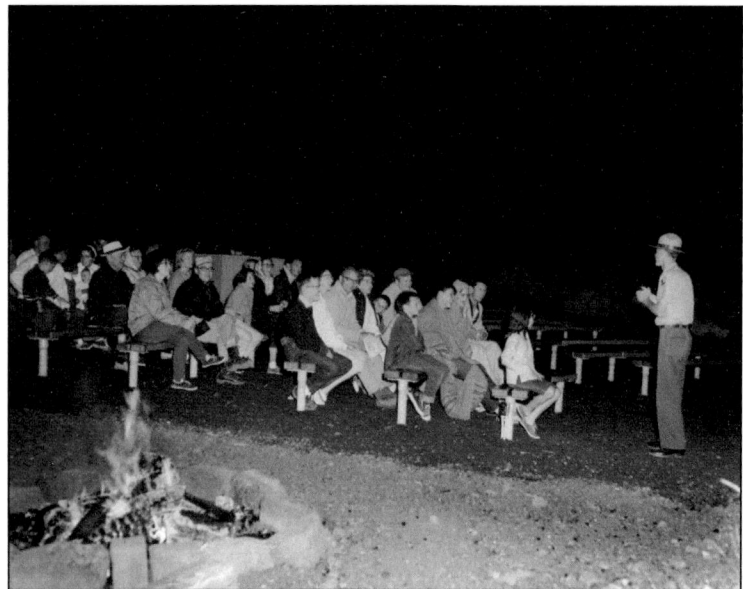

A bonfire and blankets help ward off the evening chill during a ranger-led campfire talk at the Indian Well Campground amphitheater. The nightly programs, usually given after dark, typically cover a diverse array of topics ranging from geology to human history to the region's plant life.

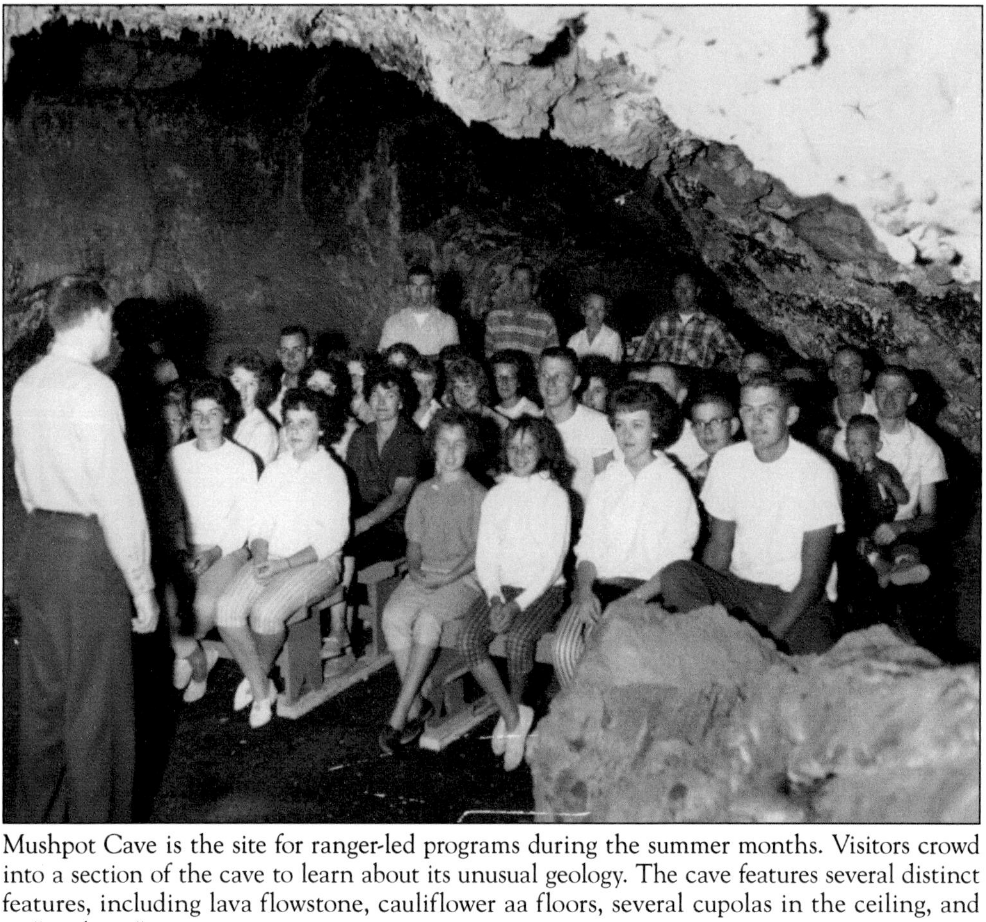

Mushpot Cave is the site for ranger-led programs during the summer months. Visitors crowd into a section of the cave to learn about its unusual geology. The cave features several distinct features, including lava flowstone, cauliflower aa floors, several cupolas in the ceiling, and its "mushpot."

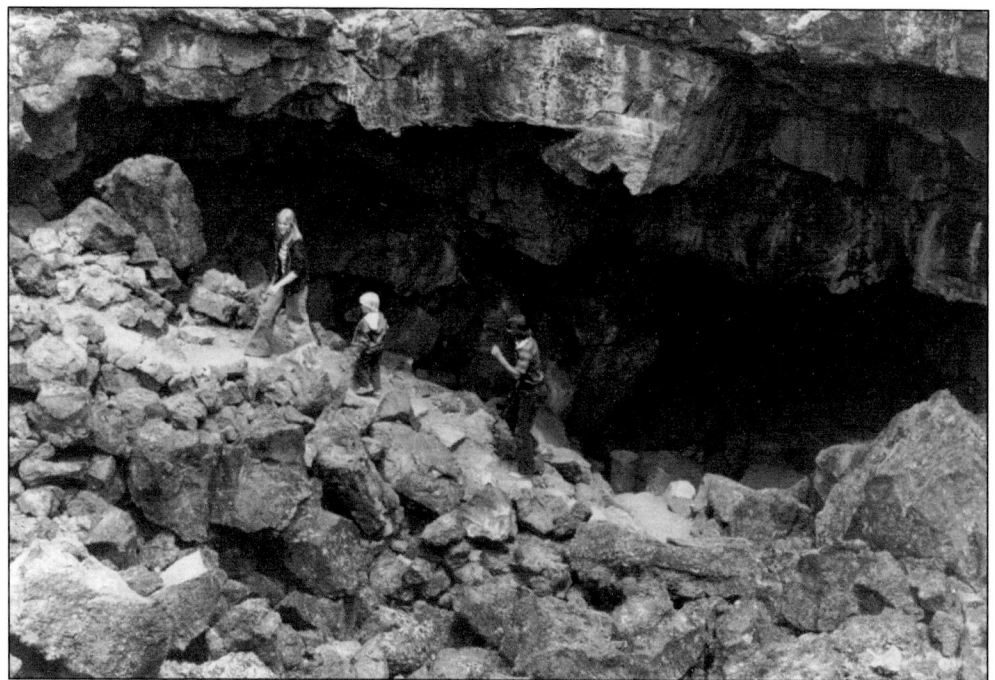

The development of trails and easy-to-access entrances to various caves, including those along the Cave Loop Road, make the monument a playground for visitors of all ages. Although ranger-led cave walks are offered during the summer, visitors can explore for themselves year-round.

Picnic tables between the monument's visitor center and Mushpot Cave offer a place for families to recharge between explorations. Some of the picnic tables, including those at Fleener Chimneys, were built by CCC work crews in the 1930s.

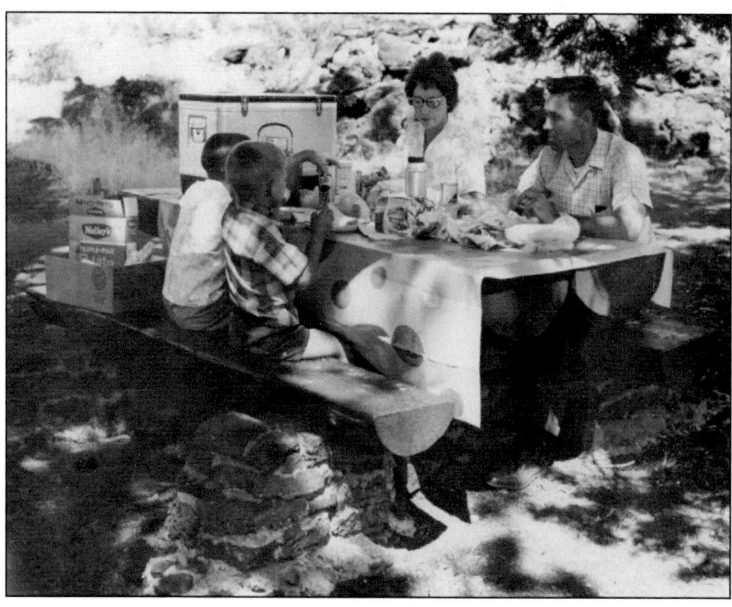

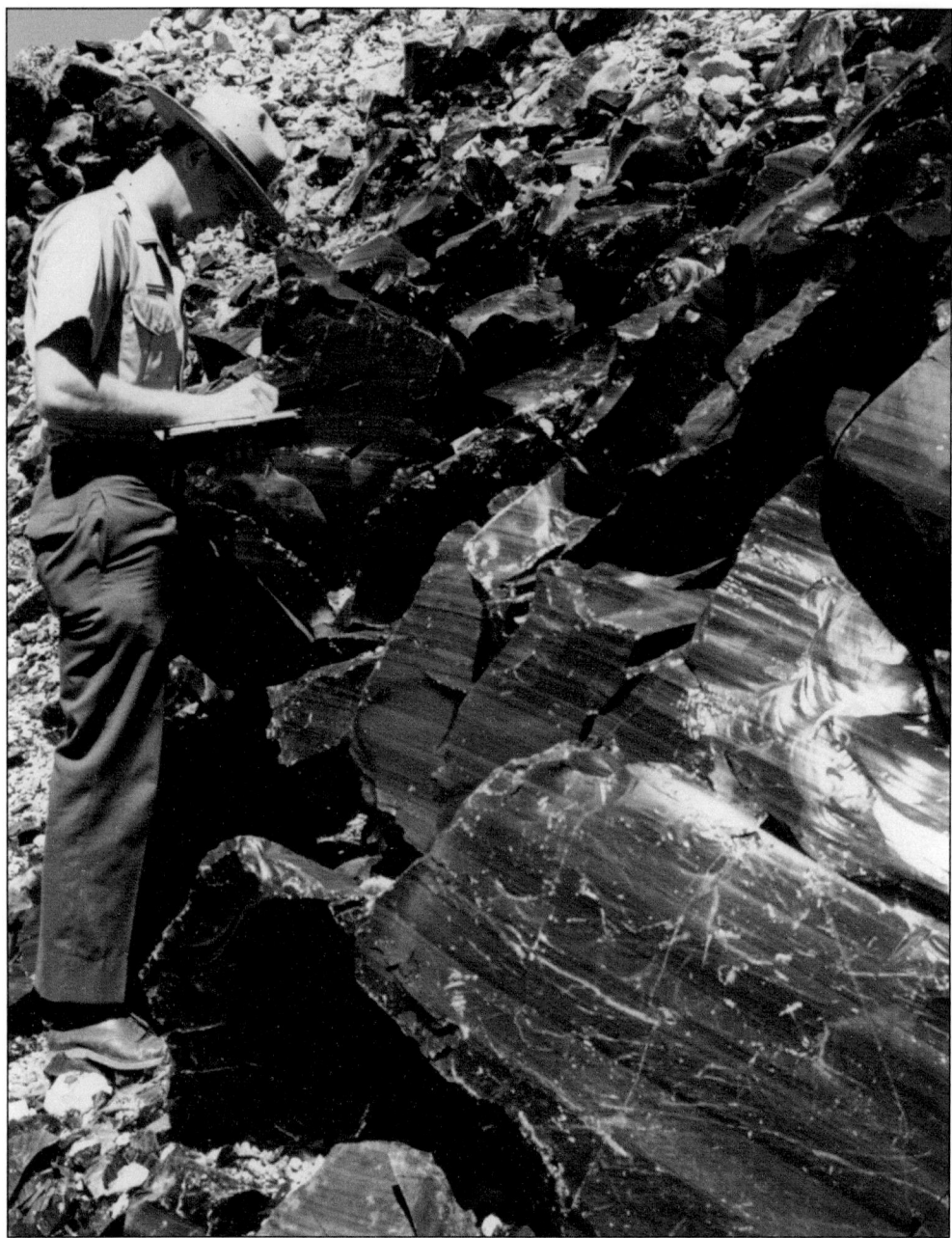

A ranger takes notes on his findings near a large obsidian outcropping. Obsidian is an acid-resistant, lustrous volcanic glass, usually black or banded, that displays curved, shiny surfaces when fractured. Large areas of obsidian are mostly found outside the monument, especially at Glass Mountain. The obsidian was used by early Native Americans and settlers to make points of varying sizes, scrapers, and other items used for hunting animals and cleaning hides. Deer, pronghorn antelope, and bighorn sheep were among the big game hunted in the Lava Beds region.

A park ranger peers into Fleener Chimneys. The pits used to be more than 100 feet deep, but they were later half-filled with rocks apparently dropped by visitors; the pits have since been cleaned out. The chimneys were named by J.D. Howard for Sam Fleener, who had a nearby homestead.

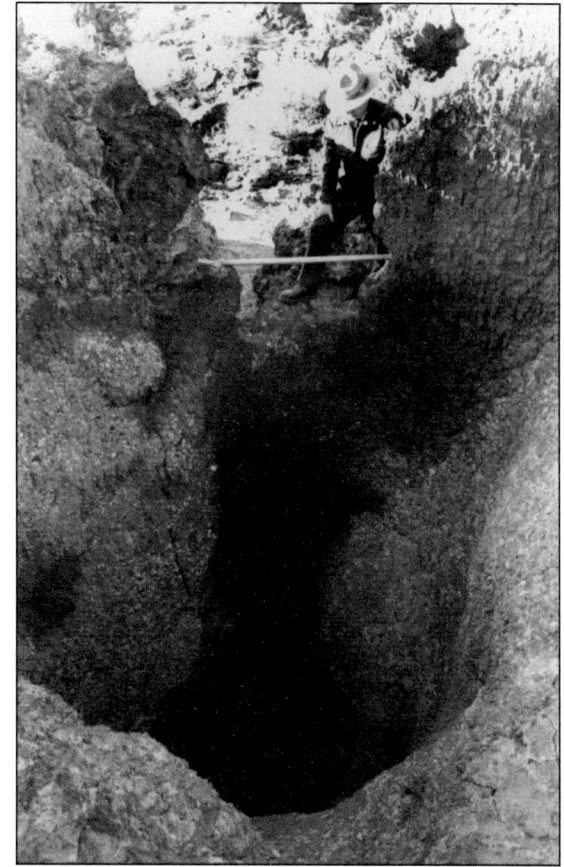

Ragged, erratically shaped rocks are characteristic of various lava flows. Note the height of the ranger next to some of the volcanic debris. There are two major flows in Lava Beds—the Devils Homestead, along the northwest boundary, and the Black Lava, along the southwest corner of the monument.

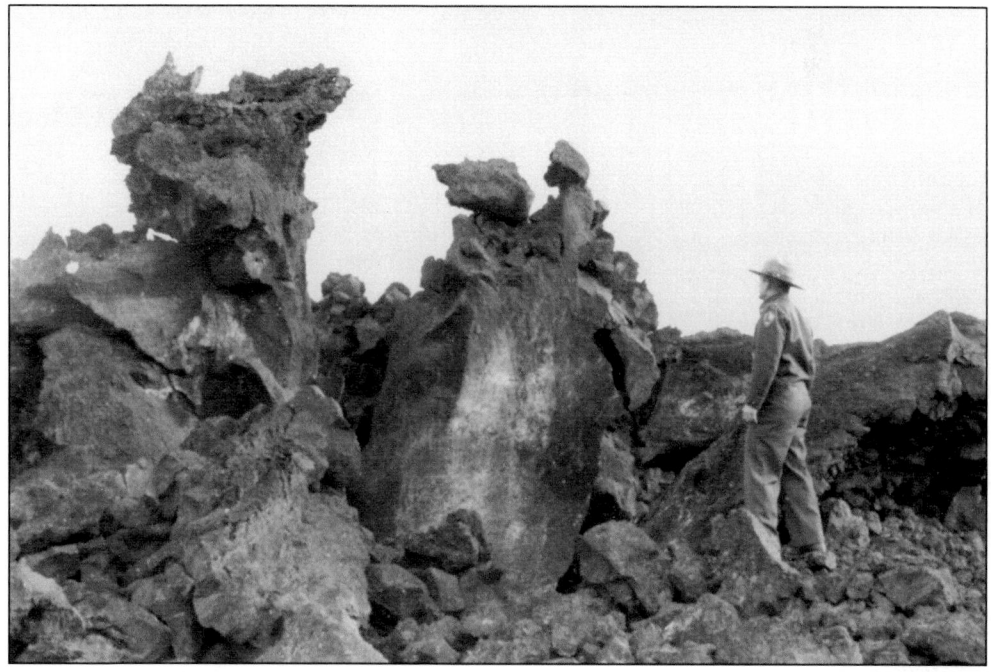

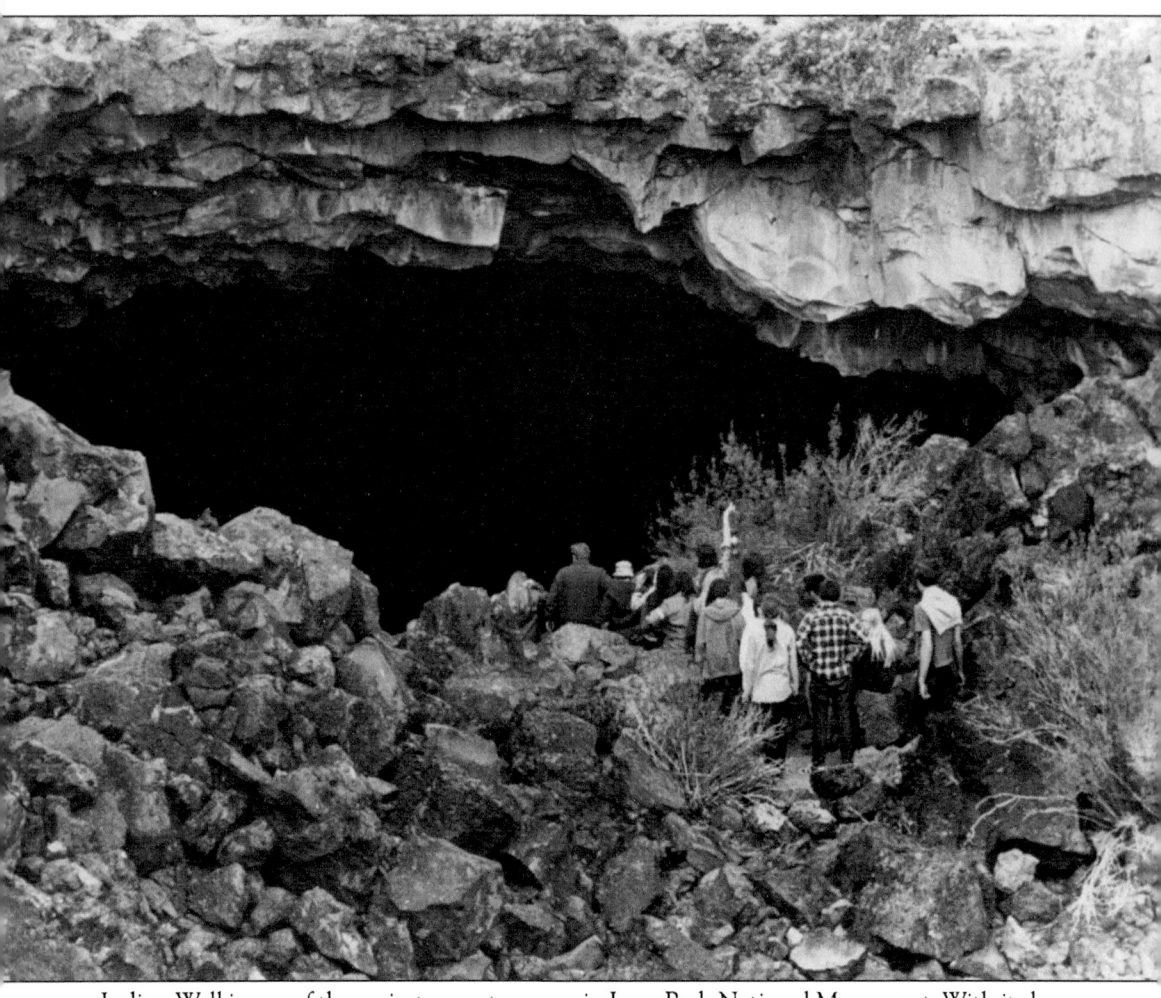

Indian Well is one of the easiest caves to access in Lava Beds National Monument. With its large entrance, wooden stairway, and frequently fascinating ice stalagmites, its wintertime displays are typically visual delights. The Modocs had their main camp near the cave, as did early cave explorer J.D. Howard. Indians used the cave to get water and, because of its wide openings, did not need to use torches. Some early reports mention Indian writings on rocks near the cave's entrance that pointed toward the pool of water. The area is centrally located, offers commanding views, and has some relatively flat areas—advantages that led to camps being built nearby by Indians and explorers. The National Park Service selected this area for the park's headquarters complex and Indian Well Campground.

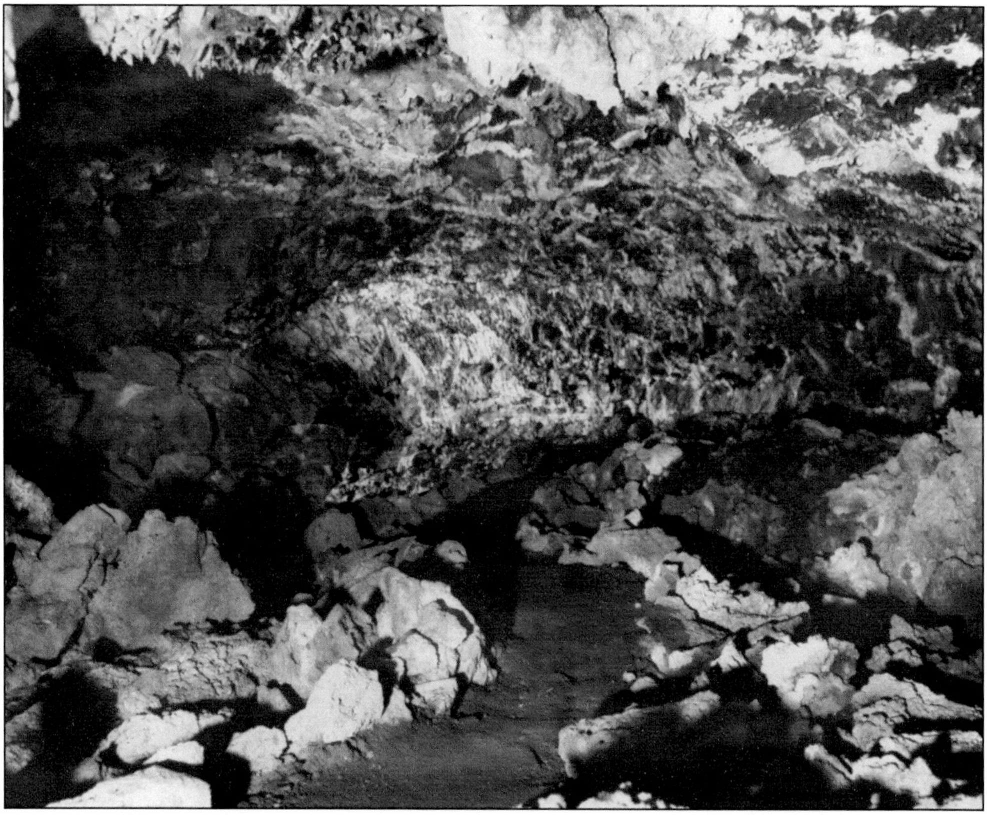

An easy-to-follow trail meanders through Blue Grotto Cave. The floor in the southern two-thirds of the cave features a raised tongue of cauliflower aa that is three feet high in places. This cave is connected to Garden Bridges and has several entrances.

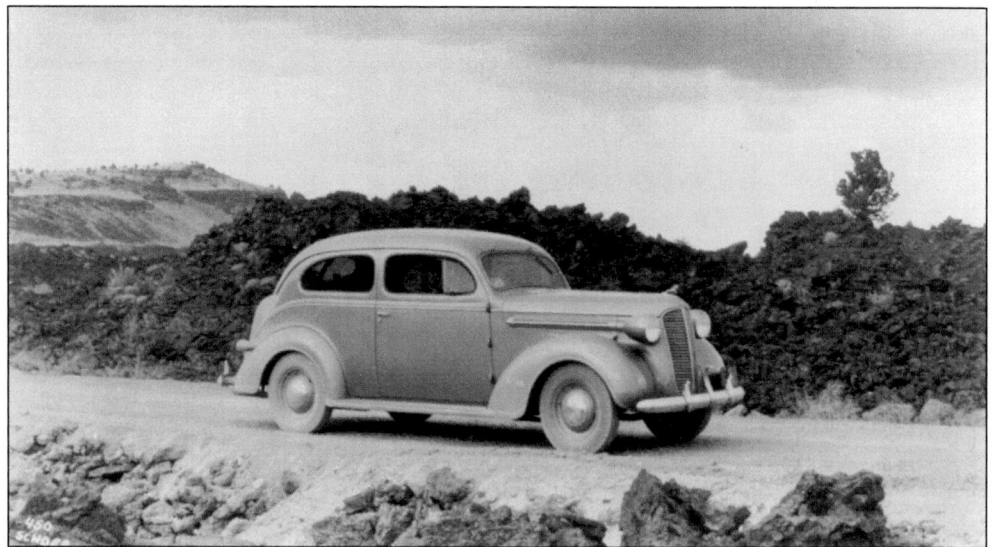

In this 1938 photograph, a car is parked alongside mounds of aa lava in the Devils Homestead flow. The main park road had not yet been paved, although Civilian Conservation Corps crews had made road improvements, and other upgrades followed over the years.

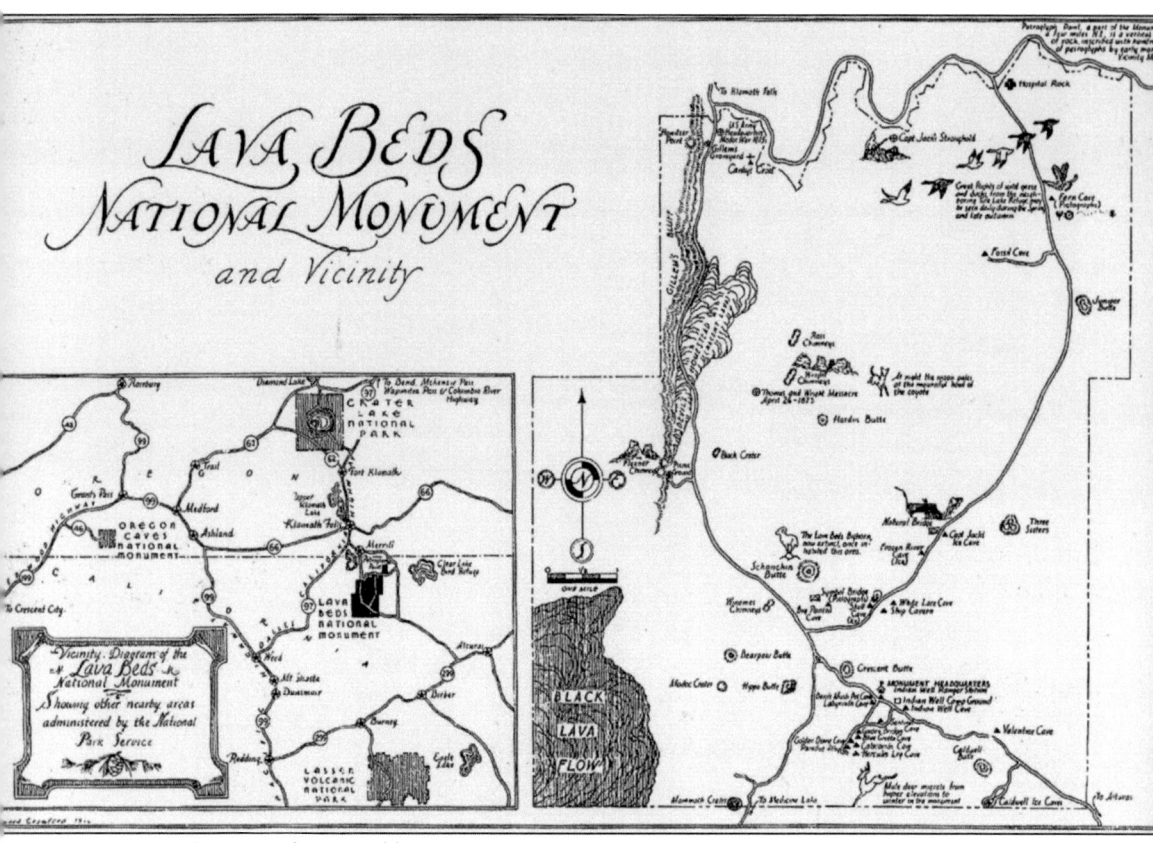

A map of Lava Beds created by CCC artist L. Howard Crawford was used in this National Park Service brochure printed in 1936. The map highlights attractions from the Modoc War, including Captain Jack's Stronghold, Canby's Cross, Gillems Camp, and the Thomas-Wright Battlefield, along with several popular caves, such as Blue Grotto, Indian Well, Catacombs, Skull and Golden Dome. An accompanying map places Lava Beds National Monument in relationship to other National Park Service sites, including Crater Lake National Park, Lassen Volcanic National Park, and Oregon Caves National Monument. Maps, brochures, and other guides helped generate interest in visiting Lava Beds.

Eight

STILL LEARNING

In a sense, Lava Beds National Monument is place where time has stood still. The lava tube caves and the historic sites from the Modoc War remain much as they were. Since becoming part of the National Park Service in 1933, subtle improvements to the park have preserved its features while making it available to a broader public.

As former Lava Beds National Monument superintendent Mike Reynolds notes, "Though the mission of the National Park Service has remained basically the same, the way in which it is interpreted by NPS managers and the American public has changed. Upon early designation in the 1920s and 30s, Lava Beds was land not civilized by man. There were early efforts to build roads and establish hotels, but it was virtually unvisited by the public at large. During the first phase of its management, the NPS began a huge development of the landscape. Roads, trails and buildings were built. Caves were signed and ladders and paths were placed." By the 1960s and 1970s, there was a shift in management practices. "It was realized at both Lava Beds and the NPS at large, that the two aspects of the mission were not balanced," Reynolds said. Visitors had the upper hand. If the NPS continued with construction and man-made development, the natural and cultural resources would not be available for future generations. Lava Beds National Monuments' two wilderness areas were designated in 1972.

Since then, efforts have focused on restoring the natural landscape from the damage done when the monument and the NPS were, according to Reynolds, "a little one-sided in their goals." More recent projects have assessed the impacts of visitors on cave ecosystems, restored old roadbeds into trails, and removed grazing sheep from the park land. "Lava Beds National Monument," Reynolds says, "will continue to welcome visitors and work to make this land better understood to the public, but the balance has been restored."

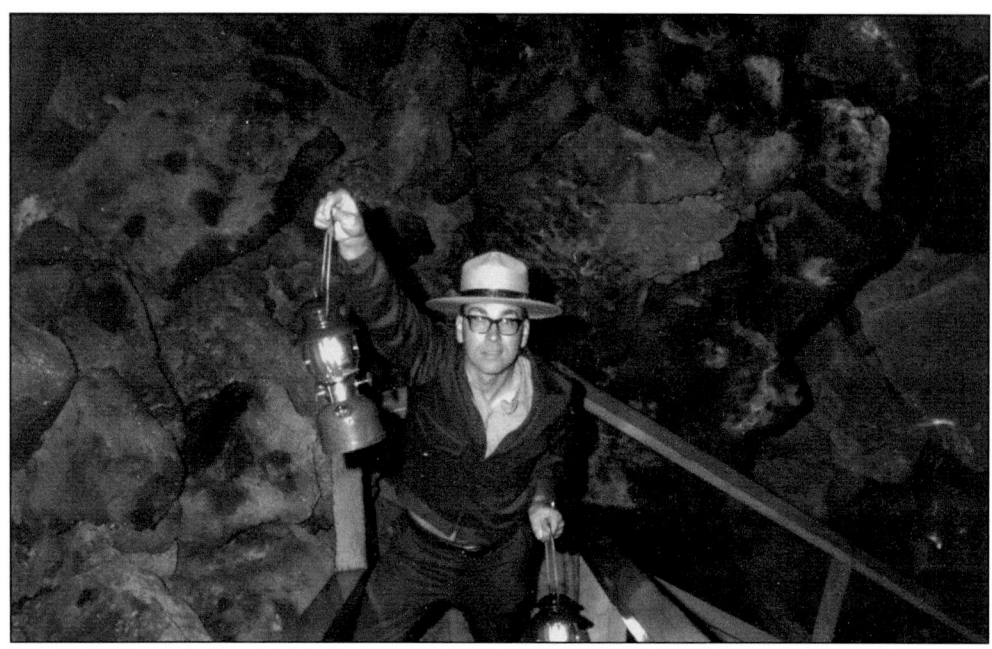

Above, a Lava Beds National Monument ranger holds a flashlight near the top of the ladder into Skull Cave. The ladders installed in recent years are a major improvement. In a note written in 1892, cave discoverer E.L. Hopkins said the first ladder he built was made from one-by-fours and bailing wire. Below, the ranger begins to make his way along a trail. The cave entrance is at the east end of a collapse trench that is about 450 feet long, and the lower level continues past a pit that connects the levels.

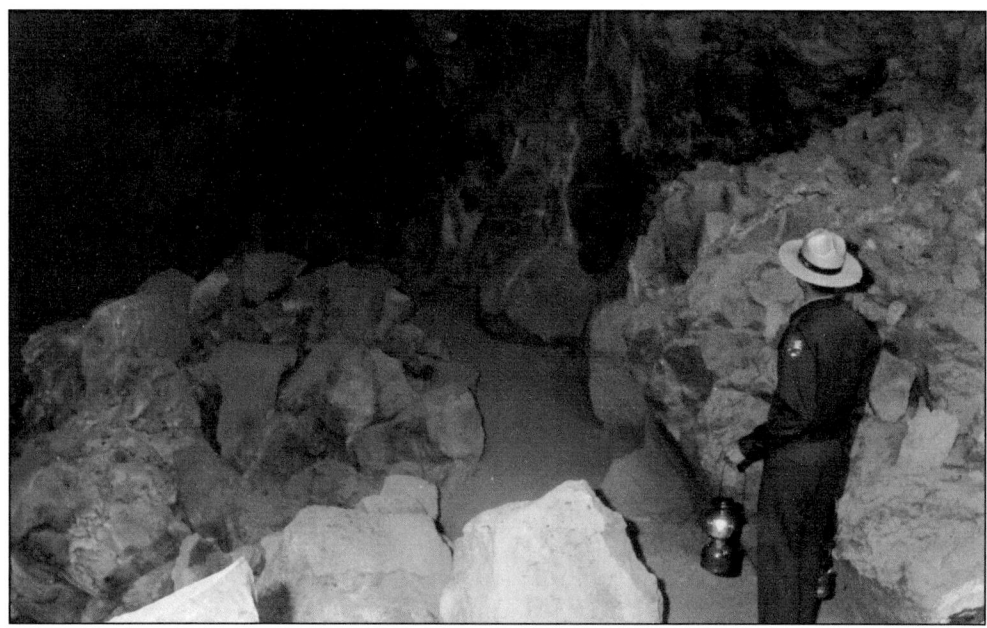

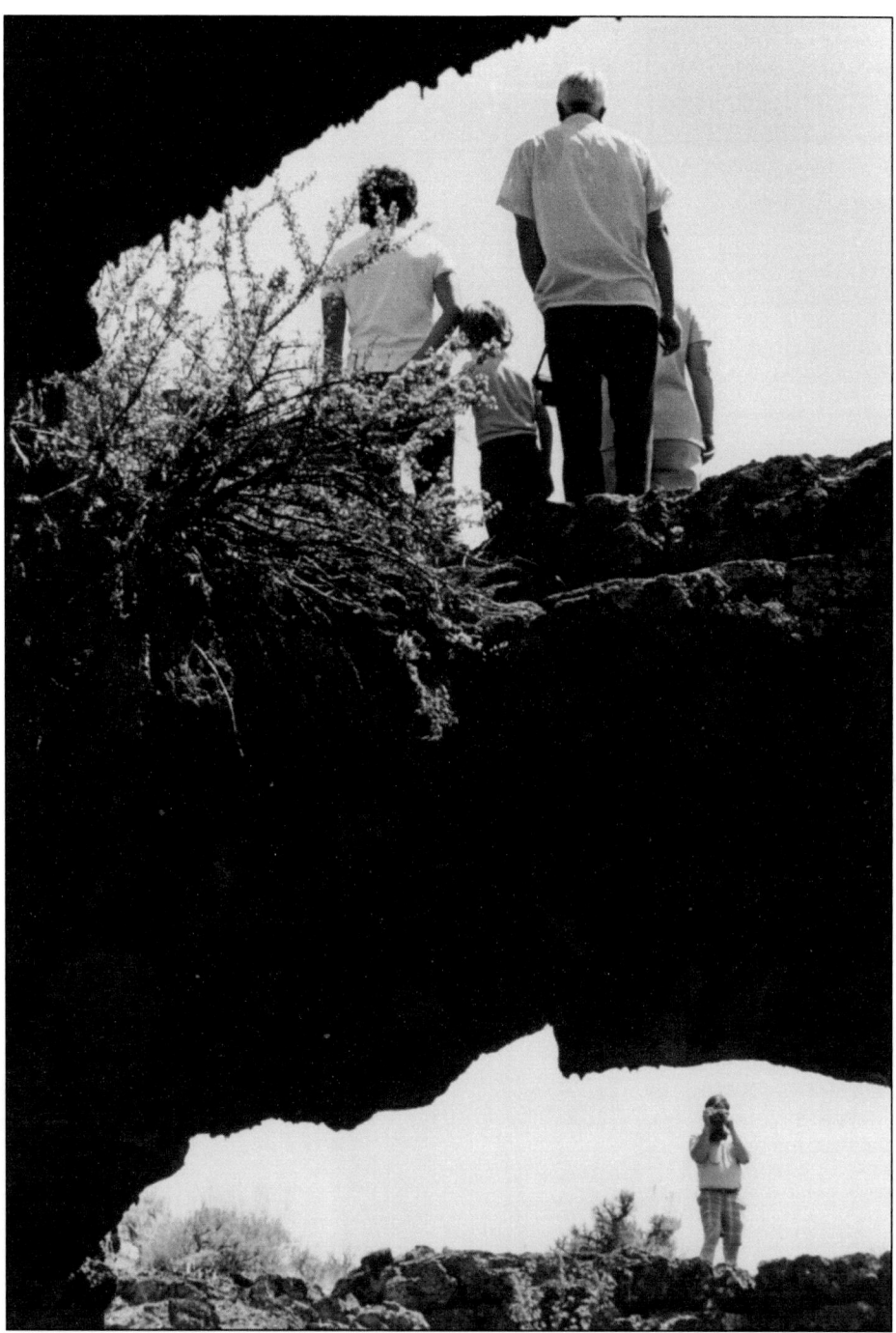

A family poses for a photograph while standing on one of the bridges at Natural Bridge Cave. The cave has no ladders or stairwells and no trails inside. People wanting to explore the cave must climb over large rocks. The cave has at least two (and probably more) levels. The upper level splits around an obstruction and spreads out to a total width of 91 feet and is divided by a large pillar. Natural Bridge is among the caves discovered by E.L. Hopkins before 1917, but it was named by J.D. Howard. Its original name, Compound Bridge, was later changed to Natural Bridge.

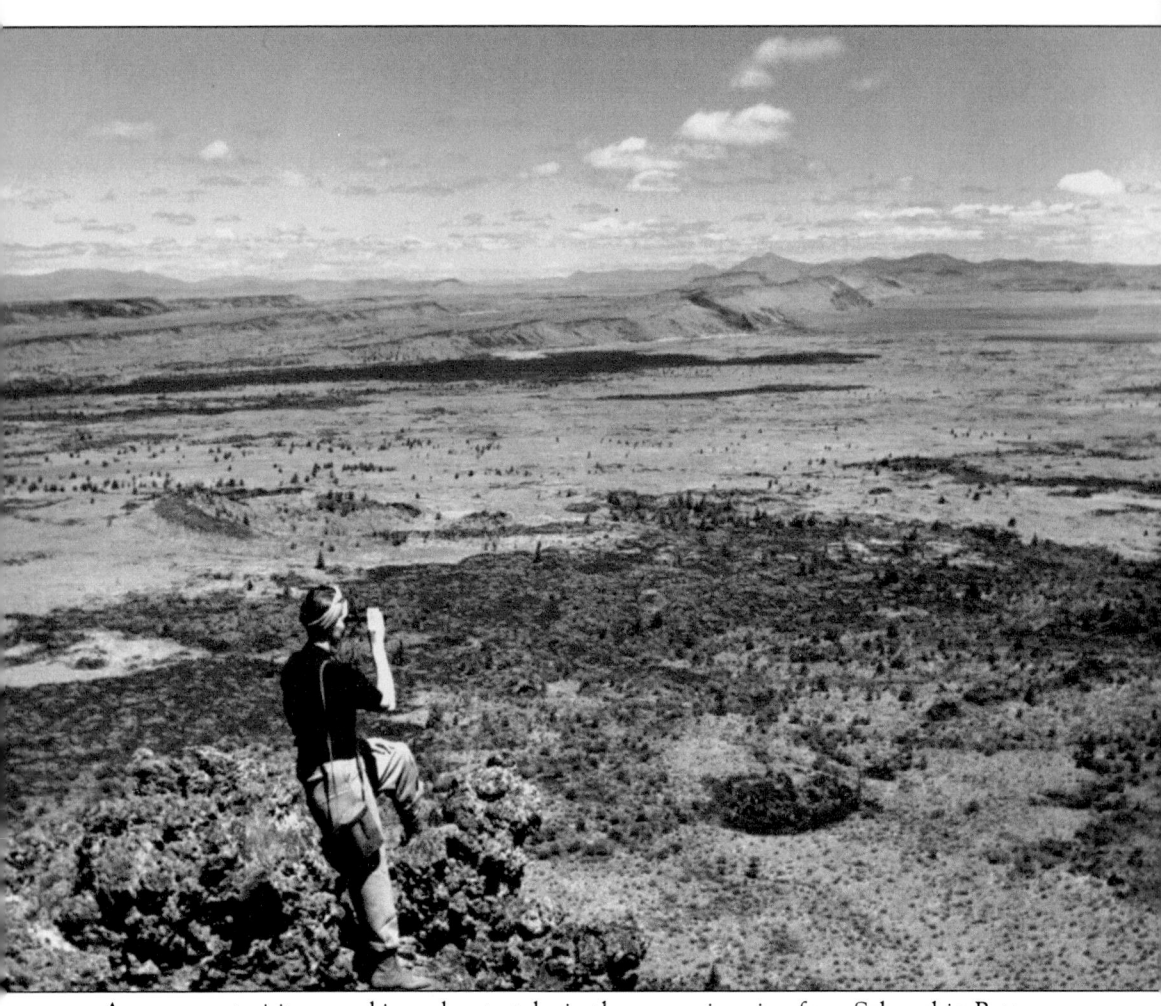

A monument visitor uses binoculars to take in the expansive view from Schonchin Butte, one of the most popular high-elevation points in the monument. The butte, which has a seasonally staffed fire lookout, offers a 360-degree panoramic view of the monument and neighboring lands. The rugged, wild landscape, including a chunky lava flow, spreads for miles in all directions. A road leads to Schonchin Butte, with the summit reachable by a well-maintained trail. Like the lookout, the trail is a remnant from the years when Civilian Conservation Corps crews worked in the monument.

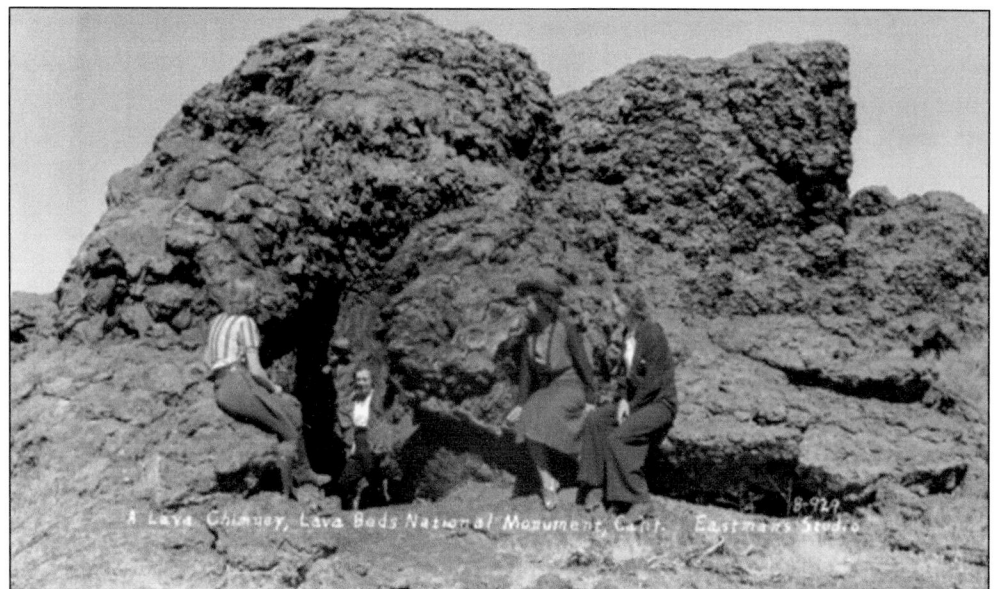

A group of women explore a lava chimney in this undated photograph taken after the National Park Service took over management responsibilities for Lava Beds National Monument in 1933. Outdoor clothing styles were different then.

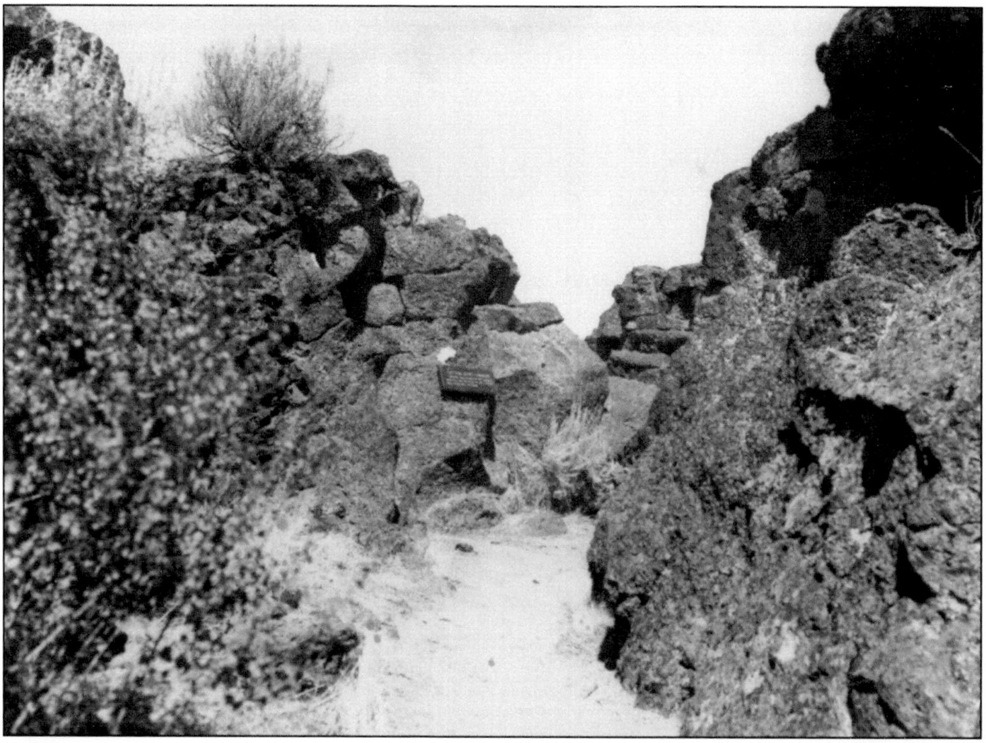

A sign near the visitor trail entrance to Captain Jack's Stronghold tells how he and other Modoc Indians lived in the rocky maze during the Modoc War in the winter of 1872–1873. The trail offers a glimpse into the natural fortress. Depending on a visitor's time and interest, they can choose to take either a short or long trail.

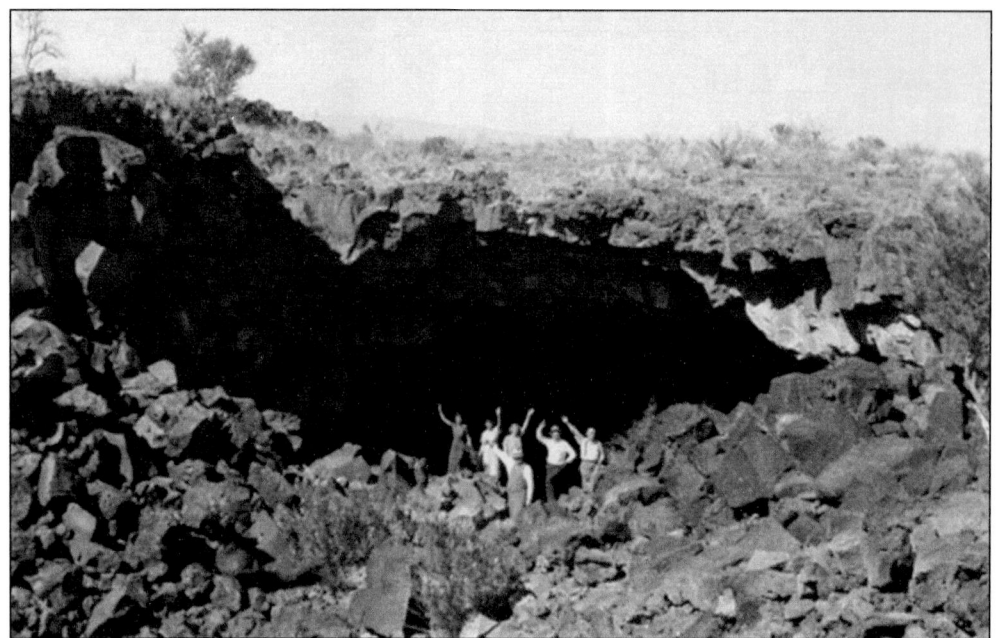

Visitors wave to the photographer near the entrance to Indian Well Cave, one of the most accessible caves in the monument. Just a short walk from the visitor center, it is especially favored during the winter months because of its unusual ice formations.

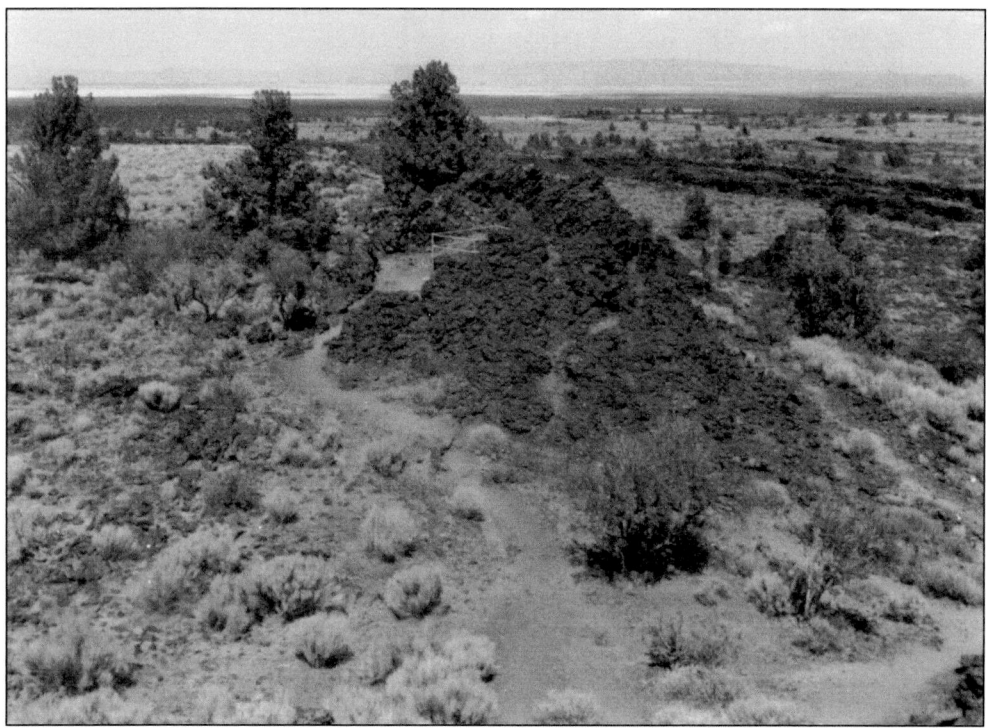

Improvements to park trails have included fences at places like Fleener Chimneys. Work began here under the direction of the US Forest Service and has been continued by the National Park Service since Lava Beds was designated as a national monument in 1925.

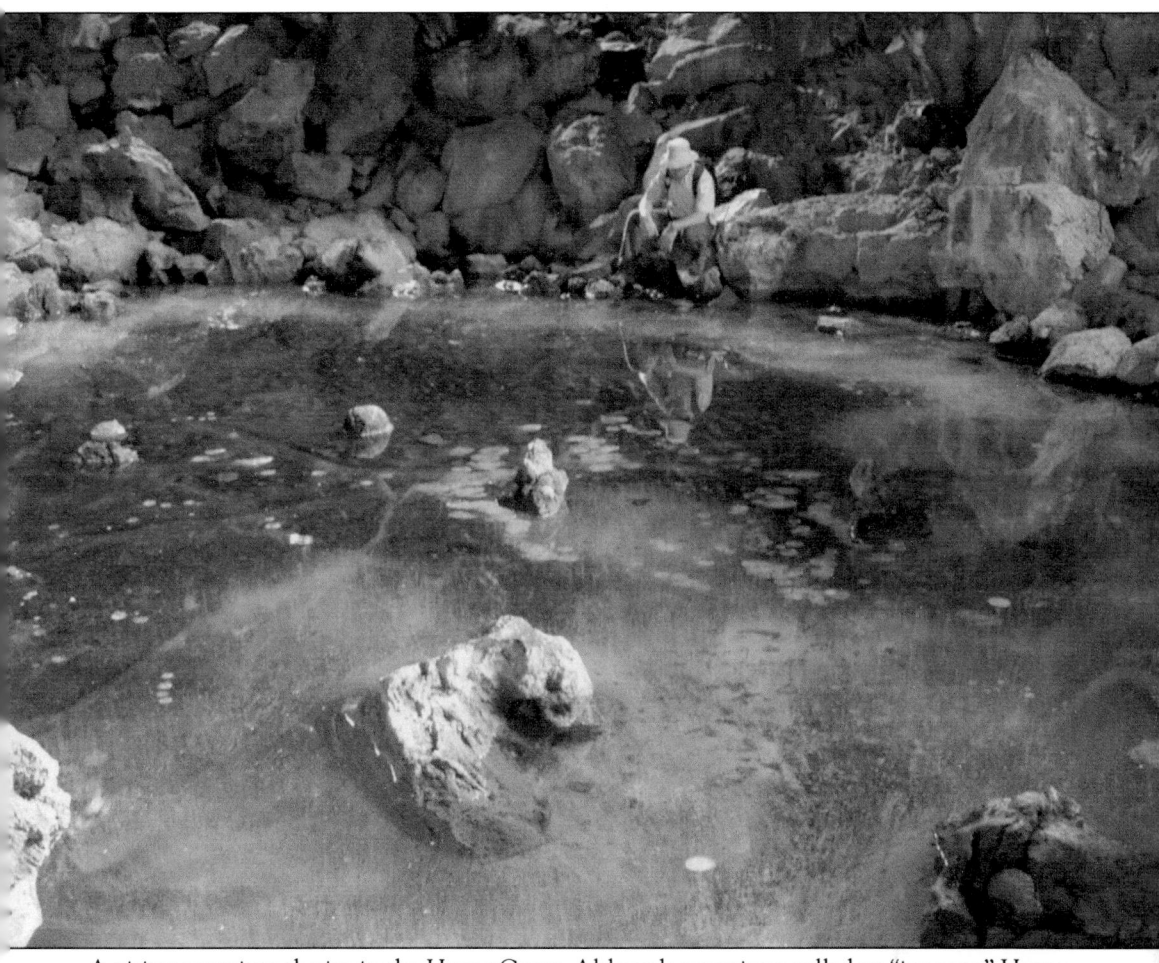

A visitor examines the ice in the Heppe Caves. Although sometimes called an "ice cave," Heppe is not known for perennial ice. At times, the pool at the bottom of the cave is the largest standing body of water in the monument and is often used by birds for drinking and bathing. It is speculated that the pool of water is perched on an impermeable layer of ice. The Heppe Caves were named by J.D. Howard for a family named Heppe that camped in the area and eventually moved to an unused barge on Tule Lake.

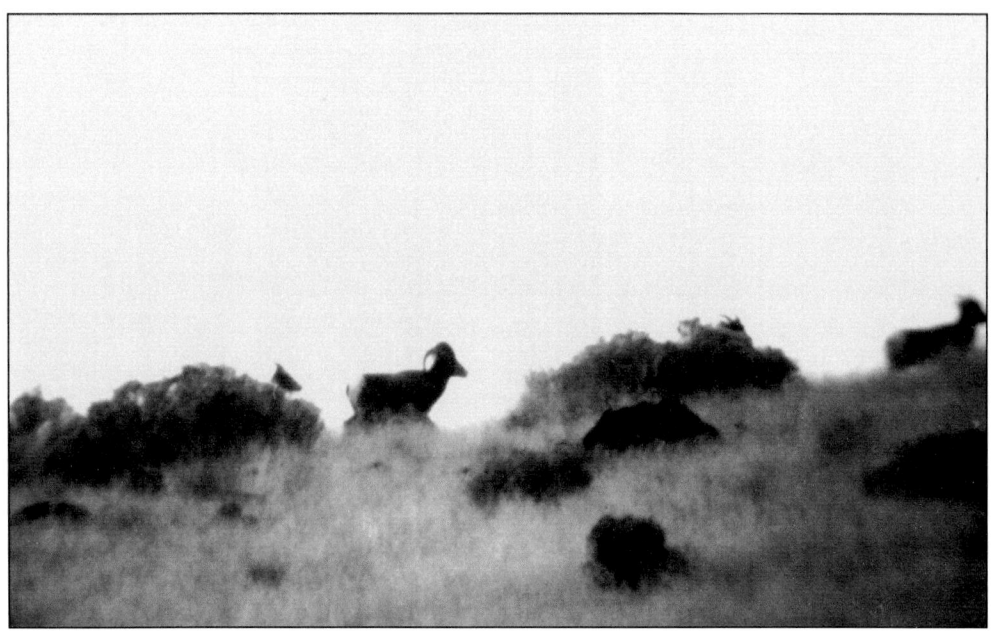

California bighorn sheep, which were found in the Lava Beds area when the region was first settled, were reintroduced to the monument in 1971. The sheep lived in a hilly fenced enclosure in the Gillem Bluff area. As populations increased, the sheep were transferred and reintroduced to other areas. During a 1980 gather, which involved people from five different state and federal agencies, stress created during the transfer killed five bighorns. Five were transferred to the Warner Mountain area in far northern California. In the summer of 1980, the remaining bighorns began to die, and by August, all 33 were dead.

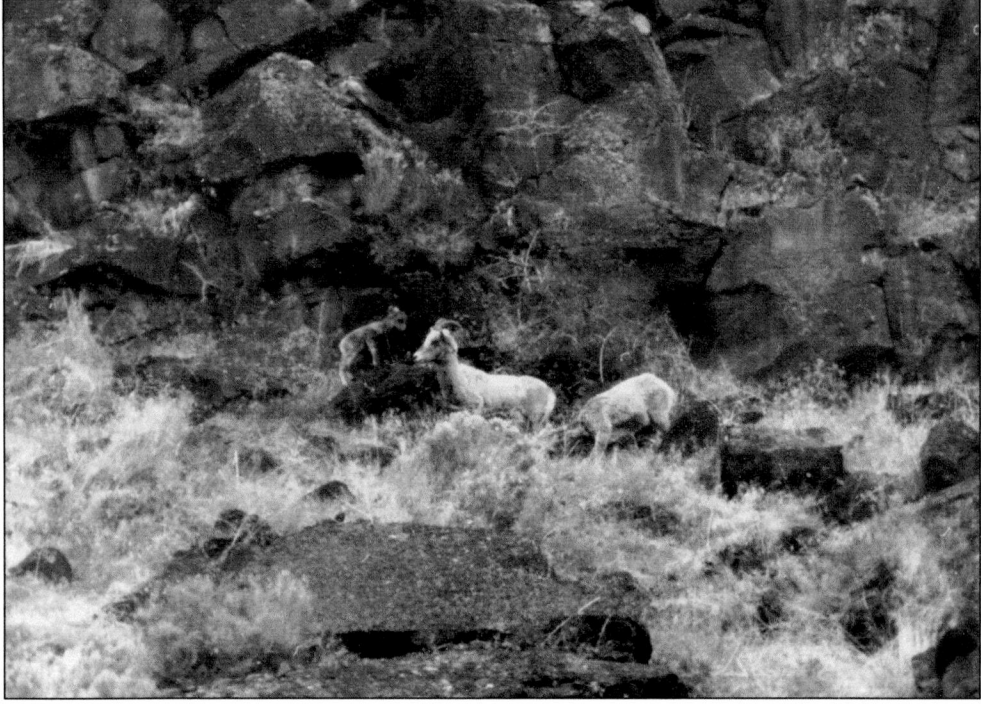

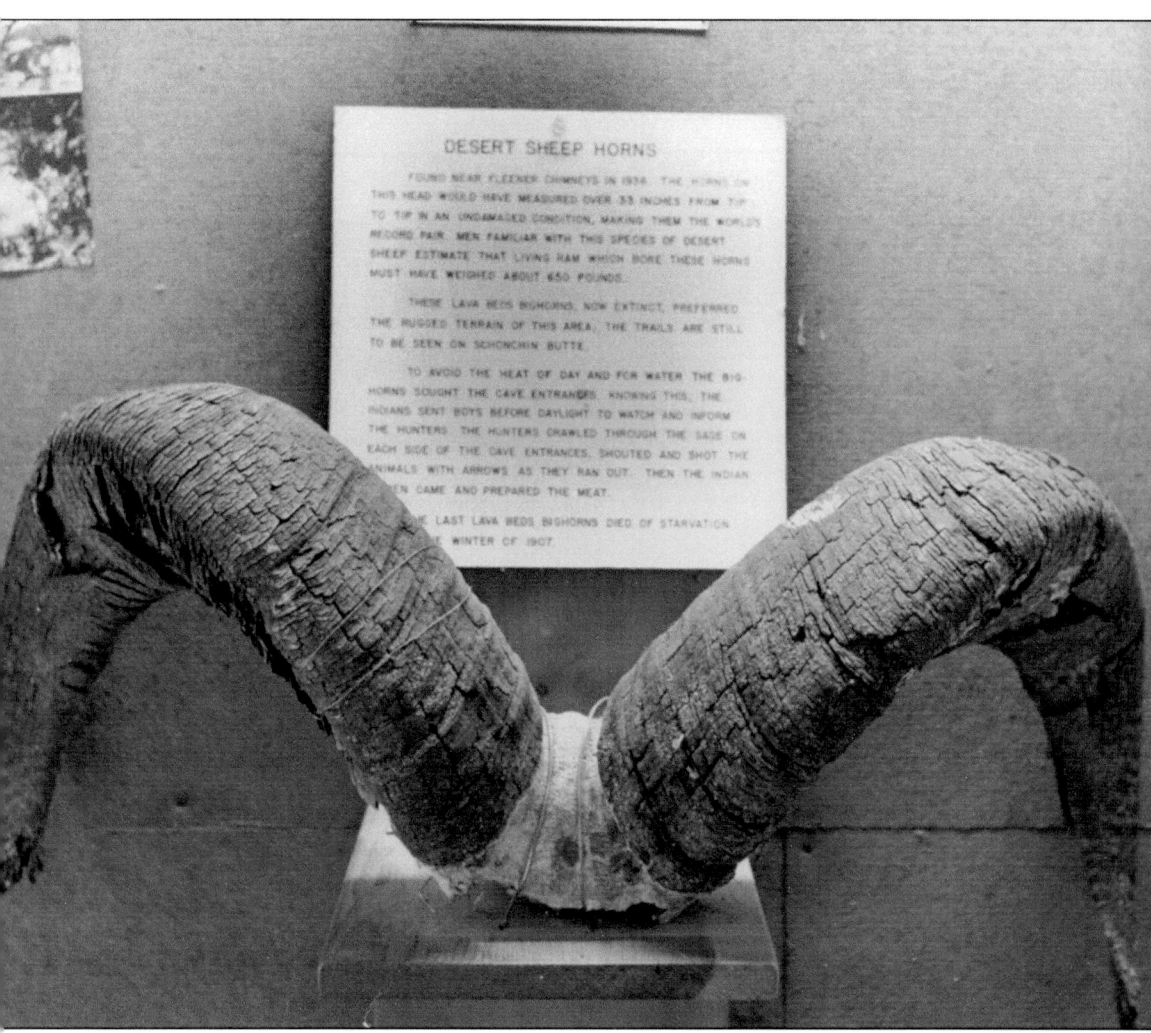

An exhibit in the monument's earlier visitor center displayed "Desert Sheep Horns" that were found near Fleener Chimneys in 1936. The plaque reads, "The width of the head would have measured over 33 inches from tip to tip in an undamaged condition, making them the world's record pair." It was estimated that this bighorn sheep would have weighed 650 pounds. The information board said that their trails could still be seen on Schonchin Butte. It is believed that during the heat of day, bighorn sought out cave entrances. After Indian scouts spotted the sheep, other Indians crawled through the sagebrush to cave entrances, where they shouted at the sheep to startle them, then shot the sheep with arrows when they tried to escape.

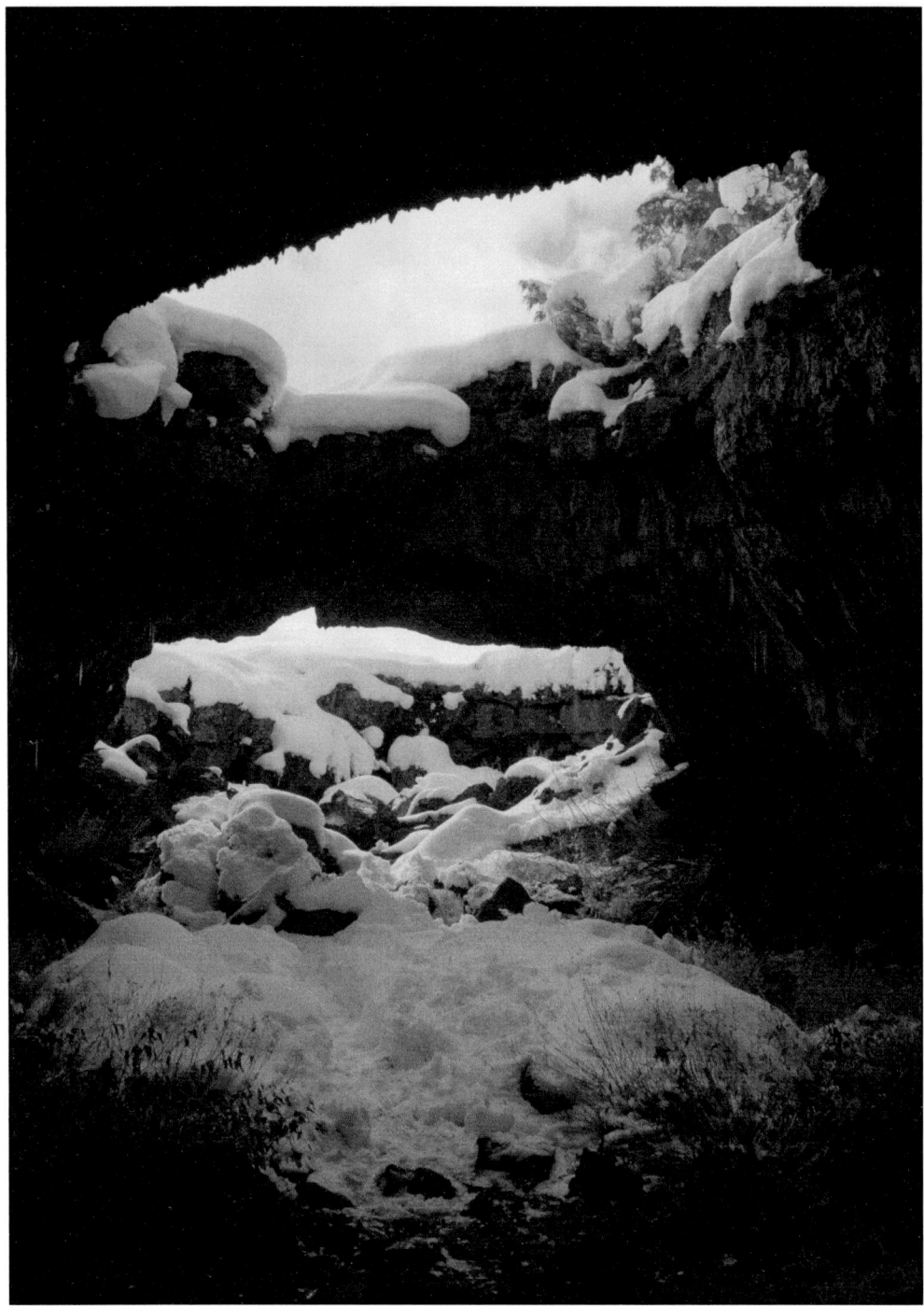

Lava Beds National Monument is a place to visit in all seasons, including winter. While snow sometimes shrouds the outside landscape, temperatures in the caves remain relatively mild—often in the mid-50s. The monument lives up to its nickname because its 72 square miles are covered with volcanic rock, with about two-thirds being basaltic lava that erupted more than 11,000 years ago. Many of the most popular caves have trails and developments aimed at insuring visitor safety.

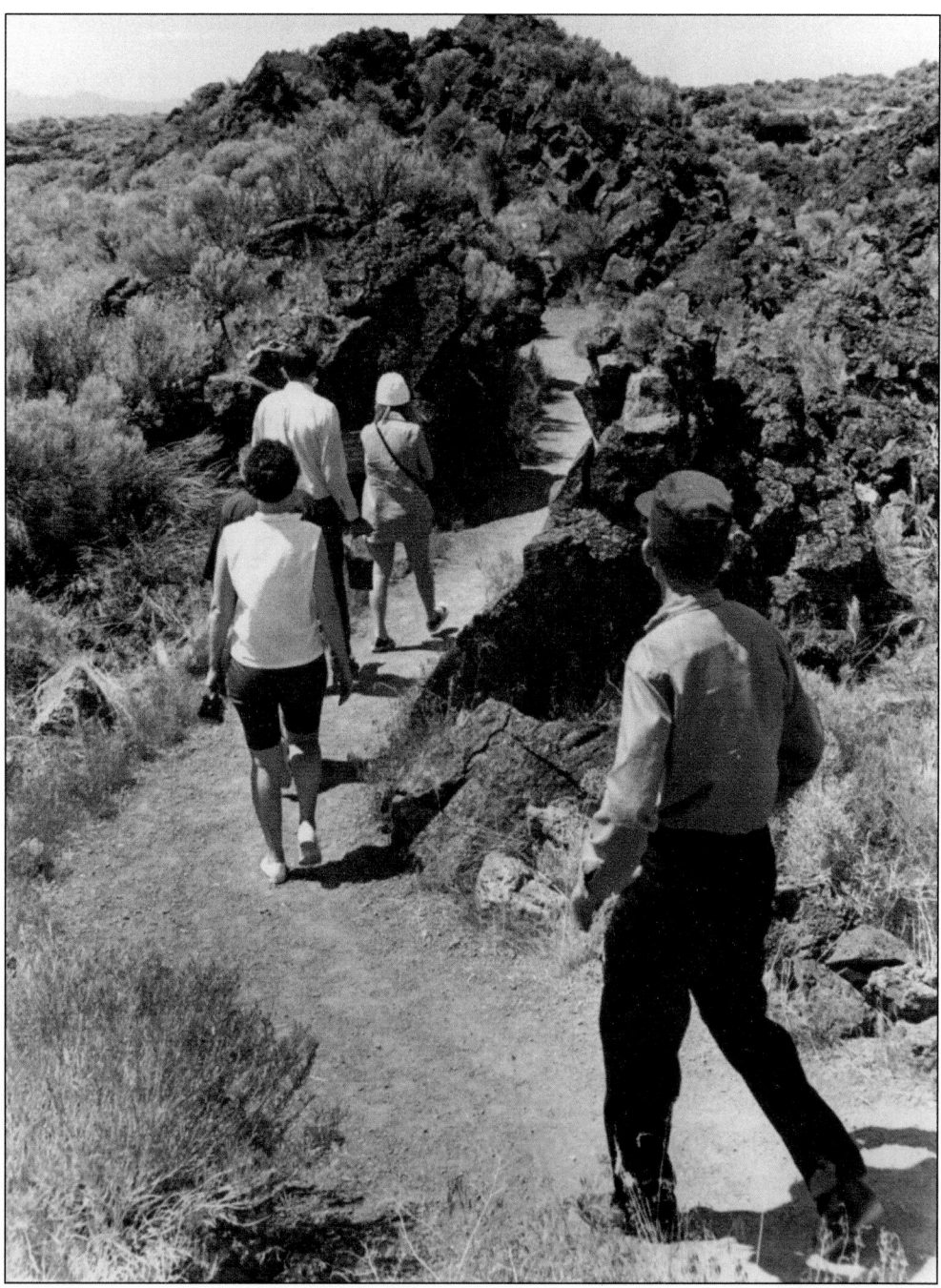
Visitors make their way through some of the open passages in Captain Jack's Stronghold. A trail weaves through the place where Modoc Indians held off far larger forces of US Army troops during the Modoc War, and a walk through the lava fortress shows how the Modocs used their knowledge of the fractured terrain to their advantage. Informative ranger-led walks through the stronghold are offered during the summer, but trail guides and signs along the route allow visitors to enjoy the area on their own at any time of year. Visitors have a choice of taking a short route that features many of the highlights of Captain Jack's Stronghold or taking a longer loop route.

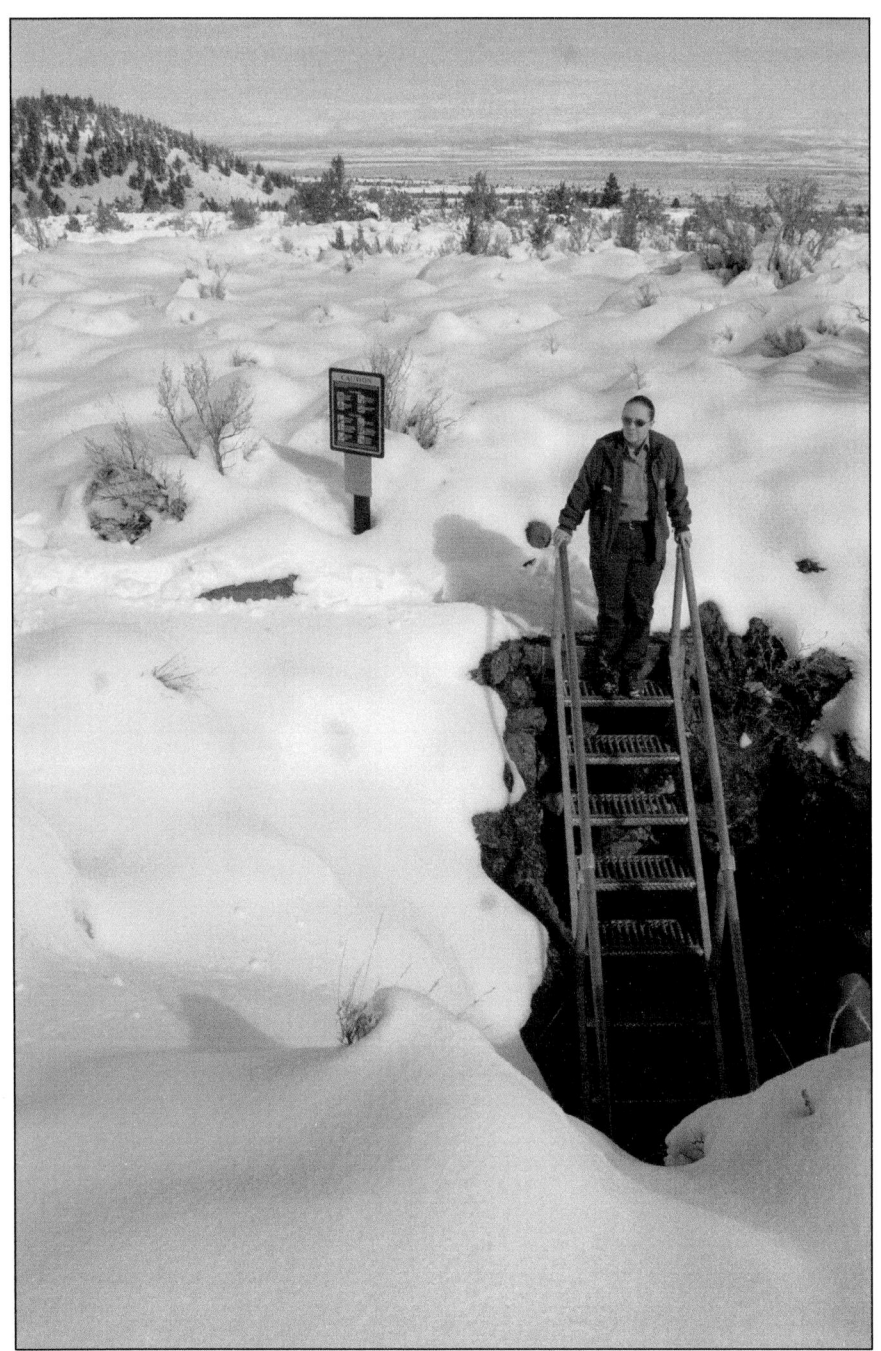

A park ranger stands at the entrance to a cave along Cave Loop Road during a break from a winter snowstorm. Winter can be an ideal season for visiting the caves at Lava Beds, because temperatures inside the lava tubes are often warmer than outside. Although cave temperatures can vary from subfreezing—in caves with ice—to those that mimic the outside air, most are in the low 50s, so the park service recommends dressing in layers. Stiff-soled shoes are recommended, and, if going through narrow passages, hard hats and kneepads can be helpful. Head-mounted lights are suggested so that visitors can keeps their hands free.

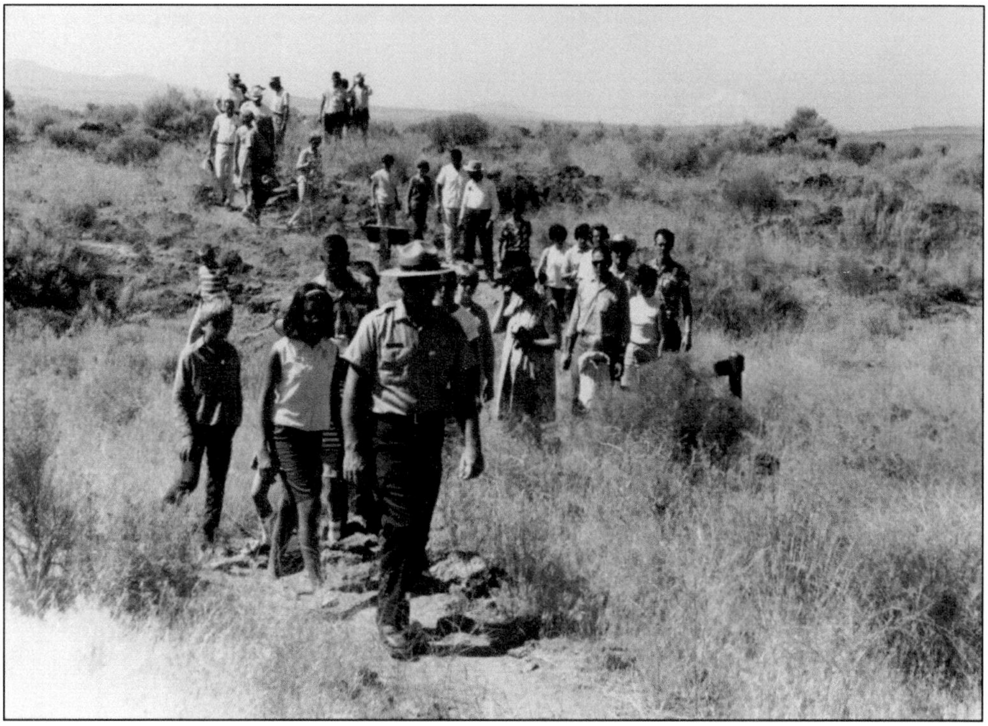

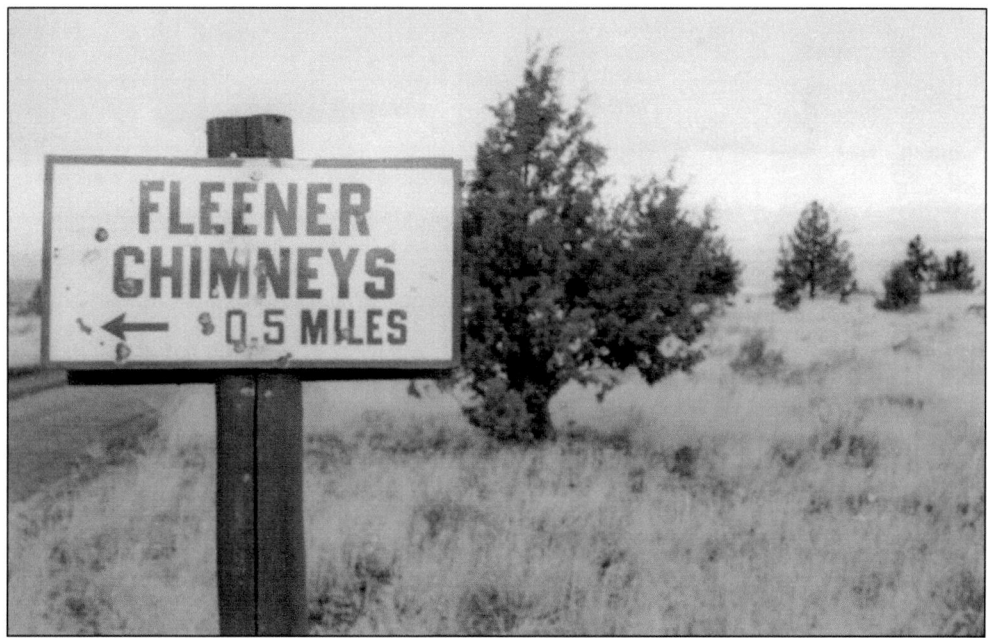

A park ranger leads a tour group along an open section of Captain Jack's Stronghold. Guided walks give visitors a chance to learn about life in the stronghold during the 1872–1873 Modoc War. Trail guides kept in a box near the trailhead also provide information.

One of the original US Forest Service signs points to Fleener Chimneys, just a half-mile off the monument's main road. The sign to the chimneys has been updated, but the site still includes picnic tables made by Civilian Conservation Corps workers.

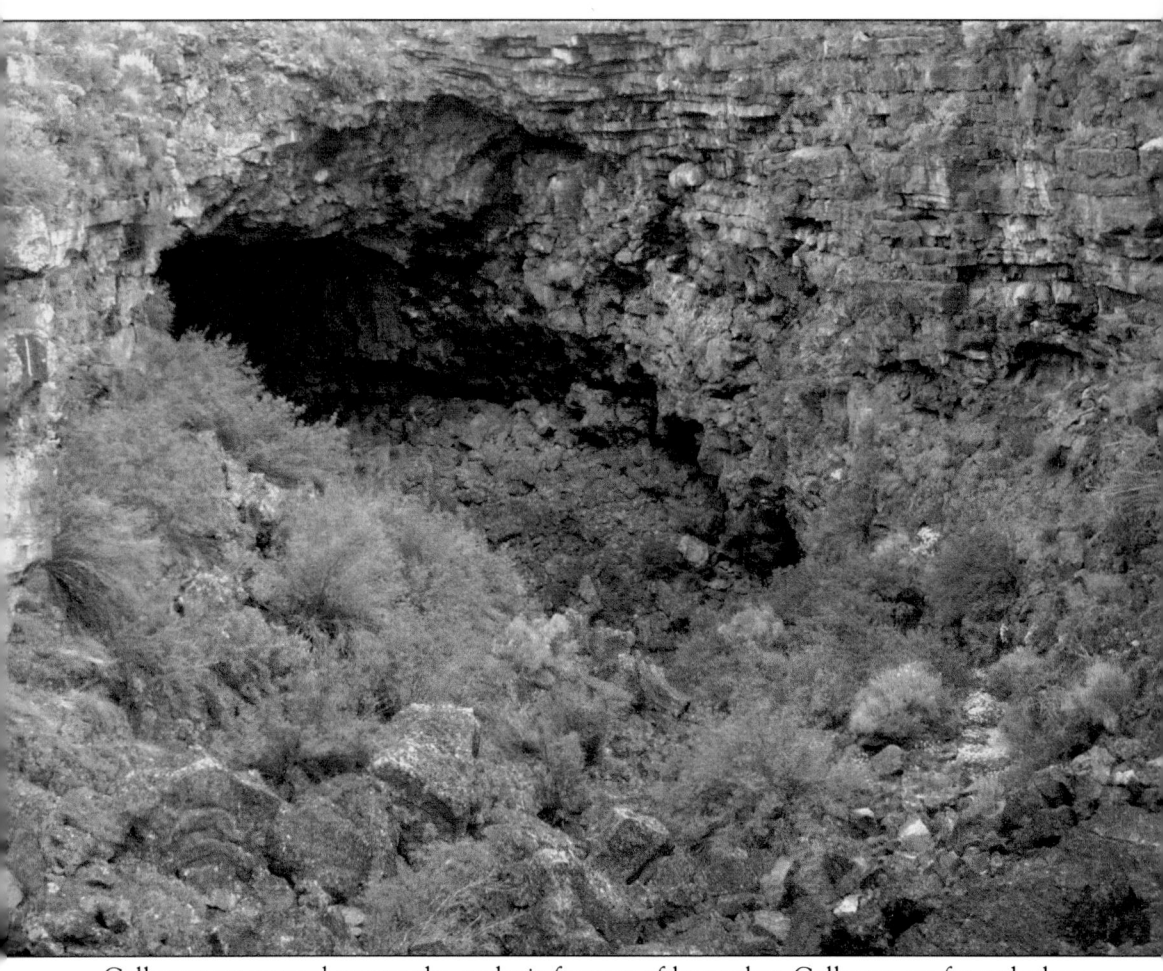

Collapses are normal among the geologic features of lava tubes. Collapses are formed when sections of a lava tube can no longer withstand gravity. Collapses may occur while lava is flowing (a primary collapse) or after the flow has ended (a secondary collapse). Evidence of collapses can be viewed at various places in the monument, including a collapse trench near the Natural Bridge parking area on Cave Loop Road. Collapses may be limited to one level or may progress through several or all levels of a lava tube system. Collapses expose pre-flow land strata, which, at the monument, is usually red cinders.

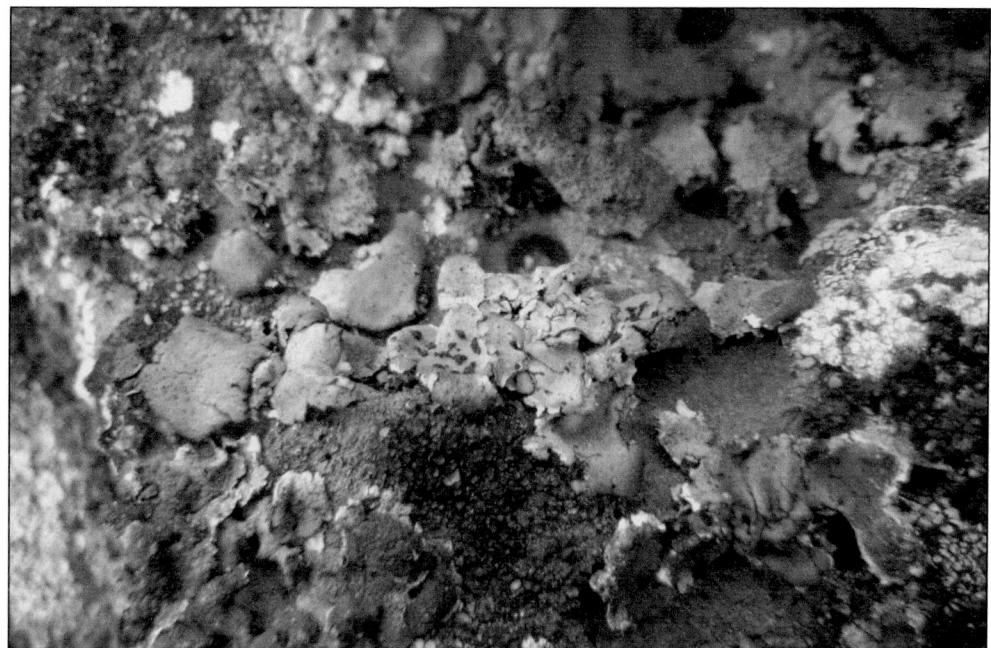

There is often more than meets the eye in caves or trenches around the monument. In recent years, researchers have identified large numbers of different lichens, including a previously unknown species. A lichen is a composite organism that emerges from algae or cyanobacteria, or both, that lives among filaments of a fungus in a mutually beneficial relationship. Lichens come in many colors, sizes, and forms. They are sometimes plant-like, but lichens are not plants. A macrolichen is a lichen that is either bush-like or leafy, while the term microlichen encompasses everything else. Lichens do not have roots that absorb water and nutrients, like plants, but produce their own food from sunlight, air, water, and minerals in their environment.

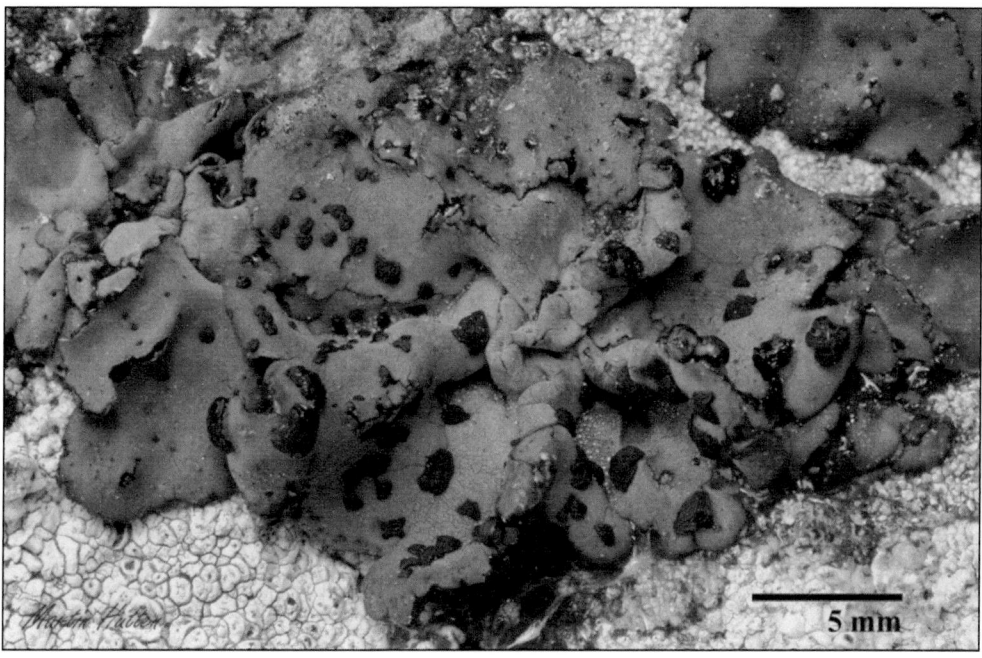

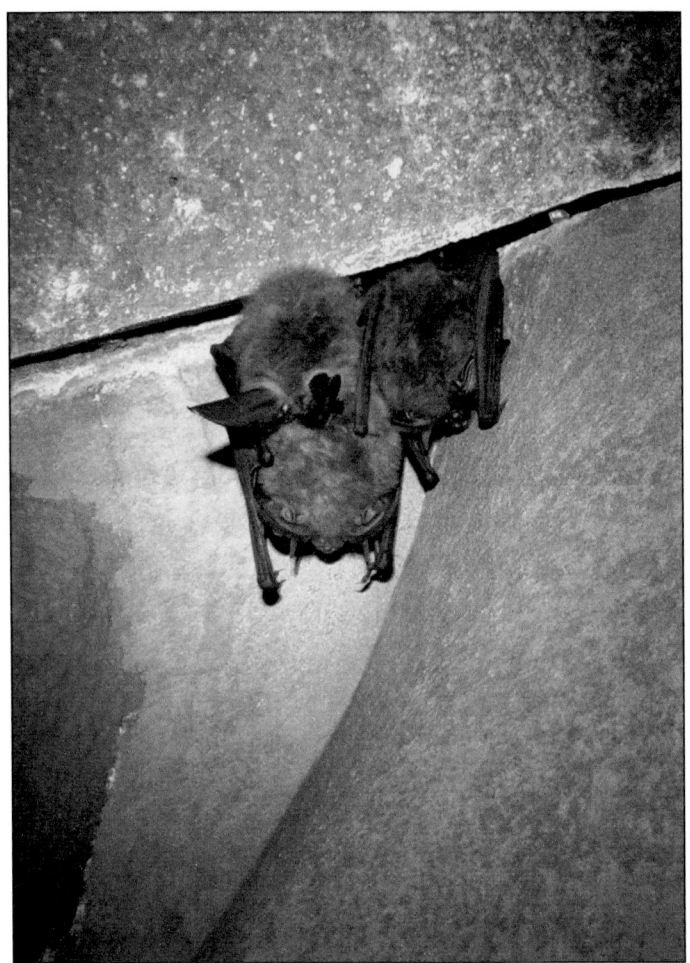

Although bats have long inhabited the caves at Lava Beds National Monument, research on them is relatively new. Undisturbed caves are used by hibernating bats during the winter, when food sources—mostly insects—are not available. Biologists have learned that bats, especially the Townsend's big-eared bats found in large numbers at Lava Beds, use their ears to keep their bodies at necessary temperatures. Some tuck their ears underneath their wings to stay warm, while others extend their ears to cool off. Despite horror stories involving bats, healthy populations are desired because they reduce insect populations, which benefits Tulelake Basin farmers.

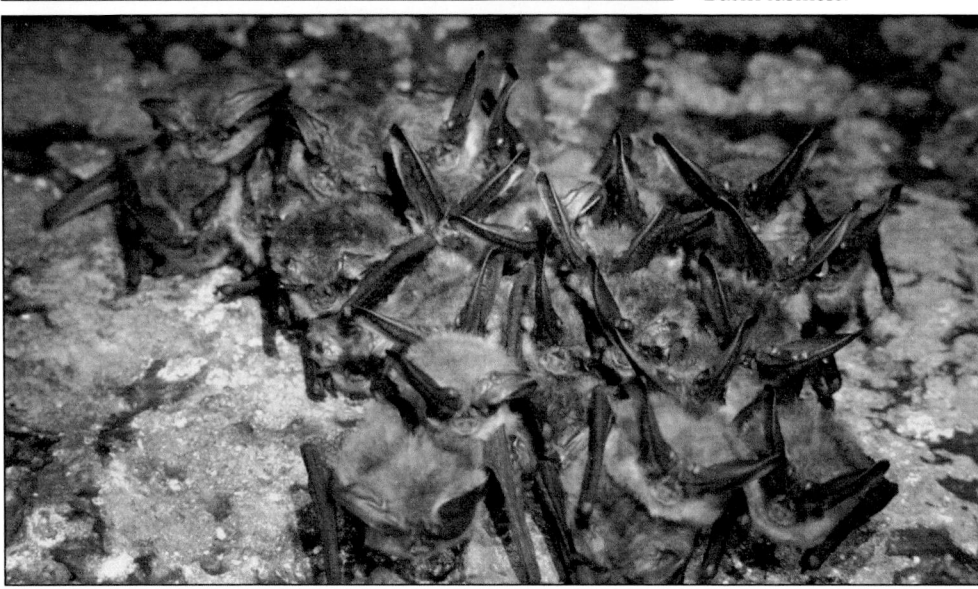

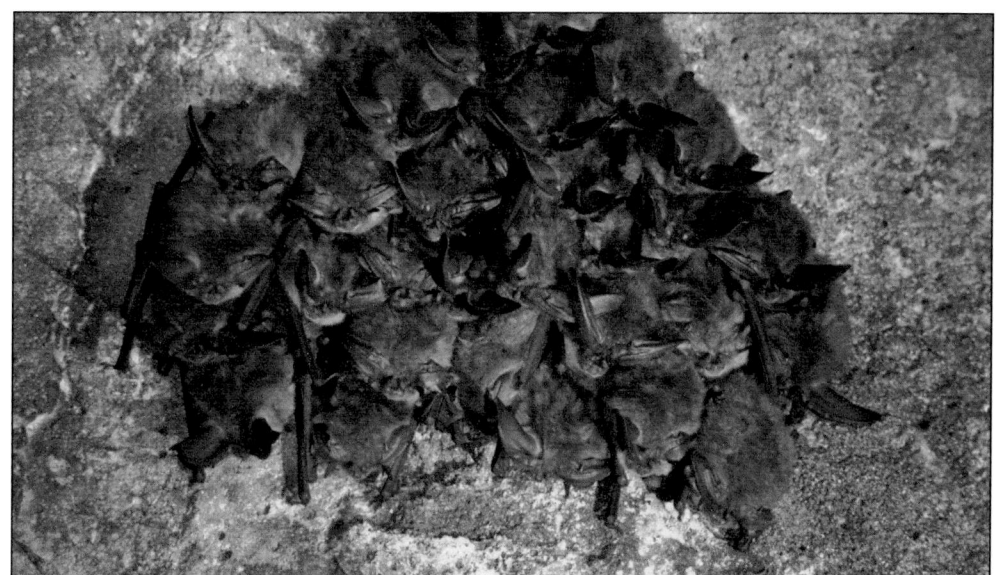

Bats have historically used caves at Lava Beds National Monument to hibernate both alone and in clusters. Above, a large cluster is shown in a photograph taken by rangers, who in recent years have done week-long surveys that typically result in counts of 1,250 to 1,450 bats, although slightly more were found in 2015. The vast majority are Townsend's big-eared bats. To protect bat habitat, the monument seasonally closes caves where bats are known to congregate.

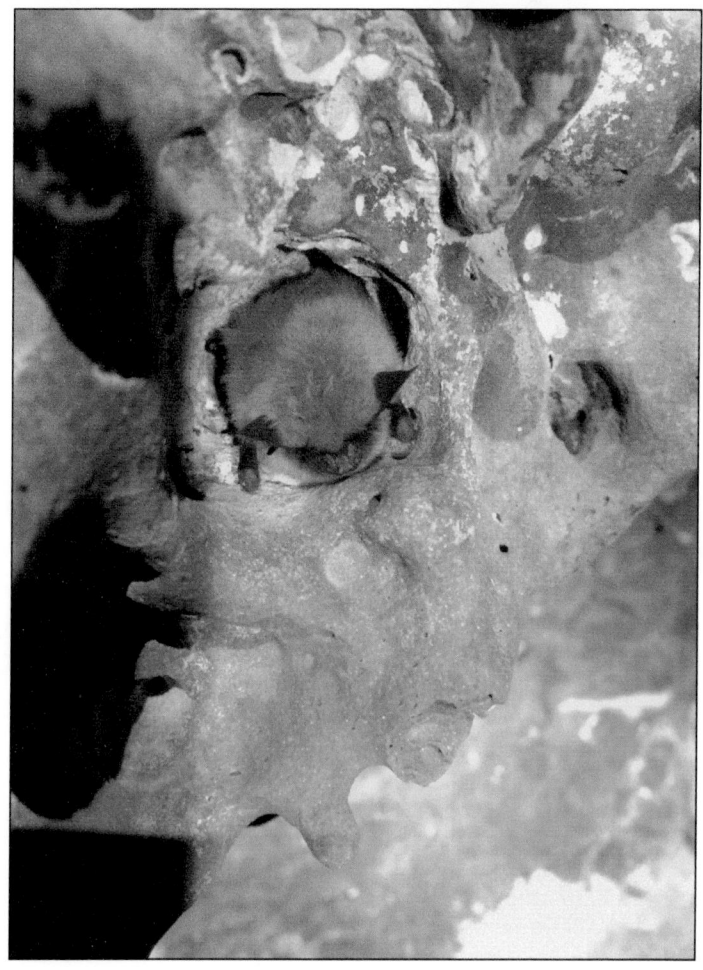

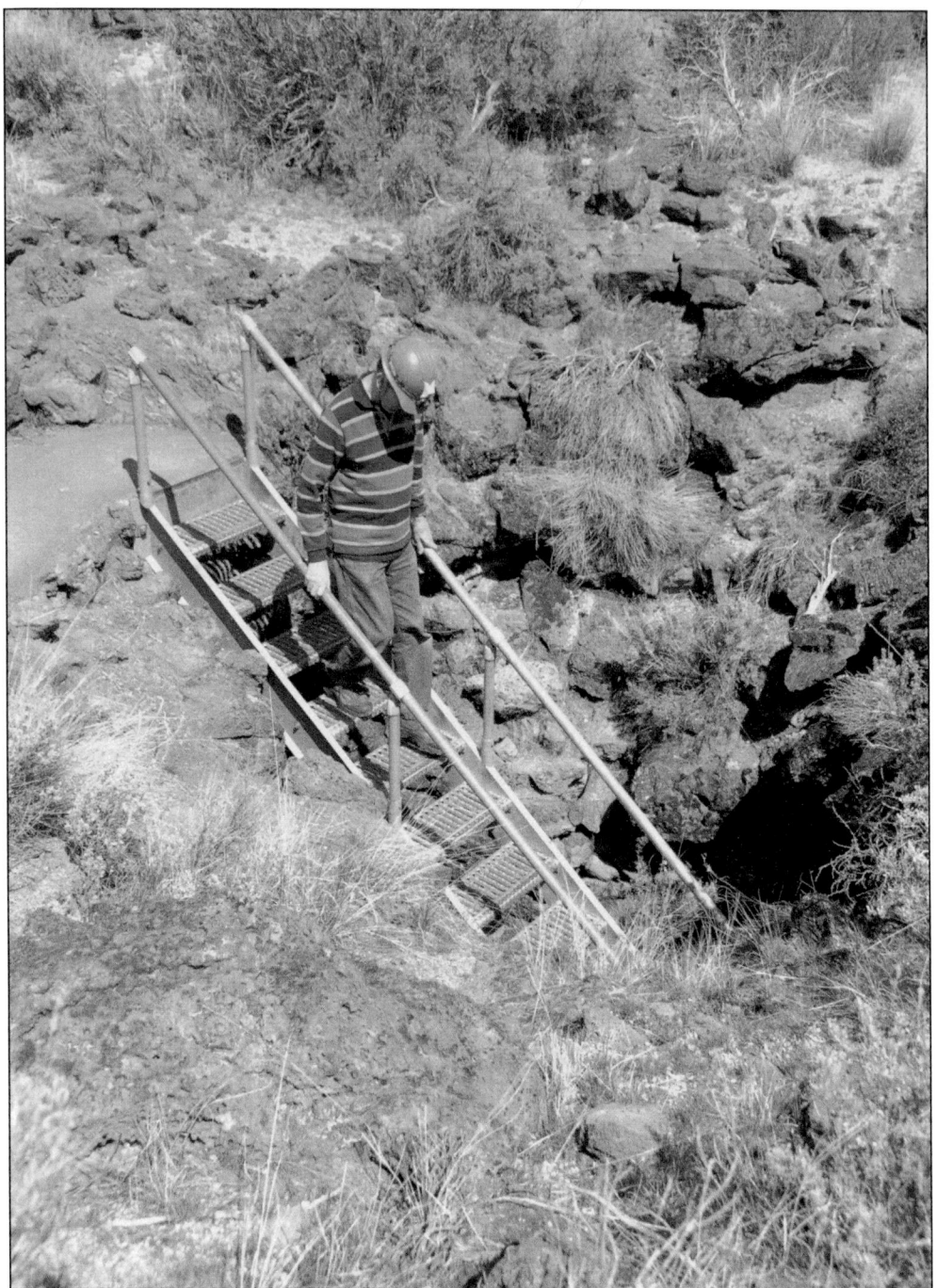

Improvements aimed at enhancing visitor experience and making it safer are ongoing at the monument. In some cases, old wooden ladders have been replaced with metal ladders that offer better gripping, which is helpful during winter months. Depending on which caves people visit, hard hats, sometimes called "bump hats," are recommended. Flashlights can be checked out at the visitor center, although experienced spelunkers often prefer headlights attached to helmets, which keep their arms free for maneuvering through narrow areas.

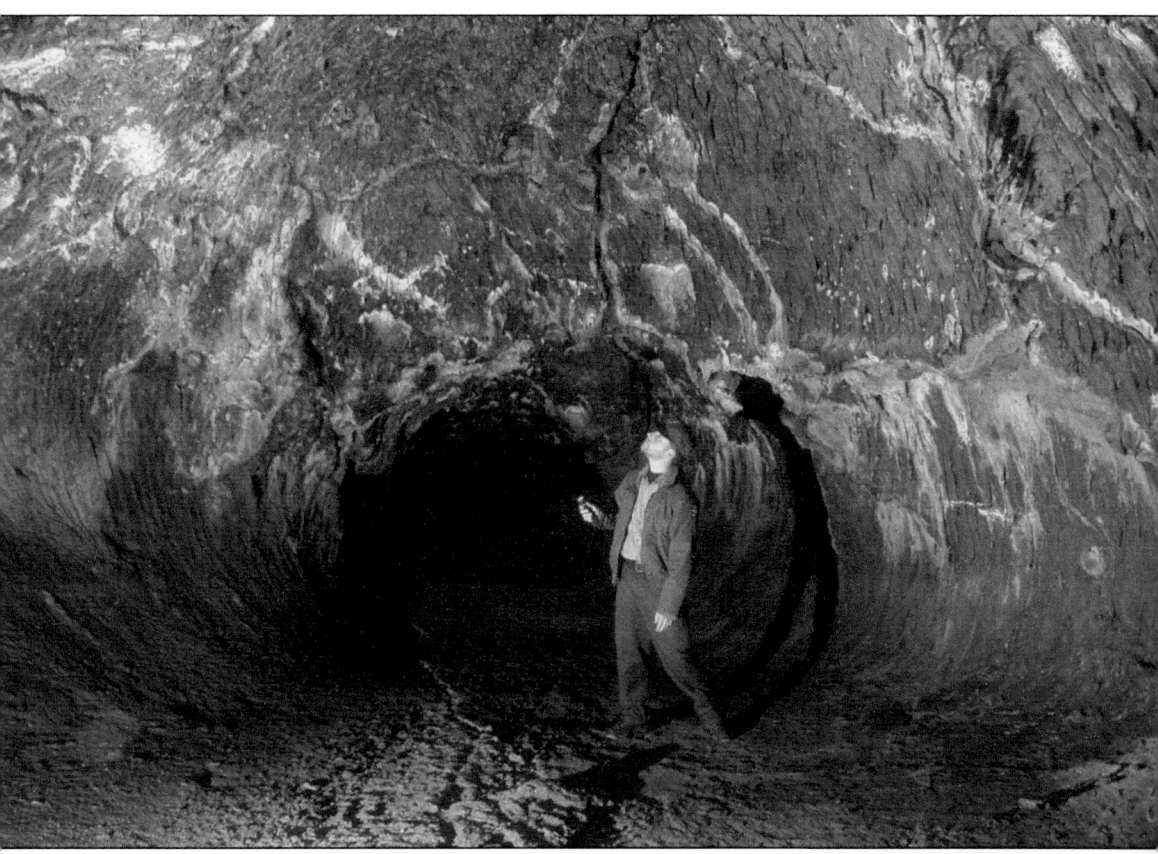

A Lava Beds ranger is shown checking out the features on the walls and sides of a large tube in the Catacombs Cave. Some of the finest examples of lava flowstone, lava stalactites, ribs, and patterns of lava flow can be seen in the cave. The cave is about 2,000 feet long, and about half that distance requires only a minimum amount of stooping. Its floors are mostly smooth with zones of cauliflower aa. J.D. Howard discovered Catacombs Cave in March 1918 when he sought shelter from a blizzard. Howard descended into a collapse, sat down on a wood rat's nest, felt air movement, tore away the nest, and enlarged a small opening that allowed him to enter the cave.

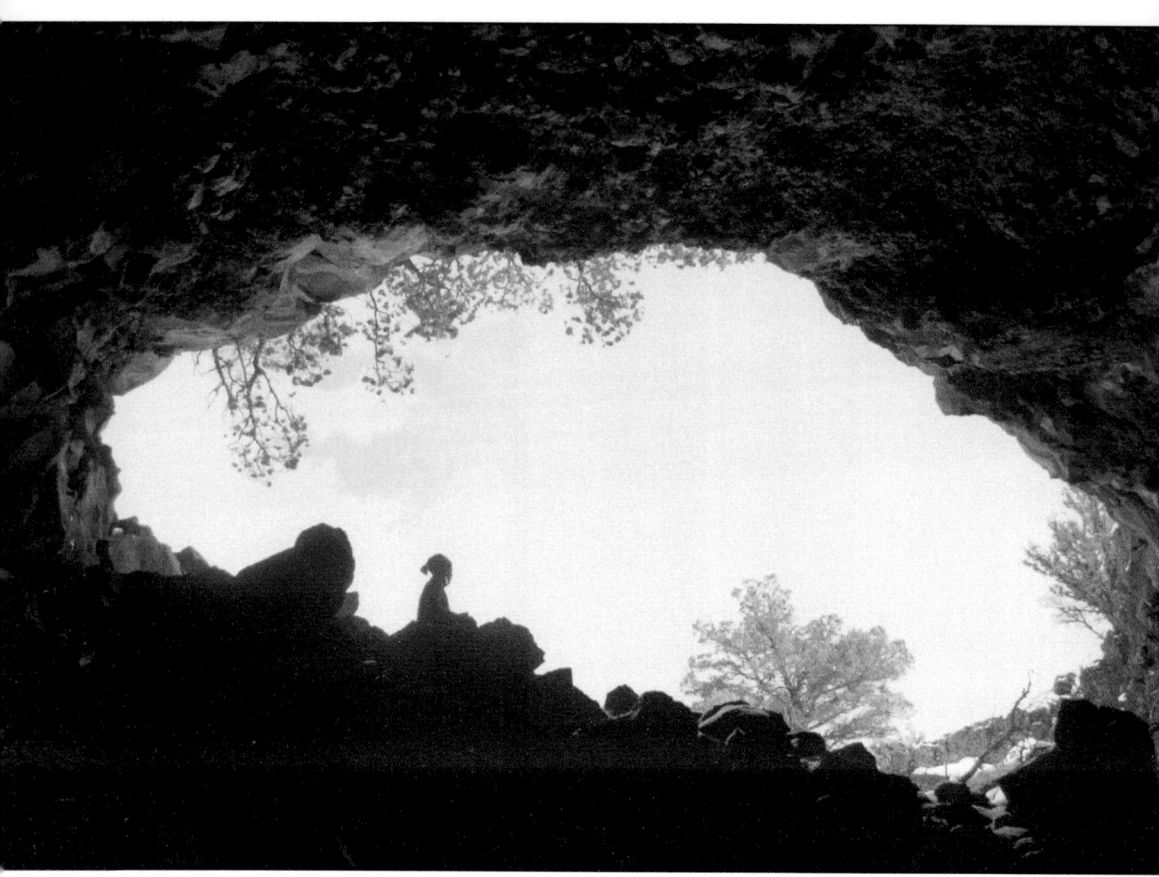

The solitude and ragged beauty of Lava Beds National Monument's sprawling landscape, the "Land of Burnt Out Fires," is something that entices visitors to make return visits. The monument is seldom crowded, and its network of trails, historic sites, and caves means that people can make multiple visits without having to retrace their steps. People making their first visit can stop at the monument's visitor center to get recommendations about caves, trails, and ranger-led activities that will match their abilities and interest levels.

Bibliography

Arnold, Charles L. *Inside the Cave*. Lava Beds, CA: Lava Beds Natural History Association, 1986.

Aslett, James, and Shelley Carman, Ann Donati, Dr. Aaron Waters. *Lava Beds Underground*. Klamath Falls, OR: Lava Beds Natural History Association, 1982.

Brown, Frederick L., "The Center of the World, The Edge of the World; A History of Lava Beds National Monument," Seattle, WA; National Park Service, 2011.

Cothran, Boyd. *Remembering the Modoc War: Redemptive Violence and the Making of American Innocence*. Chapel Hill, NC: University of North Carolina Press, 2015.

Howe, Carroll B. *Ancient Tribes of the Klamath Country*. Portland, OR: Binford & Mort Publishers, 1972.

———. *Ancient Modocs of California and Oregon*. Portland, OR: Binford & Mort Publishers, 1979.

———. *Frontier Stories of the Klamath Country*. Klamath Falls, OR: Herald and News, 1989.

James, Cheewa. *Modoc: The Tribe That Wouldn't Die*. Happy Camp, CA: Naturegraph Publishers, 2008.

Larson, Charlie and Jo Larson. *Lava Beds Caves*. Vancouver, WA: ABC Publishing, 1990.

Murray, Keith A. *The Modocs and Their War*. Norman, OK: University of Oklahoma Press, 1984.

Shaw Historical Society Journals: "Unforgiving Landscape: Lava Beds National Monument and the Modoc War," 2010; "We Can Take It: The Civilian Conservation Corps in the Land of the Lakes," 2006; "The Devil's Homestead: Celebrating 75 Years of the Lava Beds National Monument," 2000, Klamath Falls, OR; Shaw Historical Library.

Sproull, Harry V. *Modoc Indian War*. Lava Beds, CA: Lava Beds Natural History Association, 1975.

Woodhead, Daniel. *Modoc Vengeance: The 1873 Modoc War in Northern California and Southern*. San Francisco, CA: self-published, 2012.

Discover Thousands of Local History Books
Featuring Millions of Vintage Images

Arcadia Publishing, the leading local history publisher in the United States, is committed to making history accessible and meaningful through publishing books that celebrate and preserve the heritage of America's people and places.

Find more books like this at
www.arcadiapublishing.com

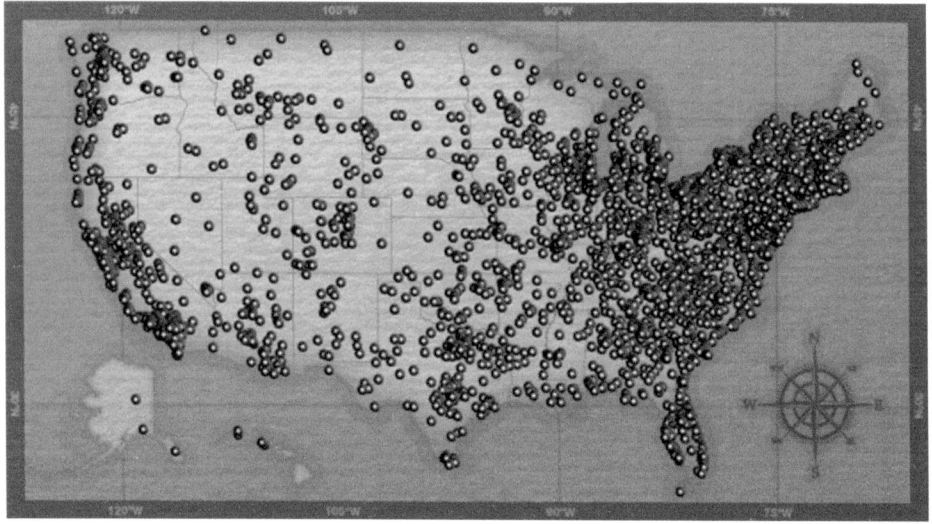

Search for your hometown history, your old stomping grounds, and even your favorite sports team.

Consistent with our mission to preserve history on a local level, this book was printed in South Carolina on American-made paper and manufactured entirely in the United States. Products carrying the accredited Forest Stewardship Council (FSC) label are printed on 100 percent FSC-certified paper.

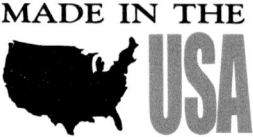